The American Revolution: New York as a Case Study

Edited by

Larry R. Gerlach

University of Utah

Wadsworth Publishing Company, Inc., Belmont, California

For T. J. and his generation

There is no substitute for documents; no documents, no history.
Langlois

He thinks I am an unprejudiced observer and will tell him the
exact truth. Now what am I to say?
Henry Adams
Esther

If we would study with profit the history of our ancestors
. . . we must never forget that the country of which we read
was a very different country from that in which we live.
Thomas Babington Macaulay
History of England

ISBN-0-534-00214-5

L. C. Cat. Card No.-72-89392

Printed in the United States of America
1 2 3 4 5 6 7 8 9 10---76 75 74 73 72

The American History Research Series

The volumes in this series are designed to allow students to work with original source materials as historians do.

The study of history can be broken down broadly into two compatible but strikingly different approaches. The student is ordinarily expected to become familiar with the facts of American history by studying a textbook, supplementary secondary materials, and lectures. He is sometimes asked to supplement this understanding of history by "doing" some history of his own—that is, examining primary source materials and coming to his own conclusions about the events of the past. Because many students do not have access to research libraries, they find this difficult, and their understanding of the past is based almost entirely on secondary accounts. The American History Research Series is an effort to give the student direct access to primary source materials on important issues.

The series is directed to the problem of how a society makes up its mind, how individuals and groups within such a society take stock of what is happening to them and of what they are becoming. Ordinarily, history courses are concerned with one phase of this problem. They take account of the many different kinds of decisions members of a society are forced to make and they take some account of the process through which these decisions are made: the election of candidates to office, the framing of new legislation, the arbitering of conflicts among groups, the revision of existing institutions, and the creation of new institutions. In general, however, the decisions studied and the assessments made are on a massive, usually national, scale: they are the decisions of governments or comparatively impersonal representatives of governments or the corporate decisions of masses of men who determine, for example, to move westward, who make their way to new American cities, or who seem to demand a vast bloodletting to regain their national honor. What the student misses is the chance to tap the thought processes of men in the course of their deliberations and on a scale that makes close observation and analysis possible.

Each of the volumes of the series has been planned with the express design of realizing this difficult general objective. Each of the problems has been selected because it is an issue which has led to disagreement among historians. None of the issues can be interpreted in a single, simple way; each one is complex and requires careful thought and weighing of evidence. In selecting topics and readings, we have been guided by considerations of focus, scale, and relatedness. We have concentrated on topics limited in time and locale; where the tactics and the process of thought are to be examined, we prefer the battle to the war. Since our object is to excite students to question historical evidence, we have tried to find bodies of documents that are closely interrelated, suggestive, and resonant of meaning. It has thus seemed preferable, for example, to present students not with a scattering of documents that illustrate the Great Awakening in all its aspects but rather to focus narrowly upon the experience of those in and around the hotseat of Yale College. Instead of trying to illustrate the critical attitudes toward the city and an industrial economy at the close of the nineteenth century, we have chosen instead to examine the thinking of a small group of writers and reformers associated with the city of Chicago and the new university founded there in the 1890s. In short, we have chosen to work microcosmically, to understand the whole of a development by the close examination of a part. We have also sought out moments of crisis, conflict, and drama where the student can observe contending ideas at play.

We have tried to compile texts that express the thinking of particular groups or communities. Wherever possible we have looked for documents that form part of an actual controversy or running debate even where the participants are little known or obscure men. For this reason, we have tried to offer whole, unabridged texts as often as we could; in other cases, a minimum of editing preserves the original design and flavor of a scholar's text.

The object of the series, in short, is to place the student in a situation where, on a limited and manageable scale, he must act the historian. By involving the student in the process of history, we hope to develop not only his inquiry skills but to provide him with a basis for judging the work of other historians.

William R. Taylor
Arthur Zilversmit

Preface

The American Revolution irrevocably shaped the course of American history. The tumultuous period from 1763 to 1789 witnessed not only the creation of a new republic but also the formulation of the nation's fundamental political and philosophical tenets. Yet despite the examination of virtually every facet of the Revolutionary era, a wide divergence of opinion still exists about even the most elementary questions. As one scholar succinctly said: "For so great an event, the American Revolution is downright elusive. Nothing seems certain about it: what it was about, how and why it happened, when or perhaps even whether it happened."[1] In short, under the skillful hands of Clio's craftsmen the Revolution has been one of the most malleable episodes in American history.

The conflicting interpretations of the Revolution stem in large measure from the duality of the event: it was the product of thirteen separate rebellions as well as a "continental" phenomenon. The transition from colony to state evoked common problems and practices throughout America, but all colonies were not equally rebellious, motivated by the same reasons, or identical in the way they instituted republican government. Moreover, after 1776 each state conducted its own experiment in independence and after 1787 opted for inclusion in "a more Perfect Union" for different reasons. Thus an understanding of the revolutionary era at the local level is essential to comprehension of the nature and significance of the American Revolution.

Perhaps nowhere was the Revolution as complex and confusing as in New York. Local circumstances complicated the prerevolutionary scene: the urban-commercial milieu of a major port contrasted with a vast agrarian hinterland; there were both

---

[1]William H. Nelson, "The Revolutionary Character of the American Revolution," *American Historical Review* 70 (July 1965): 998.

huge landed estates (including the distinctive manorial system) and widespread tenantry; the state held the largest slave population north of Maryland; the population was markedly heterogeneous; the frontier was unstable because of the presence of a powerful Indian confederacy (the Six Nations) to the west and boundary disputes with New England colonies to the east and with New Jersey to the south; and the political system was dominated by two contending family coteries—the Livingstons (predominant from 1761 to 1768 and generally supported by landed interests, lawyers, and Presbyterians) and the DeLanceys (ascendant from 1769 to 1775 and representing mainly mercantile interests and Anglicanism). New York City affairs were colored by the presence of the largest and most influential loyalist newspaper in America (James Rivington's *New York Gazetteer*) and a regiment of British soldiers assigned to North American army headquarters. During the War for Independence New York was a state divided: rebels encountered not only armed opposition from a sizable loyalist force but they also endured the British occupation of New York City from September 1776 to November 1783. After the war local conditions combined with national considerations to produce a protracted debate about the nature and future of the state and federal experiment in republicanism.

Modern historians have been as sharply divided as contemporaries in assessing the Revolution in New York. With the opening sentences of his classic *The History of Political Parties in the Province of New York, 1760-1776*, Carl Lotus Becker set the terms of the debate: "The American Revolution was the result of two general movements; the contest for home-rule and independence, and the democratization of American politics and society. Of these movements, the latter was fundamental; it began before the contest for home-rule, and was not completed until after the achievement of independence." The struggle for home rule obviously pitted rebel against royalist, but the question of who should rule at home caused a tripartite clash between a "landed and commercial aristocracy" held together by an intricate web of intermarriages, middling freeholders and freemen, and the unfranchised masses. The drama of the protest-independence movement, staged mainly in New York City, saw conservatives move progressively leftward to preempt the appeal of radicals and to maintain political hegemony. But they inadvertently opened Pandora's box by organizing the lower classes for partisan purposes: participation in extralegal activities was "the open door through which the common freeholder and the unfranchised mechanic and artisan pushed their way into the political arena." Partially submerged by the exigencies of wartime, "the latent opposition of motives and interests between the privileged and the underprivileged" reappeared during the confederation period and coalesced into the Federalist and Republican parties of the 1790s—"a revival in a slightly dif-

ferent form of the fundamental party divisions which had ex-
isted from the time of the stamp act."[2]

Becker terminated his study with the onset of independence,
but Charles Austin Beard carried the socioeconomic class conflict interpretation to its logical conclusion. To Beard there
was "no question" but that New York confirmed his view of the
Constitution as a conservative counterrevolution "originated
and carried through principally by four groups of personalty
[that is, property] interests which had been adversely affected
under the Articles of Confederation: money, public securities,
manufactures, and trade and shipping."[3] Becker's conservatives
and merchants, who had been displaced politically by radicals
and agrarian democrats during the Revolution, now regained control of the state by means of an antidemocratic constitutional
coup, thus setting the stage for the Federalist-Republican
clash of the ensuing decade.

Subsequent scholarship has turned largely on the efforts
to either confirm or confute the "Becker-Beard thesis." De-
tractors and defenders alike agree that both men overstated
their cases and that their work warrants substantive modification, but differ about the extent of revision required.[4]

Some historians have questioned Becker's fundamental as-
sumptions about prerevolutionary New York, suggesting that political life was more democratic and less dominated by an elite

---

[2](Madison, Wis.: University of Wisconsin, 1909), pp. 5, 10-11,
22, 275. Becker estimated that "over half" of the white adult
males were "without political privilege of any sort."

[3]*An Economic Interpretation of the Constitution of the United
States* (New York : Macmillan Co., 1913), p. 324. See also
Beard's *The Economic Origins of Jeffersonian Democracy* (New
York : Macmillan Co., 1915). Orin G. Libby had earlier posited
a split between commercial and noncommercial interests over the
ratification of the Constitution, observing that in New York
"the entire mass of interior counties . . . were solidly Anti-
federal, comprising the agricultural portion of the state, the
last settled and the most thinly populated," while "the Federal
area centered about New York city and county" (*The Geographical
Distribution of the Vote of the Thirteen States on the Federal
Constitution, 1787-8* [Madison, Wis.: University of Wisconsin,
1894], p. 18).

[4]See Bernard Mason, "The Heritage of Carl Becker: The Historiog-
raphy of the Revolution in New York," *New-York Historical Society Quarterly* 53 (April 1969): 127-47.

than he allowed,[5] that landlords and tenants had common as well as conflicting interests,[6] and that the lower classes were neither monolithic nor manipulated but were politically conscious and active in their own right.[7] Still others have taken exception to Becker's conceptual approach to the Revolution. To Roger J. Champagne, "the struggle over who should rule at home . . .

[5]For example, see Milton M. Klein, "Democracy and Politics in Colonial New York," *New York History* 40 (July 1959): 221-46, and "Politics and Personalities in Colonial New York," ibid. 47 (January 1966): 3-16; Nicholas Varga, "Election Procedures and Practices in Colonial New York," ibid. 41 (July 1960): 249-77; and Patricia U. Bonomi, *A Factious People: Politics and Society in Colonial New York* (New York: Columbia University Press, 1971).

[6]Sung Bok Kim, "The Manor of Cortland and Its Tenants, 1697-1783" (Ph.D. diss., Michigan State University, 1966), and "A New Look at the Great Landlords of Eighteenth-Century New York," *William and Mary Quarterly*, 3d ser., 27 (October 1970): 581-614. Endemic class conflict between landed and nonlanded interests is the theme of Irving Mark's *Agrarian Conflicts in Colonial New York, 1711-1775* (New York: Columbia University Press, 1940) and Staughton Lynd's *Anti-Federalism in Dutchess County, New York: A Study of Democracy and Class Conflict in the Revolutionary Era* (Chicago: Loyola University Press, 1962), "Who Should Rule at Home? Dutchess County, New York, in the American Revolution," *William and Mary Quarterly*, 3d ser., 18 (July 1961): 330-59, "The Tenant Rising at Livingston Manor, May 1777," *New-York Historical Society Quarterly* 48 (April 1964): 163-77, and "Capitalism, Democracy, and the United States Constitution: The Case of New York," *Science and Society* 27 (Fall 1963): 385-414. Lynd's articles appear in revised form in *Class Conflict, Slavery, and the United States Constitution: Ten Essays* (Indianapolis: Bobbs-Merrill Co., 1967).

[7]Staughton Lynd, "The Revolution and the Common Man: Farm Tenants and Artisans in New York Politics, 1777-1788" (Ph.D. diss., Columbia University, 1962) and "The Mechanics in New York Politics, 1774-1788," *Labor History* 5 (Fall 1964): 225-46; Lynd and Alfred F. Young, "After Carl Becker: The Mechanics and New York City Politics, 1774-1801," ibid., pp. 215-24; Roger J. Champagne, "Liberty Boys and Mechanics of New York City, 1764-1774," ibid. 8 (Spring 1967); and L. Jesse Lemisch, "Jack Tar vs. John Bull: The Role of New York's Seaman in Precipitating the Revolution" (Ph.D. diss., Yale University, 1962) and "Jack Tar in the Streets: Merchant Seamen in the Politics of Revolutionary America," *William and Mary Quarterly* 25 (July 1968): 371-407.

was not between the privileged and the underprivileged but was rather between two groups within the ruling aristocracy,"[8] whereas Alfred F. Young sees the Revolution as much more than a dual struggle for home rule and between home rulers. "If anything," he has suggested, "New York had not a two-way, but a three-way conflict: between Whigs and the British abetted by Loyalists, who were more numerous and powerful than in any other northern colony; between 'popular' Whigs and conservative Whigs who vied for control of the Revolution on behalf of different interests; and between tenants and 'manor lords,' both Whig and Tory, for land."[9] Still others have reexamined the overall philosophical and programatic thrust of the Revolution. Both L. Jesse Lemisch and Bernard Friedman reject the Becker idea of a radical-conservative dichotomy, but where the former sees the Revolution as "the outgrowth of a struggle between liberals and radicals,"[10] the latter emphasizes the "middle class character of Revolutionary radicalism."[11]

The most systematic assaults on the Becker thesis have come from Bernard Mason and Robert E. Brown. From his recent investigation of the independence movement in New York, Mason concludes that, among other things, Becker greatly exaggerated both the degree of class solidarity and the number of Tories and trimmers.[12] Brown, in an historiographical study of Becker, argues that not only was there "an absence of internal revolution" in New York but Becker's own evidence, properly evaluated, "points to a middle-class, democratic society living under an

---

[8]"The Sons of Liberty and the Aristocracy in New York Politics, 1765-1790" (Ph.D. diss., University of Wisconsin, 1960), p. iv.

[9]*The Democratic-Republicans of New York: The Origins, 1763-1797* (Chapel Hill, N.C.: University of North Carolina Press, 1967), p. 11.

[10]"New York's Petitions and Resolves of December 1765: Liberals vs. Radicals," *New-York Historical Society Quarterly* 49 (October 1965): 326. A similar analysis of later events is Roger J. Champagne, "New York and the Intolerable Acts, 1774," ibid. 45 (April 1961): 195-207, and "New York's Radicals and the Coming of Independence," *Journal of American History* 51 (June 1964): 21-50.

[11]"The Shaping of the Radical Consciousness in Provincial New York," *Journal of American History* 56 (March 1970): 800.

[12]*The Road to Independence: The Revolutionary Movement in New York, 1773-1777* (Lexington, Ky.: University of Kentucky Press, 1966); see also "The Heritage of Carl Becker" (footnote 4).

imperial system which the people opposed when the British attempted to make it effective." The question of home rule, then,
was fundamental: New York waged a war for independence "to preserve the kind of democracy it enjoyed, not to achieve a new
kind of lower-class democracy."[13] Yet for all the revisions,
refinements, and repudiations, Becker's, as the sole comprehensive study of New York during the prerevolutionary decade, remains the standard history of the period.

Although Charles Beard did not deal specifically with the
confederation era, by implication it was not a "critical period"
and the Articles of Confederation constituted a viable, if
somewhat defective, instrument of government. E. Wilder Spauld-
ing provided confirmation of this view by arguing that for New
York the half decade 1783-88 was "not a period of static futil-
ity, but one of movement, of vigorous reconstruction" that left
the state "well recovered" from the dislocations of the war and
"on the way toward vigorous maturity." The politics of the era,
which culminated in the contest over the Constitution, was the
saga of "the supremacy of George Clinton, with his following of
small, democratic farmers, and its challenge by Alexander Hamilton and his party of merchants and great proprietors."[14]
Forrest McDonald, an ardent critic of Beard, agrees that "New
York's experiment in independence was eminently successful" and
that the state "had little reason to adopt any plan for a general government" because "it was prosperous and contended with
the government it had." Nonetheless, he contends that an "economic interpretation of the constitution does not work" in New
York because "neither party to the conflict had a monopoly on
economic interests of any kind." Although it was capable of
maintaining an independent existence exclusive of union, the
state finally succumbed to external pressures (including ratification by other states) and internal threats (primarily secession by New York City.)[15] A recent study of the ratifica-

---

[13]*Carl Becker on History and the American Revolution* (East
Lansing, Mich.: Spartan Press, 1970), p. 57.

[14]*New York in the Critical Period, 1783-1789* (New York: Columbia University Press, 1932), pp. 3-4. Thomas Cochran, *New York
in the Confederation: An Economic Study* (Philadelphia: University of Pennsylvania Press, 1932), and Clarence E. Miner, *The
Ratification of the Federal Constitution by the State of New
York* (New York: Columbia University Press, 1921), also offer
traditional Beardian analyses.

[15]*We the People: The Economic Origins of the Constitution* (Chicago: University of Chicago Press, 1958), pp. vii, 296, 300,
417.

tion row explicitly rejects an economic format. Finding the
evidence for a socioeconomic interpretation to be "especially
scanty and contradictory," Linda Grant De Pauw interprets the
struggle as a political-constitutional issue. Her analysis of
the campaign for the Constitution "reveals that Antifederalism,
in New York State at least, was compatible with a strong attachment to the Union and a sincere desire to augment the power of
the central government, and that the final vote at the Poughkeepsie Convention was probably as much a victory for the Antifederalists as for the Federalists."[16]
    There is also disagreement over the extent to which pre-
revolutionary issues and alignments persisted after independence. Both Alfred F. Young and Staughton Lynd point to con-
tinuities in personnel, principles, and interests among the
conservative Whigs, nationalists, and Federalists on the one
hand, and the radical Whigs, Antifederalists, and Democratic-
Republicans on the other.[17] But according to Linda Grant De
Pauw, "New York State politics were much more heated in the
nineties than they had been in the Confederation decade," and
"parties drew new lines that cut across far too many old loyal-
ties to be considered mere continuations of the Federalist-Anti-
federalist division."[18]
    Alexander C. Flick once predicted that "any one who will
take the pains to study the original sources of the State during the Revolutionary period will realize that the Revolution
was not a simple struggle but [was] tremendously complex and
kaleidoscopic."[19] So that the student might experience the
agony and the ecstasy of the historian, I have assembled representative documents illustrating the causes, course, and consequences of the Revolution in New York. In so doing I have proceeded on the assumption that the reader possesses a general
knowledge of the period from 1763 to 1789 and on his own will
provide a larger context for the New York material. The volume
has a twofold purpose: to impart increased understanding of and
empathy for the revolutionary era through a rather intensive
investigation of the experience of a single state, and, as Carl

---

[16]*The Eleventh Pillar: New York State and the Federal Constitution* (Ithaca, N.Y.: Cornell University Press, 1966) p. xiii.

[17]Young, *Democratic-Republicans of New York*, pp. 32, 566-67;
Lynd, *Anti-Federalism in Dutchess County*, pp. 3-4.

[18]*The Eleventh Pillar*, p. 279.

[19]*The American Revolution in New York: Its Political, Social,
and Economic Significance* (Albany, N.Y.: University of the
State of New York, 1926), p. 1.

Becker would have it, to enable every man to be his own historian.

Historians, professional and amateur alike, encounter two pervasive problems in assaying the records of the past. First, the historian must weigh the evidence. What do the documents say and what is left unsaid? How can contradictory material be resolved? Are all sources equally valid? Which conclusions follow logically from the facts? Second, and more important, the historian must refine the raw data by asking appropriate questions. Is the relationship between events sequential or consequential? What relative importance should be assigned to political, economic, and social factors, to mundane and metaphysical considerations? Is there a discrepancy between rhetoric and reality? What is the role of chance and circumstance as opposed to calculation and conviction? What do the documents reveal about human behavior and the process of history? What is the meaning of such descriptive terms as *conservative, moderate, liberal,* and *radical*? More specifically, what was the origin and outcome of the Revolution? Which term best describes the imperial conflict—*revolution, civil war,* or *war for independence*? How revolutionary was the Revolution? What is the salient feature of the period from 1763 to 1789—change or continuity, conflict or consensus? Does the federal Constitution represent the culmination of the Revolution or a betrayal of the principles of '76? The documents in this collection will not solve all these problems; indeed, they will undoubtedly raise as many questions as they answer. In the final analysis the historian is limited as much by the quality of his queries as by the quantity of extant evidence.

A few words concerning the nature of this collection are in order. Because the historical record belongs primarily to the victors instead of to the vanquished, students are familiar with the thoughts and deeds of the Founding Fathers but are unfamiliar with those of the Loyalists and the Antifederalists. The resultant perspective often produces a distorted picture of Revolutionary America. To sharpen the focus the selections are weighted slightly in favor of those who opposed independence and the federal Constitution. Because it is impracticable to provide balanced coverage of the entire revolutionary era, I have concentrated on three pivotal episodes—the Stamp Act crisis, the transition from royal to republican government, and the constitutional controversy of 1787-88. Materials of intercolonial or national character—for example, the Continental Association of 1774, the Declaration of Independence, and the Constitution—have been excluded on the grounds that they are readily available elsewhere. Nor are documents pertaining to the military conduct of the war or the British occupation of New York City included. And because it is difficult to trace socioeconomic developments through literary sources, the selections are mostly political. Finally, it is impossible in a compilation of this kind to capture the pathos of the period—the hopes and fears, the suffering and sacrifice, the temerity and timidity, the vision and venality of a people who experienced nearly a quarter century of civil disorder, armed conflict, economic dislocation, and the momentous transformation from dependent colony to independent state and nation.

The selections that follow are for the most part excerpts rather than full texts. Deletions within sentences and paragraphs are designated by an ellipsis (. . .); five dots indicate the deletion of an entire paragraph or more. Because suggestive introductions and headnotes would violate the spirit and negate the purpose of both this volume and the series of which it is a part, I have provided only the minimum chronology and background information necessary to place the documents in proper historical perspective. For readers who are interested in further research on the subject, the selected bibliography contains references to the basic published collections of source material.

Three friends have made this a better book. I should like to thank Arthur Zilversmit for his encouragement and editorial assistance, Sung Bok Kim for his wise counsel and warm comradeship, and Ronald M. Gephart for sharing his bibliographic expertise.

The American History Research Series

William R. Taylor
State University of New York at Stony Brook

Arthur Zilversmit
Lake Forest College

General Editors

The American Revolution: New York as a Case Study
Larry R. Gerlach, University of Utah

Salem-Village Witchcraft: A Documentary Record of Local Conflict in Colonial New England
Paul Boyer and Stephen Nissenbaum,
University of Massachusetts, Amherst

The Great Awakening at Yale College
Stephen Nissenbaum, University of Massachusetts,
Amherst

The Response to John Brown
Richard Scheidenhelm

Lincoln on Black and White: A Documentary History
Arthur Zilversmit, Lake Forest College

Forthcoming

Thomas Mott Osborne and Prison Reform
Jack M. Holl, Williams College

The Passaic Textile Strike
Paul L. Murphy, University of Minnesota

The Negro in the New Deal
Paul B. Worthman, Wellesley College, and
Linda Gratz Worthman

Contents

General Chronology

1764:	April 5	Sugar Act of 1764 enacted
1765:	March 22	Stamp Act signed (effective November 1)
	October 7-25	Stamp Act Congress meets in New York City
1766:	March 18	Stamp Act repealed; Declaratory Act passed
	June 6	Revenue Act of 1766 enacted
1767:	June 29	Townshend duties enacted
1770:	March 5	Boston "Massacre"
	April 12	Townshend duties repealed except the tax on tea
1773:	May 10	Tea Act passed
	December 16	Boston "Tea Party"
1774:	March 31-June 2	"Coercive Acts" passed
	September 5-October 26	First Continental Congress meets in Philadelphia
	October 20	Congress adopts the Continental Association
1775:	April 19	Battles of Lexington and Concord
	May 10	Second Continental Congress convenes in Philadelphia
	June 17	Battle of Bunker Hill
1776:	July 4	Congress adopts the Declaration of Independence

1777:	October 17	General Burgoyne surrenders at Saratoga
	November 15	Congress adopts the Articles of Confederation
1778:	February 6	Franco-American alliance consummated
1781:	March 1	Articles of Confederation ratified
	October 19	Lord Cornwallis surrenders at Yorktown
1782:	November 30	Preliminary articles of peace signed
1783:	September 3	Treaty of Paris signed; ratified by Congress January 14, 1784
1787:	May 25– September 17	Constitutional Convention meets in Philadelphia
1788:	June 21	Constitution operative with the assent of New Hampshire

Chapter one:

Prologue to Rebellion, 1764-66

The struggle between Great Britain and France from 1756 to
1763, the last of a series of wars for colonial hegemony in
North America, ranks as one of those momentous historical
events that deserve the label *turning point*. For the war—
whether designated the Seven Years War, the French and Indian
War, or the Great War for the Empire—was the catalyst that
precipitated the deterioration of Anglo-American relations,
which eventually led to the first successful anticolonial war
for independence in modern history. Although in the long run
the removal of the French threat gave greater latitude to colonial action vis-à-vis the mother country, the immediate import
of the war for the coming of the Revolution was the exposure of
serious defects in the imperial administrative system and the
subsequent attempts by the British government to resolve those
problems.

To deal with the exigencies of postwar America, the British appointed two superintendents for Indian affairs to regu-
larize Indian-white relations, issued the Proclamation of 1763
to systematize westward expansion, dispatched 7,500 troops to
the trans-Appalachian west to pacify hostile Indians and con-
quered Frenchmen, extended the annual Mutiny Act to North
America to provide for the governance and maintenance of the
army, enacted the Currency Act of 1764 to stabilize currency,
and reorganized the customs service to facilitate enforcement
of commercial regulations.

However, it is one thing to formulate a program of reform
and quite another to finance it. Faced with an unprecedented
national debt of approximately £140,000,000 (a near twofold
increase since 1755) and an already overtaxed citizenry, the
British ministry not surprisingly looked to America for an
additional source of income. To raise sufficient revenue to
defray one-third of the estimated £350,000 required to finance
the army, the two Indian departments, and the civil governments

of Nova Scotia, Florida, and Georgia, Parliament enacted the
Sugar Act of 1764 and the Stamp Act of 1765.

Americans opposed both exactions. But whereas opposition
to the threepence per gallon excise on foreign molasses took
the form of petitions and remonstrances, the tax on publications and legal documents, enacted in March and scheduled to
take effect on November 1, engendered widespread violent protest. In New York the press criticized the act throughout the
summer, stamp distributor James McEvers resigned on August 30
because of threats to his person and property, and the Sons of
Liberty took to the streets in October to persuade merchants to
boycott British goods and lawyers to transact business without
stamped paper. And from October 7 to 25 the Stamp Act Congress,
composed of delegates from nine colonies, met in New York City
to present a united intercolonial front against the act. In
the wake of intransigent colonial opposition and at the urging
of the newly formed Rockingham ministry, Parliament rescinded
the Stamp Act in March 1766 but coupled repeal with the passage
of the Declaratory Act, which unequivocally asserted the legislative authority of Parliament over the colonies "in all cases
whatsoever."

1

GENERAL ASSEMBLY PETITION TO THE HOUSE OF COMMONS
October 18, 1764

. . . . .

THAT from the Year 1683, to this Day, there have been
three Legislative Branches in this Colony; consisting of the
Governor and Council appointed by the Crown, and the Representatives chosen by the People, who, besides the Power of making
Laws for the Colony, have enjoyed the Right of Taxing the Subject for the Support of the Government. . . .

. . . . .

It is therefore with equal Concern and Surprize, that they
have received Intimations of certain Designs lately formed, if

*Journal of the Votes and Proceedings of the General Assembly of
the Colony of New York, 1691-1765*, 2 vols. (New York: Hugh
Gaine, 1764-66), 2: 776-79.

possible, to induce the Parliament of *Great-Britain*, to impose
Taxes upon the Subjects *here*, by Laws to be passed *there;* and
as we who have the Honour to represent them, conceive that this
Innovation, will greatly affect the Interest of the Crown and
the Nation, and reduce the Colony to absolute Ruin; it became
our indispensible Duty, to trouble you with a seasonable Representation of the Claim of our Constituents, to an Exemption
from the Burthen of all Taxes not granted by themselves, and
their Foresight of the tragical Consequences of an Adoption of
the contrary Principle, to the Crown, the Mother Country, themselves and their Posterity.

Had the Freedom from all Taxes not granted by ourselves
been enjoyed as a *Privilege*, we are confident the Wisdom and
Justice of the *British* Parliament, would rather establish than
destroy it, unless by our abuse of it, the Forfeiture was justly incurred; but his Majesty's Colony of *New-York*, can not only
defy the whole World to impeach their Fidelity, but appeal to
all the Records of their past Transactions, as well for the
fullest Proof of their steady Affection to the Mother Country,
as for their strenuous Efforts to support the Government, and
advance the general Interest of the whole *British* Empire.

. . . . .

On no Occasion can we be justly reproached for withholding a necessary Supply, our Taxes have been equal to our
Abilities, and confessed to be so by the Crown; for Proof of
which we refer to the Speeches of our Governors in all Times of
War; and though we remember with great Gratitude, that in those
grand and united Struggles, which were lately directed for the
conquest of *Canada*, Part of our Expenses was reimbursed, yet
we cannot suppress the Remark, that our Contribution surpassed
our Strength, even in the Opinion of the Parliament, who under
that Conviction, thought it but just to take off Part of the
Burthen, to which we had loyally and voluntarily submitted; in
a Word, if there is any Merit in facilitating on all Occasions,
the publick Measures in the remote Extremes of the national
Dominion, and in preserving untainted Loyalty and chearful Obedience, it is ours; and (with Submission) unabused, nay more,
well improved Privileges cannot, ought not, to be taken away
from any People.

Nor will the Candour of the Commons of *Great Britain*, con-
strue our Earnestness to maintain this Plea, to arise from a
Desire of Independency upon the supreme Power of the Parliament.
Of so extravagant a Disregard to our own Interests we cannot be
guilty.—From what other Quarter can we hope for Protection?
We reject the Thought with the utmost Abhorrence; and a perfect
Knowledge of this Country will afford the fullest Proof, that
nothing in our Temper can give the least Ground for such a
Jealousy.

. . . . .

The Authority of the Parliament of *Great-Britain*, to model
the Trade of the whole Empire, so as to subserve the Interest
of her own, we are ready to recognize in the most extensive and
positive Terms. Such a Preference is naturally founded upon
her Superiority, and indissolubly connected with the Principle
of Self-Preservation. . . .

But a Freedom to drive all Kinds of Traffick in a Subordination to, and not inconsistent with, the *British* Trade; and an
Exemption from all Duties in such a Course of Commerce, is humbly claimed by the Colonies, as the most essential of all the
Rights to which they are intitled, as Colonists from, and connected, in the common Bond of Liberty, with the uninslaved Sons
of *Great-Britain*.

For, with Submission, since all Impositions, whether they
be internal Taxes, or Duties paid, for what we consume, equally
diminish the Estates upon which they are charged; what avails
it to any People, by which of them they are impoverished?
Every Thing will be given up to preserve Life; and though there
is a Diversity in the Means, yet, the whole Wealth of a Country
may be as effectually drawn off, by the Exaction of Duties, as
by any other Tax upon their Estates.

And therefore, the General Assembly of *New-York*, in Fidelity to their Constituents, cannot but express the most earnest
Supplication, that the Parliament will charge our Commerce with
no other Duties, than a necessary Regard to the particular
Trade of *Great-Britain*, evidently demands; but leave it to the
legislative Power of the Colony, to impose all other Burthens
upon it's own People, which the publick Exigences may require.

Latterly, the Laws of Trade seem to have been framed without an Attention to this fundamental Claim.

. . . . .

The honourable House will permit us to observe next, that
the Act of the last Session of Parliament, inhibiting all Intercourse between the Continent and the foreign Sugar Colonies,
will prove equally detrimental to us and *Great-Britain*.—*That*
Trade, gave a value to a vast, but now alas unsaleable Staple,
which being there converted into Cash and Merchandize, made
necessary Remittances for the *British* Manufactures we con-
sumed. . . . And when we consider the Wisdom of our Ancestors
in contriving Trials by Juries, we cannot stifle our Regret,
that the Laws of Trade in general, change the Current of Justice from the common Law, and subject Controversies of the utmost Importance to the Decisions of the Vice-Admiralty Courts,
who proceed not according the old wholesom Laws of the Land,
nor are always filled with Judges of approved Knowledge and
Integrity.—To this Objection, the aforementioned Statute will
at first View appear to be so evidently open, that we shall
content ourselves with barely suggesting, that the amazing Confidence it reposes in the Judges, gives great Grief to his

Majesty's *American* Subjects; and pass on to a few Remarks on that other Law of the same Session, which renders our Paper Money no legal Tender.

The Use of this Sort of Currency in procuring a speedy Supply on Emergencies, all the Colonies have often experienced.—We have had Recourse to this Expedient in every War, since the Reign of King *William* the Third; and without it we could not have co-operated so vigorously in the Reduction of *Canada*, that grand stroke which secured to *Great-Britain*, the immense Dominion of the Continent of *North-America*. We had no other Alternative but *that*, or the taking up Money upon Loan, Lenders could not have been easily found, and if they were, the Interest upon all the Sums raised in that Way, would have exceeded our Ability now to discharge. Happy for us, therefore, that we fell upon the Project of giving a Credit to Paper, which was always supported by seasonable Taxes on our Estates; the Currency of the Bills being prolonged only till we were able to burn up the Quantity from Time to Time emitted.—Our Laws, or the Copies transmitted to the Plantation Office, will evince that of the numerous Emissions we have made since the first, which was on the 8th of *June*, 1709, all were for the urgent Service of the Crown. . . . We wish his Majesty's Service may suffer no Impediment, by this new Restraint in an Article which has been of so much Utility.—The Traffick of the Colony certainly will, for want of a competent Medium; and on that Account, and in behalf of those miserable Debtors, whose Estates, through the Scarcity of legal Cash, must be extended by Executions, and hastily sold beneath their true Value, to the Ruin of many Families, permit us to implore your tender Commiseration.

The General Assembly of this Colony have no desire to derogate from the Power of the parliament of *Great-Britain*; but they cannot avoid deprecating the Loss of such Rights as they have hitherto enjoyed, Rights established in the first Dawn of our Constitution, founded upon the most substantial Reasons, confirmed by invariable Usage, conducive to the best Ends; never abused to bad Purposes, and with the Loss, of which Liberty, Property, and all the Benefits of Life, tumble into Insecurity and Ruin: Rights, the Deprivation of which, will dispirit the People, abate their Industry, discourage Trade, introduce Discord, Poverty and Slavery; or, by depopulating the Colonies, turn a vast, fertile, prosperous Region, into a dreary Wilderness; impoverish *Great-Britain*, and shake the Power and Independency of the most opulent and flourishing Empire in the World.

. . . . .

2

WILLIAM SMITH, JR., TO GENERAL ROBERT MONCKTON
New York, May 30, 1765

. . . . .
The new Tax gives the highest Disgust.—Considered in itself the Duties are thought to be beyond all reasonable
Bounds.—The Poverty of our People, and the frequent Transfer
of Lands in this Country, extendable also by Act of Parliament
even for simple Contract Debts, 'tis imagined, were good Reasons for lower Duties here than in great Britain: And the Restrictions upon our Commerce, as they shorten our Purses, ought
to have reduced the Stamps to so small a Duty, as to be inferior to the first Imposition of that sort in the Mother Country.—These now enacted, unless a freer Vent is given to our
Staple, I am perswaded will soon draw out all the little silver
and gold we have or can procure, distress us to an Extremity
and frustrate the very End of the Law.—But when the Americans
reflect upon the Parliament's Refusal to hear their Representations—when they read Abstracts of the Speeches within Doors,
and the Ministerial Pamphlets without, and find themselves
tantalized and contemned, Advantage taken of their Silence
heretofore, and Remonstrances forbidden in Time to come; and
above all, when they see the Prospect of innumerable Loads,
arising from their Connection with an over-burdened Nation, interested in shaking the Weight off their own Shoulders, and
commanding Silence in the oppressed Beast upon which it is
cast, what can be expected but Discontent for a while, and in
the End open Opposition.—The Boldness of the Minister amazes

William H. W. Sabine, ed., *Historical Memoirs from 16 March to
12 November 1783, of William Smith*, 3 vols. (New York: Colburn
and Tegg, Publishers, 1956, 1958, 1971), 1: 29. Reprinted with
permission of the publisher. Perhaps the preeminent New York
attorney of his day, Smith (1728-93) held numerous prestigious
offices including chief justice (1763-76) and councillor
(1767-76). A leader of the Presbyterian Whigs along with William Livingston and John Morin Scott, Smith actively partici-
pated in the protest movement but could not support independence. He left for England when the British evacuated New York
City in 1783 and emigrated to Canada, where he served as chief
justice from 1785 to 1793. Monckton (1726-82), who gained high
military honors as a general during the Great War for the Empire, served as governor of New York from 1761 to 1763.

our People.—This single Stroke has lost Great Britain the Affection of all her Colonies. . . .

3

NEW YORK CITY BOYCOTT AGREEMENT   October 31, 1765

At a general Meeting of the Merchants of the City of New-
York, trading to Great-Britain, . . . to consider what was necessary to be done in the present Situation of Affairs, with
respect to the STAMP ACT, and the melancholy State of the
North-American Commerce, so greatly restricted by the Impositions and Duties established by the late Acts of Trade: They
came to the following Resolutions, viz.

FIRST, That in all Orders they send out to Great-Britain,
for Goods or Merchandize, of any Nature, Kind or Quality whatsoever, usually imported from Great-Britain, they will direct
their Correspondents not to ship them, unless the STAMP ACT be
repealed: It is nevertheless agreed, that all such Merchants as
are Owners of, and have Vessels already gone, and now cleared
out for Great-Britain, shall be at Liberty to bring back in
them, on their own Accounts, Crates and Casks of Earthen Ware,
Grindstones, Pipes, and such other bulky Articles, as Owners
usually fill up their Vessels with.

SECONDLY, It is further unanimously agreed, that all Orders already sent Home, shall be countermanded by the very
first Conveyance; and the Goods and Merchandize thereby ordered,
not to be sent, unless upon the Condition mentioned in the
foregoing Resolution.

THIRDLY, It is further unanimously agreed, that no Merchant will vend any Goods or Merchandize sent upon Commission
from Great-Britain, that shall be shipped from thence after the
first Day of January next, unless upon the Condition mentioned
in the first Resolution.

FOURTHLY, It is further unanimously agreed, that the foregoing Resolutions shall be binding until the same are abrogated
at a general Meeting hereafter to be held for that Purpose.

[Signed by upwards of 200 "principal Merchants"]
In consequence of the foregoing Resolutions the Retailers
of Goods of the City of New York subscribed a Paper in the
Words following, viz.

We, the under-written Retailers of Goods, do hereby promise and oblige ourselves not to buy any Goods, Wares, or Merchandizes of any Person or Persons whatsoever that shall be
shipped from Great-Britain after the first day of January next
unless the STAMP ACT shall be repealed. . . .

4

ROBERT R. LIVINGSTON TO ROBERT MONCKTON

New York, November 8, 1765

Your Excellency's esteemed favour of the 12th of May,
which I had the great pleasure of receiving some time ago,
would not have emboldened me so much as to be troublesome to
you again by another long letter . . . if events of the most
extraordinary nature, and such as, I believe, you would chuse
to receive a full information of, had not lately happened.
They were such as had liked to have reduced this City to a
State, the most deplorable & shocking imaginable; and God only
knows, how dismal the consequences yet may be. At present, it
bears the face, rather of a Comedy, than of a Tragedy. Your
Excellency will doubtless hear, long before this comes to your
hands, with what a general disgust the first Act, imposing Internal Taxes on the Colonies, was received. The distributors
appointed for all the Colonies have resigned their offices, or
have been obliged to desist from all attempts to carry the Act
into execution. M^r McEvers appointed for this office, finding
it odious to his fellow-citizens, resigned early; and by that
means, prevented those compulsions, which were made use of in

Aspinwall Papers, Collections, 4th ser., 9-10 (Boston: Massachusetts Historical Society, 1871), 10: 559-67. The only son
of Robert Livingston, proprietor of Clermont, Livingston Manor,
Robert R. Livingston (1718-75) served from 1758 to 1768 as
assemblyman from Dutchess County and from 1763 until his death
as puisne justice of the supreme court. A Whig, he opposed the
thrust of post-1763 British imperial policy.

the neighboring Colonies. In this, we thought ourselves happy & those, who were fond of peace & were real friends to the
prosperity of the Country hoped, that we should be free from
all further disturbances and remain in perfect quiet; but when
the stamped paper began to be expected, about the beginning of
September, the Lieut-Governour ordered a Man-of-war to guard
the Ship, in which they were to come, and began to fortify the
Fort for their reception. These proceedings (as every thing
done by this man has long been odious, from an excessive personal hatred to him) very much irritated the minds of the
Citizens, already too much inflamed by a number of Publications
in the Newspaper, which the Government did not dare to punish,
for fear of adding still more fuel to a very dangerous Fire.
When the Ship with the Stamps arrived, which was the 23d of
October, it was announced to the City by the firing of several
cannon from one of the Men-of-war, at about 10 o'clock at night,
and the next day the ship was convoyed into the harbor by a
Man-of-War and a tender, with great parade. A vast number of
people beheld this sight, and, it is said, appeared most furi-
ously inraged. In the mean time the Fort was constantly endeavoured to be rendered more & more respectable by additional
preparations for defence, which the citizens continued to look
on as an Insult. Whether this put it in the heads of some rash
men to form a design of attacking the fort, I know not, neither
is it absolutely certain, that such a design was formed. About
a day or two after Davis's arrival with the stamps, Papers were
posted up in the night in several parts of the Town, entitled
Vox Populi, bidding the persons who first made use of Stamped
papers, to take care of *House, Person, & Effects*, which appeared by the hand, tho' a disguised one, to be written by a
person not very ill educated. A number of such publications
followed this and threatened vengeance, in terms, the most
terrifying imaginable, till the first of November approached;
which was termed the last day of Liberty. On the day preceding
it, the Merchants of the City met at Barns's Tavern, the House
of James Delancy . . . and came to a Resolution, to send for no
goods from England, and sell none, should they be consigned to
them, except the Stamp act was repealed. At the door of this
house, a number of boys & sailors appeared, imagining that
there was a design to execute some foolish ceremony of burying
Liberty; which it seems had been talked of; but when they found
that the Merchants peaceably separated, and that there was no
shew to be exhibited, they proceeded through the streets, in a
mobbish manner, whistling and hurraing. This ended without
mischief, except the breaking of a few glass windows. On the
night of the first of November, there passed through the
streets a mob, the most formidable imaginable. The Mayor & Aldermen had met at the City Hall, in order to prevent any thing
of the sort, and at its commencement, endeavored to oppose it

with their Constables, & threw down the Effigy they were carrying, but the persons attending ordered it to be taken up
again in the most Magisterial manner, and told the Mayor &c^a,
they would not hurt them, provided they stood out of their way.
They were obliged to yield, and the mob proceeded,—the numbers
of the Actors and Spectators were inconceivably great,—and
they went on with the greatest order, carrying candles and
torches in their hands, and now & then firing a pistol at the
Effigy, which was carried in a chair.   As I was convinced no
good was to be done by going out, (for it was supposed to design no more than to expose a man universally odious, nobody
would have assisted in suppressing them), I saw no more of all
this nights transaction, than their passing twice by my door.
The second time with the Governors Chariot, taken out of the
Coach house at the Fort.   While this was doing, a number of
other men were employed in making a gallows and hanging thereon
the effigy of the Governor and the Devil.   This they went from
the common to the Fort with, and there placed it, as the Lieut.
Governor has since told me, within ten feet of the Fort walls.
Here it is impossible sufficiently to admire and commend the
patience & temper of the officers and soldiers.   The Populace
knocked at the gate, placed their hands on the top of the Ram-
parts, called out to the guards to fire, threw bricks & stones
against the Fort and notwithstanding the highest provocation
was given, not a word was returned to the most opprobrious
language.   From this description, you will perhaps conclude
that it was the design of the people to provoke a fire.   I must
leave you to judge from appearances.   I can do no more.
     After this, the gallows with the Effigies were carried in-
to the Bowling Green, where they were burnt with the Chariot &
chair, belonging to another person, and almost every moveable,
they could find in the Stables.   The fire was kindled with the
boards of that part of the Fort fence, which faces Broadway.
This had been broke down before by the Garrison in order to expose the Assailants to the fire of the Fort, and was a new
cause of dissatisfaction to the People.   From thence, after the
Execution, they went to Major James's house, who was become an
object of their hatred for having said, as was reported that he
would cram down the Stamp Act upon them with a hundred men.
They brought out of his house all they could find, drank his
liquors, and burnt and destroyed every thing else before the
door.   I hear he computes his loss at Fifteen Hundred pounds
sterling.   Thus, with an attack on some bawdy houses, the mischief ended for this night.   And here we hoped all farther designs would have been dropped.   But the next day, it was pub-
lickly reported, that an attack would be made, at night, on the
Fort, and that nothing would satisfy them, but the delivery of
the Stamps.   This, I own, surprized me much.   I heard the Mayor
and Aldermen were met in order to consult the peace of the Town,

at the City Hall. Thither I went a volunteer, sent for the
Mayor out, and told him that if they were on that business, I
came to offer them all the assistance in my power. He received
the offer with great cordiality, and immediately introduced me.
I found the whole body extremely dejected, and I could not find,
that they had formed any one design, except that of waiting for
a message from the Council who were to tell them what concessions the Governor would make, to quiet the minds of the people.
Proposals were then made, to draw out the militia, and to form
an Association. But despondency and irresolution prevailed
over all, and the power of the Magistrate was sunk. At last
came a message from the Governor, acquainting the Corporation,
that he would distribute no Stamp papers, except they were
called for, and was willing to put them aboard a Man-of-War, if
Capt. Kennedy would take them; and this was all he would condescend to say, in order to quiet the Ferment, he had been so
imprudently instrumental in raising. He has since told me, in
the presence of several other gentlemen, that he had wrote to
the Ministry a fortnight before, that he should not meddle with
those papers, till he received farther directions. Had he con-
descended to say this, in time, all would have been quieted,
and he would even have acquired some degree of popularity, instead of those gross and mortifying affronts, he has received,
and the City would have continued in peace, at least till a new
Distributor was appointed. However, this being all he conde-
scended to say, we agreed to put it in as favorable a light, as
we could, and to endeavor, with this, to quiet the people; and
also, by shewing them the folly of attacking the Fort, if such
a thing was really intended. For this purpose, Mr Duane put
me I think, on the most prudent measure, and what contributed
more than any other thing to success. He observed, that as the
disturbances had & would probably begin amongst the Sailors,
the most likely method would be to apply ourselves to those
captains that had commanded privateers. This we immediately
put in execution and with good success, tho' we found the minds
of several much inflamed. One came immediately into our measures. With him we went round to every part of the Town, spoke
to many persons, found the highest resentment against the Lieut.
Governor every where prevailing, and every now and then had
hints of the intended design, tho' we could no where find any
number assembled. The party, however by many gentlemen's taking the same measures, speaking to and persuading all they met,
was certainly divided. After patrolling in this manner for
some time, seeing no collection of men any where we supposed
all would be quiet. At last resolving to go to Major James's
house, where the mischief ended, out of one of the houses on
the Church ground, facing the Commons, we saw seven or eight
men issue, with candles lighted, and a Barbers Block, on a pole,
dressed up with a parcel of Raggs. We immediately ran up to

them, and soon prevailed on one half of the number to desist.
The others continued obstinate and in a very short time, a
strange sett poured in, from all quarters, so that we soon had
about us above two hundred men. We divided them. Some were
for going on, others for desisting as the Governor had now
given satisfaction enough. Thus we continued a long time prevailing with some, while others made attempts to proceed. Expressions dropped, which shewed but too plainly, they had all
met to execute this mad project. Never before this, could I
think that this was really intended. While we remained in this
suspense, at last came from the Governor a Declaration of his
in Council, that he would not meddle with the Stamps at all.
This divided them in such a manner, that we at last defeated
the purposes of the most turbulent. During all this time it
was not thought advisable to exert the authority of the Magis-
tracy. The next day, being Sunday, a letter was wrote to the
Custom House officers, threatening destruction, if they did not
clear out vessels as usual, deliver up all the money & notes,
they had taken for duties. Another was put up at the Coffee
House, telling them they must not mind the peaceable orators,
who had prevented them on Saturday night, that they should be
resolute, they would be commanded by men, who had given proofs
of their courage, in the defence of their country. This was
subscribed *The Sons of Neptune*, and plainly fixed the time for
the assault, to the fifth of November, which was Tuesday. It
was high time, now, for those inclined to keep the peace of the
City, to rouse their sleeping courage. A meeting was appointed
for that purpose, to be on Monday, and all the Citizens were
invited to be at the Coffee House at about ten o'clock. There
tho' all came to form a union, few cared openly to declare the
necessity of it; so intimidated were they at the secret unknown
party which, had threatened such bold things, and had put the
Fort in such terrors, that every day new measures were taken to
put it in a posture of defence. This continual adding to the
strength of the Fort kept up the dissatisfaction of the people
and made every report of the strength and preparations of the
party who, it was said, designed to attack it, more credible.
I ventured however, to tell them that it was high time to form
a resolution to keep the peace, and to enter into an engagement
for that purpose, and set before them, in as strong a light as
I could, all the terrors of a Mob Government, in such a city as
this. All agreed to this, tho' some dreading the secret party,
who called themselves *Vox Populi*, thought I declared my sentiments too freely. I soon after heard I was threatened. However, what was said made its due impression, and that evening
many of those that determined to keep the peace met and went
out into the Common to quell any new disturbances and at night
several Captains of Vessels and others met together at a tavern,
and sent word to the Mayor and Corporation, that they were

resolved to join in the design to keep the peace, but hoped the
Governor, for the quieting mens' minds perfectly, would execute
his first purpose of putting the Stamps on board a Man-of-war.
They, to whom these cruel papers had occasioned so much uneasiness, had sent to Capt. Kennedy, to desire him to receive them;
but he refused; and the next morning, being the 5th of November,
the day, which all feared, as we did not know, but, by an attack on the Fort, an open Rebellion would be commenced, tho'
we could not tell by whom or how formidable this *Vox Populi*
was. The Corporation met, and proposals were made in writing
to the Governor, to take the Stamps into their own custody, in
consequence of a question he had asked the Mayor, to wit;
whether he would take them and a desire at the same time that
proposals might be made him in writing. And tho' the Governor
has since confessed to me, that the proposal was agreeable to
him, and all the inhabitants were collected at the City Hall,
at 4 o'clock, in the afternoon, to know whether tranquillity
would be restored by his agreement, yet he would not signify
his consent till the evening, nor then, till he had got the
General to signify his assent to a matter, he had nothing to do
with. This the General however readily did, for he knew the
security for them by the Corporation was quite sufficient; for
all agreed to protect them in their hands, and the Government
would have got more by their destruction, than by their preservation. Thus at last, tranquillity is restored by the humanity
of one gentleman, which was so unnecessarily disturbed by the
perverseness of another. As many different accounts of this
matter will go home, I thought it necessary to be thus prolix.
Your Excellency will see by this account, that the enforcing
the Stamp Act will be attended with the destruction of all Law
Order & Government in the Colonies, and ruin all men of property, for such is the temper of people's minds, from one end of
the Continent to the other, that whoever carries his opposition
to this Act, to the greatest excess, will be most followed, and
will force the rest into their measures. Therefore, we beg, as
for life and all its comforts, from every person that can aid
us, that this Act may be repealed. If it be not, it is impossible for the wisest man on earth to tell how far its mischievous consequences will extend. Britain will suffer more by it,
in one year, in her trade, than this tax, or any other,—should
others be imposed,—can ever recompence. Merchants have resolved to send for no more British manufactures, Shopkeepers
will buy none, Gentlemen will wear none,—our own are encouraged, all pride in dress seems to be laid aside, and he that
does not appear in Homespun, or at least a turned coat, is
looked on with an evil eye. The Lawyers will not issue a writ.
Merchants will not clear out a vessel. These are all facts not
in the least exaggerated; and it is of importance that they
should be known. But the worst of all is this; that should the

Act be enforced there is the utmost danger, I speak it with the greatest concern imaginable, of a civil war. . . .

5

GENERAL ASSEMBLY STAMP ACT RESOLVES   December 18, 1765

The General Assembly of the Colony of *New-York*, taking into their most serious Consideration, several Acts of Parliament lately passed, granting Stamp, and other Duties to his Majesty, and restricting the Trade of this Colony, apprehending an Abolition of that Constitution under which they have so long and happily enjoyed the Rights and Liberties of *Englishmen*, and being clearly of Opinion that it is the Interest of *Great-Britain*, a Dependence on which they esteem their Felicity, to confirm them in the Enjoyment of those Rights, think it their indispensible Duty to make a Declaration of their Faith and Allegiance to his Majesty King GEORGE the Third, of their Submission to the Supreme Legislative Power; and at the same Time to shew that the Rights claimed by them are in no Manner inconsistent with either: For which Purpose they are come to the following Resolutions, *that is to say:*
    Resolved, Nemine Contradicente, That the People of this Colony owe the same Faith and Allegiance to his Majesty King GEORGE the Third, that are due to him from his Subjects in *Great-Britain*.
    Resolved, . . . That they owe Obedience to all Acts of Parliament not inconsistent with the essential Rights and Liberties of *Englishmen*, and are intitled to the same Rights and Liberties which his Majesty's *English* Subjects both within and without the Realm have ever enjoyed.
    Resolved, . . . That his Majesty's Subjects in *England*, are secured in the superior Advantages they enjoy principally, by the Privilege of an Exemption from Taxes not of their own Grant, and their Right to Trials by their Peers.—The First secures the People collectively from unreasonable Impositions; and without the Second, Individuals are at the arbitrary Disposition of the executive Powers.

Resolved, . . . That the Colonists did not forfeit these essential Rights by their Emigration; because *this* was by the Permission and Encouragement of the Crown; and that they rather merit Favour, than a Deprivation of those Rights, by giving an almost boundless Extent to the *British* Empire, expanding its Trade, increasing its Wealth, and augmenting that Power which renders it so formidable to all *Europe.*

Resolved, . . . That the Acts of Trade giving a Right of Jurisdiction to the Admiralty Courts, in Prosecutions for Penalties and Forfeitures, manifestly infringes the Right of Trials by Jury; and that the late Act for granting *Stamp Duties,* not only exposes the *American* Subjects to an intolerable Inconvenience and Expence, by compelling them to a Defence at a great Distance from Home; but, by imposing a Tax, utterly deprives them of the essential Right of being the *sole* Disposers of their own Property.

Resolved, . . . That all Aids to the Crown, in *Great-Britain,* are Gifts of the People by their Representatives in Parliament, as appears from the Preamble of every Money Bill, in which the Commons are said to give and grant to his Majesty.

Resolved, . . . That it involves the greatest Inconsistency with the known Principles of the *English* Constitution, to suppose that the honourable House of Commons of *Great-Britain,* can without divesting the Inhabitants of this Colony of their most essential Rights, grant to the Crown their, or any Part of their Estates for any Purpose whatsoever.

Resolved, . . . That from the first Settlement of the Colonies, it has been the Sense of the Government at Home, that such Grants could not be constitutionally made; and therefore Applications for the Support of Government, and other publick Exigencies, have always been made to the Representatives of the People of this Colony; and frequently during the late War by immediate Orders from the Crown, upon which they exerted themselves with so much Liberality, that the Parliament thought proper to contribute to their Reimbursement.

Resolved, . . . That if the People of this Colony should be deprived of the *sole* Right of Taxing themselves, or presenting such Sums as the publick Exigencies require, they would be laid under the greatest Disadvantages, as the united Interest of the Electors, or Elected, which constitute the Security of his Majesty's Subjects in *Great-Britain,* will operate strongly against them.

Resolved, . . . That the Impracticability of inducing the Colonies to grant Aids in an equal Manner, proportioned to their several Abilities, does by no Means induce a Necessity of divesting the Colonies of their *essential Rights.*

Resolved, . . . That it is the Duty of every Friend to *Great-Britain,* and this Colony to cultivate a hearty Union between them.

Resolved, . . . That if the honourable House of Commons insist on their Power of Taxing this Colony, and by that Means deprive its Inhabitants of what they have always looked upon as an undoubted Right, though this Power should be exerted in the mildest Manner, it will teach them to consider the People of *Great-Britain*, as vested with absolute Power to dispose of all their Property, and tend to weaken that Affection for the Mother Country, which this Colony *ever had*, and is *extremely* desirous of retaining.

Resolved, . . . That in order to keep the Colonies in due Subjection to, and Dependence upon *Great-Britain*, it is not necessary to deprive them of the Right they have long enjoyed, of Taxing themselves; since the same Right has been enjoyed by the Clergy within the Realm, and by all the Subjects of *Great-Britain* without the Realm, until the late Innovation.

Resolved, . . . That the Duties lately imposed by Act of Parliament on the Trade of this Colony, are very grievous and burthensome; and in the Apprehension of this House, impossible to be paid: Have already greatly diminished the advantageous Traffic heretofore carried on with the foreign Islands in the *West-Indies*; and in consequence, must render us unable to purchase the Manufactures of *Great-Britain*.

6

GENERAL THOMAS GAGE TO HENRY SEYMOUR CONWAY
New York, December 21, 1765

In my Letter [of December 8] I had the honor to acquaint you of the Riots which had happened here on Account of the Stamp Act. Since that Time they have been employed to devise Means to carry on their Business in Trade and Law Proceedings

Clarence E. Carter, ed., *The Correspondence of General Thomas Gage . . . 1763-1775*, 2 vols. (New Haven, Conn.: Yale University Press, 1931, 1933), 1: 78-79. Reprinted with permission of the publisher. Gage (1721-87) was commander in chief of the British army in North America from 1763 to 1775. Himself a former general, Conway (1719-95) was secretary of state for the Southern Department from 1765 to 1766 and thus exercised jurisdiction over the American colonies.

without the Stampt Papers. Various Seditious and Treasonable
Papers have been Struck up, and appeared in their Gazettes en-
couraging the People to every violence, and appointing Meetings
of the Citizens to resolve upon violent Measures. The Inferior
Sort, ready for any Mischief, were for obliging the Provincial
Assembly to pass an Act to annull the Stamp Act, and afterwards
to force the Governor and Council to confirm it. They also proposed to force the Lawyers to do Business in Comtempt of the
Stamp Act. This was going too far for the better Sort to join
them, who fearing the Consequence of such Extreams, by their
Numbers and Influence quashed these Attempts of the inferior
Burgers, who Seeing themselves deserted by those who had raised
them, were obliged to desist. No Law Proceedings have been
carried on, and the Genius of the Lawyers [is] put to the Rack
to find out Pretences and means to evade or Set the Act aside.

. . . . .

The Plan of the People of Property has been to raise the
lower Class to prevent the Execution of the Law, and as far as
Riots and Tumults went against Stamp-Masters and other obstruc-
tions to the Issuing of the Stamps, they encouraged, and many
perhaps joined them. But when they tended towards Proceedings
which might be deemed Treasonable or Rebellious, Persons and
Propertys being then in Danger, they have endeavored to restrain them. They have wrote many Letters to their Correspondents in England, in which they throw the Blame upon the unruly
Populace, Magnifying the Force and determined Resolution of the
People to oppose the Execution of the Law by every Means, with
the View to terrify and Frighten the People of England into a
Repeal of the Act. And the Merchants having Countermanded the
Goods they had Wrote for unless it was repealed, they make no
Doubt that many Trading Towns and principal Merchants in London
will assist them to accomplish their Ends.

The Lawyers are the Source from whence the Clamors have
flowed in every Province. In this Province Nothing Publick is
transacted without them, and it is to be wished that even the
Bench was free from Blame. The whole Body of Merchants in general, Assembly Men, Magistrates, &c. have been united in this
Plan of Riots, and without the Influence and Instigation of
these the inferior People would have been quiet. Very great
Pains was taken to rouse them before they Stirred. The Sailors
who are the only People who may be properly Stiled Mob, are
entirely at the Command of the Merchants who employ them.

. . . . .

7

GENERAL THOMAS GAGE TO THE DUKE OF RICHMOND
New York, August 26, 1766

Since my Letter . . . of the 15th of July fresh Disturbances have happened in the County of Albany in this Province, which has occasioned further Applications to Me from the Civil Power for Military Aid. A Detachment from the 66th Regiment of 100 Men under the Command of Captain Clarke, was ordered into the said County, and put under the Direction of the Civil Magistrates. These Insurrections have arisen from Disputes between the Landholders and their Tenants, the latter not choosing to Submit the Decision of their Rights to Civil Judicatures, have had Recourse to open Force and violence. The Rioters moved from the Troops as they approached them, but kept in armed Body at a Distance appearing in Several parts of the Country to the great Terror of the Inhabitants. It was found in vain to pursue them, and that the best way was to post the Troops at the Rioters Habitations, which would put them under the Alternative of Surrendering to Justice, or losing their Harvest, which was ready for Reaping: This obliged many of them to fly who took Refuge in the Government of the Massachusett's Bay, into which the Troops had Orders not to pursue them, unless attended by the Civil Magistrates of that Province. . . . Before the Limits were ascertained between the Governments of Massachusett's Bay and New York, the Country where many of the Rioters live was claimed by the former, and many of them hold under the Authority of that Government; I dont know whether it is for that Reason only that they would protect the Rioters, for I find many of the lower Class in this and other Provinces who defend them, by saying that they have been ill treated by their Landlords, and complain of the steps taken by the Government here to Suppress them: At the same Time they make no Account of their resisting the Civil Authority, of their Assembling in armed Bodys, of their disturbing the Peace of the Country, and committing Outrages. Your Grace will judge from thence of the Licentious Spirit which too generaly prevails.

Carter, ed., *Correspondence of General Thomas Gage*, 1: 102-4. Reprinted with permission of the publisher. A soldier by profession, Charles Lennox (1735-1806), third Duke of Richmond, was secretary of state for the Southern Department for the brief period from May to July 1766.

There has been some Disturbance in this Place between the
People and the Soldiers: The latter were accused of cutting
down a [Liberty] Pole set up in an open Place near the Barracks;
It appears upon Enquiry that it was no general Act of the Sol-
diery, but there is Reason to Suspect some of them, as well as
some of the People of the Town, were concerned in it. A Mob
assembled to erect the Pole again, and a Drumer passing, words
ensued; They fell upon him and afterwards upon a Corporal who
came to his Assistance and pursued both to the Barrack Gate,
from whence Twenty or more Soldiers Sallied, and drove the Mob
a considerable Distance. Some Officers being near got up in
Time to force the Soldiers back to their Barracks, tho' in
passing the Mob some were beat, and the whole grossly abused.
The Mob afterwards in Presence of the Magistrates Surrounded
the Barracks, and vented so much abuse and provoking Language,
that some of the better Sort of People who had assembled there,
did not think it possible that the Officers could command themselves, or restrain the Fury of their Men and pressed the Magistrates to Support their own Dignity and disperse the Mob.
The Soldiers were however kept quiet and no Mischief ensued,
nor is there any Person much hurt except the Corporal. The
Populace resented highly the Check they had received, and drew
up a Paper that the Soldiers might be ordered out of the City;
but finding that no Person of Consequence or Reputation would
sign it they fixed up a Paper inviting the People to drive them
out by Force, but these were immediately pulled down. The
Meaning of all these Proceedings is, that the Populace are not
willing to part with the Power and Authority they have so long
usurped, to which they think the Soldiers may give some Ob-
struction: The better Sort tired of the Anarchy and Confusion
which has so long prevailed want to have Order restored and the
Laws put in Force, which they judge the Presence of the Soldiers is Necessary to bring about. The Magistrates See the
Necessity of checking the Mutinous Spirit in the People, but
they depend so much upon them for their Elections into the Mag-
istracy or General Assembly, that they act with Timidity, and
even Suffer themselves to be insulted. It became Necessary to
take more than usual Care of the Behavior of the Soldiers on
this Occasion, and such a readiness has been Shewn to deliver
up every Soldier guilty of committing Disorders, to the Civil
Power; Or to punish them by Military Law, that the People Seem
disarmed of all Complaints against them.
    . . . . .

Chapter two:

The Die is Cast, 1767-74

The repeal of the Stamp Act ended the turmoil in the colonies, but the British government still faced a serious pecuniary problem. The Revenue Act of 1766, a one-penny tariff on all imported molasses explicitly enacted to answer the same ends as the Stamp Act, created as little revenue as it did opposition. Therefore, a year later, in June 1767, Parliament levied a series of graduated duties on a long list of imports, including paper, tea, printers' ink, glass, and paints. This time, however, the colonials demonstrated against the exactions, using the increasingly familiar technique of constitutional protestation, economic sanction, and, when necessary, physical coercion. In April 1768 New York merchants agreed to comply with a general boycott of British goods inaugurated by Bostonians, provided their Philadelphia counterparts did likewise; and a nonimportation agreement was announced in August. Anglo-American tensions eased once again when Parliament in April 1770 revoked all the levies except the tax on tea, which remained as a generally ignored symbol of imperial authority.

Despite the outbreak of such localized incidents as the Boston Massacre of March 1770 and the burning of the revenue schooner *Gaspee* off the coast of Rhode Island in June 1772, relations between England and America remained quiescent from 1770 to 1773. But in New York, as elsewhere, latent tensions threatened to erupt at any time. Much of the uneasiness that afflicted New Yorkers on the eve of the Revolution stemmed from sources other than taxation. Religious Dissenters, mainly Presbyterians, had become increasingly aroused in the 1760s at the prospect—more imagined than real—of the creation of an American bishop and the concomitant establishment of the Anglican church as the state church. Moreover, the presence of troops was a constant irritant because of the competition between soldiers and citizens for jobs and women and because of the traditional English aversion to standing armies and professional soldiers. Although it was never implemented, the suspension of the provincial legislature by Parliament in June 1767 for refusing to comply with the letter of the Mutiny Act exacerbated civilian-military relations and heightened the appearance of political repression. A series of tenant uprisings and bitter political competition between the Livingston and DeLancey factions, in which imperial issues were used for partisan purposes, created additional anxiety. Finally, parliamentary authorization in 1770 for the legislature to issue £120,000 in paper money did not immediately alleviate the fiscal problems arising from a shortage of specie caused by the proscriptions of the Currency Act six years before.

Peaceful relations ended abruptly in May 1773, when Parliament exempted East India Company tea sold in America from normal marketing procedures and export duties in order to alleviate the financial plight of the company. Because East India tea could now be sold even cheaper than the smuggled variety, colonials were faced not only with complying with the excise on tea but also with supporting the virtual monopoly enjoyed by company merchants. Opposition to the Tea Act, especially strong in mercantile communities, reached fruition on December 17, when Boston radicals signified their disapprobation by staging an unceremonious tea party. The British response was immediate and resolute. Partly to punish the obstreperous Bostonians and partly to prevent the recurrence of similar disorders in the Bay Colony, in the spring of 1774 Parliament passed a series of statutes (the so-called Intolerable or Coercive Acts), the most famous, albeit least important, of which closed the port of Boston pending indemnification for the destroyed tea.

The American reaction was equally swift and determined. Extralegal committees, such as the New York City Committee of Fifty-one, were formed to contravene the British action and to correspond with counterparts in other colonies. In September delegates from New Hampshire to Georgia met in Philadelphia to discuss the entire question of Anglo-American relations and to determine a course of action to resolve the conflict. The action taken by the First Continental Congress, especially in fashioning the Continental Association in October, represented the culmination of a decade of intercolonial protest and provided the crucial impetus for the transition from dependent colony to independent state.

8

GOVERNOR HENRY MOORE TO THE EARL OF HILLSBOROUGH
New York, May 12, 1768

. . . . .
It would give me great pleasure if I could boldly assert that the inflammatory Publications in the printed News Papers here . . . had been treated with the contempt they really deserve, but I am afraid the bad effects of them are but too sensible already, and that the doctrine they would endeavour to establish is without the least reluctance adopted by all Ranks and conditions of People here; The Provinces of Massachusets and Pensylvania furnish us so plentifully with Papers of this kind that we have no occasion for any Writers of our own on the subjects they handle with so much freedom, and if the attempts to promote Sedition had been confin'd to the Limits of their particular Provinces I should not have thought it so much my duty to mention to your Lordship what would in the common course of Business have been communicated by the respective Governors of those Colonies but when they are extended so far as to endanger the tranquillity of the Province committed to my charge, I think I am partiucularly call'd upon to exert myself in opposition to measures which can only tend to make a breach between the Mother Country and the Colonies. The Inhabitants of Boston not satisfy'd with the Associations enter'd into among themselves, which they took care to make as public as possible, wrote letters to the Merchants of this Town whom they desired to joyn with them in the Plan form'd for distressing Great Britain by not importing any English Goods or Manufactures into America after a stated time, In consequence of this Advertisements were publish'd appointing the time and place for the Meeting of all persons concern'd in Trade, and much pains taken to carry the propos'd plan into execution: But as I could not help being alarm'd at such a proceeding, I took the first

---

E. B. O'Callaghan and Berthold Fernow, eds., *Documents Relative to the Colonial History of New York* . . . , 15 vols. (Albany, N.Y.: Weed, Parsons,and Co. 1853-87), 8: 68-69. (Hereafter cited as *New York Colonial Documents.*) Former governor of Jamaica (1755-62), Sir Henry Moore (1713-69) served as governor of New York from his arrival in November 1765 until his death in September 1769. Wills Hill (1718-93), the first Earl of Hillsborough, served as president of the Board of Trade (1763-66) and first secretary of the American Department (1768-72).

opportunity of laying my sentiments before his Majesty's Council, expressing at the same time my apprehension of the Evil Tendency of these Meetings, which in the eye of the Law are look'd upon to be illegal and might be productive of fresh commotions in the Province; The Council differ'd in opinion from me and saw this in no other light than that a certain number of People had assembled together to consider & establish among themselves certain Rules of Œconomy, and were of opinion that as they were Masters of their own Fortunes they had a right to dispose of, and lay out their money in whatever manner they should think would be most agreable to themselves, and afterwards added that, they were not under the least apprehension of the tranquillity of the Province being disturb'd by such meetings, from the known characters of many who had assembled on the occasion; I was far from being satisfy'd with this answer, for it appear'd to me that when the association was once begun many people who had at present no inclination to joyn in it might be afterwards intimidated, and compell'd to set their hands to an engagement they were actually averse to. . . .

. . . . .

9

NEW YORK CITY MERCHANT BOYCOTT RESOLVES   August 27, 1768

    I. THAT we will not send for from Great-Britain, either upon our own Account or on Commission this Fall, any other Goods than what we have already ordered.
    II. THAT we will not import any kind of Merchandize from Great-Britain . . . nor purchase from any Factor or others, any kind of Goods imported from Great-Britain directly or by Way of any other Colonies, or by Way of the West-Indies, that shall be shipped from Great-Britain after the First Day of November, until the forementioned Acts of Parliament imposing Duties on Paper, Glass, &. be repealed; except only the Articles of Coals, Salt, Sail-Cloth, Wool-Cards, and Card-Wire, Grindstones, Chalk, Lead, Tin, Sheet Copper and German Steel.

New York Journal, September 8, 1768. The published version of the resolutions concludes: "Subscribed by nearly all the Merchants and Traders in Town." An informal boycott of British goods had been agreed to in April.

III. WE further agree, not to import any kind of Merchandize from Hamburgh and Holland, directly from thence, nor by
any other Way whatever, more than what we have already ordered
(except Tiles and Bricks).

IV. WE also promise to countermand all Orders given from
Great-Britain, on or since the 16th Inst. by the first Conveyance, ordering those Goods not to be sent unless the aforementioned Duties are taken off.

V. AND we further agree, that if any Person or Persons,
Subscribers hereto, shall take any Advantage by importing any
kind of Goods that are herein restricted, directly or indirectly contrary to the true Intent and Meaning of this Agreement;
such Person or Persons shall by us be deemed Enemies to their
Country.

VI. LASTLY, we agree, that if any Goods shall be consigned
or sent over to us, contrary to our Agreement in this Subscription; such Goods so imported, shall be lodged in some public
Ware-House there to be kept under Confinement until the
forementioned Acts are repealed.

10

NEW YORK CITY TRADESMEN AGREEMENT September 5, 1768

REFLECTING on the salutary Measures entered into by the
People in Boston, and this City, to restrict the Importation of
Goods from G. Britain, until the Acts of Parliament laying
Duties on Paper, Glass, &c. are repealed. And being animated
with a Spirit of Liberty, and thinking it our Duty to exert
ourselves by all lawful Means to maintain and obtain our just
Rights and Privileges, which we claim under our most excellent
Constitution as Englishmen, not to be taxed but by our own
Consent or Representatives: And in Order to support and
strengthen our Neighbours, the Merchants of this City.—We the
Subscribers, uniting in the common Cause, do agree to and with
each other, as follows:

Ist. THAT we will not ourselves, purchase, or take any
Goods or Merchandize imported from Europe, by any Merchant directly or indirectly, contrary to the true Intent and Meaning

New York Journal, September 15, 1768.

of an Agreement of the Merchants of this City, on the 27th of August last.

II. THAT we will not ourselves, or by any other Means, buy any Kind of Goods from any Merchant, Store-keeper, or Retailer, (if any such there be) who shall refuse to join with their Brethren in signing the said Agreement: But that we will use every lawful Means in our Power to prevent our Acquaintance from dealing with them.

III. THAT if any Merchant, in or from Europe, should import any Goods in Order to sell them in this Province, contrary to the above Agreement, that we ourselves, will by no Means deal with such Importers; and as far as we can, by all lawful Means, endeavour to discourage the Sale of such Goods.

IV. THAT we will endeavour to fall upon some Expedient to make known such Importers or Retailers as shall refuse to unite in maintaining and obtaining the Liberties of their Country.

V. THAT we, his Majesty's most dutiful and loyal Subjects, Inhabitants of the City of New-York, being filled with Love and Gratitude to our present most gracious Sovereign, and the highest Veneration for the British Constitution, which we unite to plead as our Birth-Right; and are always willing to unite, to support and maintain, give it as our Opinion, and are determined to deem those Persons who shall refuse to unite in the common Cause, as acting the Part of any Enemy to the true Interest of Great-Britain and her Colonies and consequently not deserving the Patronage of Merchants or Mechanicks.

11

GENERAL ASSEMBLY DECLARATION OF RIGHTS December 31, 1768

The general assembly agrees to these resolutions: "As it is not only the common birthright of all his Majesty's subjects,

---

Journal of the Votes and Proceedings of the General Assembly of the Colony of New-York . . . [1768-69] (New York: Hugh Gaine, 1769), pp. 70-71. On February 11 the Massachusetts House of Representatives sent a circular letter to the speakers of the other North American assemblies urging that the colonies follow the example of the Bay Colony in petitioning the king against the Townshend Duties. On April 21 Lord Hillsborough instructed

but it is also essential to the preservation of the peace,
strength and prosperity of the British empire; that an exact
equality of constitutional rights, among all his Majesty's subjects in the several parts of the empire, be uniformly and
invariably maintained and supported; and as it would be inconsistent with the constitutional rights of his Majesty's subjects in Great Britain, to tax them either in person or estate,
without the consent of their representatives in parliament assembled. It is therefore,

"Resolved, *Nemine Contradicente*, "That . . . as his most
gracious Majesty is the common father of all his good subjects,
dispersed throughout the various parts of the British empire;
And as the commons of Great Britain in parliament assembled,
do enjoy a constitutional right of humbly petitioning his Majesty, as the common father of his people there, for constitutional benefits and the redress of grievances. The representatives of this colony, in general assembly convened, lawfully
may, and ought to exercise the same constitutional right, when,
and as often as to them shall seem meet.

"Resolved, "That . . . this colony lawfully and constitutionally has and enjoys an internal legislature of its own, in
which the crown and the people of this colony, are constitutionally represented; and that the power and authority of the
said legislature, cannot lawfully or constitutionally be suspended, abridged, abrogated, or annulled by any power, authority or prerogative whatsoever, the prerogative of the crown
ordinarily exercised for prorogations and dissolutions only
excepted.

"Resolved, *Nemine Contradicente*, "That . . . this house
has an undoubted right, to correspond and consult with any of
the neighboring colonies, or with any other of his Majesty's
subjects out of this colony, or belonging to any part of his
Majesty's realm or dominions, either individually or collectively on any matter, subject or thing whatsoever, whereby they
shall conceive the rights, liberties, interests or privileges
of this house, or of its constituents, are, or may be affected."

(Cont'd.) each governor to prevent the legislatures from acting
upon the Massachusetts missive by persuasion if possible and by
prorogation or dissolution if necessary. Upon conclusion of
regular business, the New York assembly on December 31 adopted
three pointed resolutions and took up the Massachusetts letter;
Governor Moore dissolved the legislature on January 2, 1769.

12

PETER VAN SCHAACK TO HENRY VAN SCHAACK
                              New York, December 20, 1769

. . . . .
On Sunday, a good deal of noise was made on account of
some anonymous papers, filled with the most violent and inde-
cent expressions, charging a combination between the Governor,
Council, and the ascendent party in the House of Assembly, the
DeLanceys, to trample upon the liberties of the people, in
order, as they said, on the part of the Lieutenant Governor, to
keep his peace at home, and on the part of the DeLanceys, to
prevent a dissolution. The mighty occasion of this was that a
vote had passed the House (*nemine con.*) to grant to the troops
two thousand pounds; one thousand thereof to be taken out of
the treasury, the other one thousand to be drawn out of the
money expected to be emitted in a short time by law. One of
those papers contained an invitation to the TRUE SONS OF FREE-
DOM to meet at the Liberty pole on Monday morning, and from
thence to repair to the House of Assembly, to oblige the
House to retract their vote. A number, to the amount of about
three or four hundred men, met and appointed a committee to
draw up instructions to their members to the above effect. The
people who met were not of the more respectable part of
town. . . . They have this morning delivered their instructions.
It is not expected the members will regard those instructions
because they were not the sentiments of the major, or the more
respectable part of the city. Much is said on both sides of
the question, and people's minds are heated to a great degree.

Henry C. Van Schaack, *Memoirs of the Life of Henry Van Schaack,
Embracing Selections from His Correspondence during the American Revolution* . . . (Chicago: A. C. McClurg & Co. 1892), pp.
17-19. Peter Van Schaack (1747-1832), a 1766 graduate of
King's College and a Kinderhook lawyer, warmly opposed imperial
policy in the decade after 1763 but recoiled at the thought of
independence. Banished from the state for refusing to sign a
loyalty oath, he was repatriated after the war largely because
of his friendship with such men as John Jay, Egbert Benson, and
Gouverneur Morris. Henry Van Schaack, Peter's eldest brother,
was postmaster of Albany. The libelous pamphlet referred to is
Alexander McDougall's *To the Betrayed Inhabitants of* . . . *New
York*, published on December 16. McDougall was incarcerated but
never tried because of the death of the principle witness.

The minority allege that troops are a useless expense to the colony; that their residence here is a burden to the city; is productive of luxury, and tends to enhance the prices of provisions in an intolerable manner; that they are a tax upon us, and may perhaps be instrumental in enforcing the most unconstitutional acts of Parliament.

The other party say that these are the mere suggestions of a malevolent, disappointed faction; that in a FORMER ADMINIS-TRATION, when a CERTAIN PARTY prevailed, those moneys were granted without murmur; that they have been granted at a time when we were threatened, in the over-bearing terms of ministe-rial language, to have our House of Representatives annihilated unless we complied; that a requisition could never be complied with promising greater advantage to this colony; for that now we had the highest assurances that a compliance will procure us that so-long-wished-for object, a paper currency, for which the country cries aloud, and which has been thought so highly nec-essary that an address has been presented to Sir Henry Moore, most earnestly begging him to solicit his Royal Master for leave to give his assent to a bill for the purpose; and that Sir Henry has been extolled to the skies for exercising his in-fluence to effect this; that an additional reason for a paper currency now is, that the colony is indebted, through means of the deficiencies of the late treasurer, in the sum of thirty thousand pounds, which, unless we have an emission (which being by loan will enable the colony to replace this deficiency in a manner least burdensome), must be supplied by a tax on the colony; that besides, of the two thousand pounds now granted, one half is to pay off the arrearages already incurred, and that if no money is granted to the troops, without which no emission will take place, individuals, who have trusted the troops upon the faith of the government, must suffer. But if the granting a supply now is so disagreeable, why, when the matter has been under consideration near three weeks, were no objections before raised? Why endeavor to fix a stigma on the House after passing a vote which they knew would take place and took no pains to prevent? Why attempt to reduce the city mem-bers to the disagreeable dilemma of receding from this vote, or of drawing upon them the unjust censure of disregarding the sentiments of their constituents?

These considerations have operated so powerfully, that the dream is over, and men are come to their senses, and those who favored the scheme are now ashamed of it. The House has voted those papers scandalous libels, and addressed his Honor to offer a reward of two hundred pounds for any person discovering the author, etc.

. . . . .

13

"BRUTUS," *TO THE PUBLICK*   New York, January 15, 1770

WHOEVER seriously considers the impoverished State of this
City, especially of many of the poor Inhabitants of it, must be
greatly surprized at the Conduct of such as employ the Soldiers,
when there are a Number of the former that want Employment to
support their distressed Families. Every Man of Sense amongst
us knows, that the Army is not kept here to protect, but to
enslave us; notwithstanding our Assemblies have given vast Sums
of Money to provide them with such Necessaries which many of
the good Burghers want.
     These Supplies are paid by a Tax on the Colony, a Third of
which is the Quota for this City and County. Add to this Burthen the heavy Duty we pay on Sugar, &c. which so greatly distresses our Trade, and has so impoverished this City, that many
of its former Inhabitants have removed, and others that remain,
are, for want of Employ, unable to support themselves, and are
thereby become a public Charge.
     This might, in a great Measure, be prevented, with Comfort
to their distressed Families, and a Saving to the Community, if
the Employers of Labourers would attend to it with that Care
and Benevolence that a Citizen owes to his Neighbour, by employing him. Is it not enough that you pay Taxes for Bil-
leting-Money to support the Soldiers, and a Poor-Tax, to maintain many of their Whores and Bastards in the Work-house,
without giving them the Employment of the Poor, who you must
support if you do not employ them, which adds greatly to swell
your Poor-Tax? I hope my Fellow Citizens will take this Matter into Consideration, and not countenance a Sett of Men who
are Enemies to Liberty, and at the Beck of Tyrants to enslave;
especially when it will bring on you the just Reproaches of the
Poor. Experience has convinced us, that good Usage makes Soldiers insolent and ungrateful; all the Money that you have
hitherto given them, has only taught them to despise and insult
you. This is evident, in a great Number of them attempting
last Saturday Night to blow up the Liberty-Pole; which they had
near effected, if some of the Inhabitants had not discovered

This anonymous broadside appears in the *Supplement to the Pennsylvania Gazette* of February 15, 1770, as part of an account of
the "Battle of Golden Hill," a free-for-all between soldiers
and citizens on January 19 which culminated a series of minor
brawls fought ostensibly over the erection of liberty poles.

them. They had Time to saw the Braces, and bore a Hole in the
Pole, which they filled with Powder, and plugged it up, in order to set Fire to it; which was discovered by a Person at Mr.
Montanye's: They in Resentment broke 76 Squares of his Windows,
entered his House, and stopped him in the Passage with Swords,
and threatened if he stirred to take his Life; which so much
intimidated the People in the House, that they were induced to
go out of the Windows. Not satisfied with this atrocious
Wickedness, they broke two of his Lamps, and several Bowls; and
that they might the better accomplish their Designs, they
posted Centinels in the Roads, that lead to Liberty-Pole, to
prevent their being discovered. This and worse would be the
Treatment we might expect, if there were a greater Number of
them. It is hoped that this Conduct, with the former Considerations, will be sufficient to prevent any Friend to Liberty
from employing any of them for the future. There is a Matter
of the utmost Importance to the Liberties of the good People of
this Colony and the Continent, now before the Assembly. All
the Friends to Liberty, that incline to bear a Testimony
against a literal Compliance with the Mutiny Act [otherwise
called the Billeting Act] are desired to meet at Liberty-Pole,
at 12 o'Clock, on Wednesday next, which will be on the 17th Instant, where the whole Matter shall be communicated to them.

14

BRITISH ARMY BROADSIDE   New York, January 19, 1770

God and a Soldier all Men doth adore
In Time of War, and not before:
When the War is over, and all Things righted,
God is forgotten, and the Soldier slighted.

WHEREAS an uncommon and riotous Disturbance prevails
throughout this City, by some of its Inhabitants, who stile
themselves the S--s of L-----y, but rather may more properly be
called real Enemies to Society; and whereas the Army, now quartered in New-York, are represented in a heinous Light, to their
Officers and others, for having propagated a Disturbance in

Supplement to the Pennsylvania Gazette, February 15, 1770.

this City, by attempting to destroy their Liberty-Pole, in the
Fields; which being now completed, without the Assistance of
the Army, we have Reason to laugh at them, and beg the Public
only to observe how chagrined those pretended S--s of L-----y
look as they pass through the Street, especially as these great
Heroes thought their Freedom depended on a Piece of Wood. . . .
And altho' those shining S--s of L-----y have boasted of their
Freedom, surely they have no Right to throw an Aspersion upon
the Army, since it is out of the Power of Military Discipline,
to deprive them of their Freedom: However, notwithstanding we
are proud to see these elevated Geniuses reduced to the low
Degree of having their Place of general Rendezvous made (a Gallows Green) a vulgar Phrase for a common Place of Execution for
Murderers, Robbers, Traitors, and R----s, to the latter of
which we may compare those famous L-----y B--s, who have nothing to boast of but the Flippancy of Tongue, altho' in Defiance
of the Laws and good Government of our most gracious Sovereign,
they openly and r------y assemble in Multitudes, to stir up the
Minds of his Majesty's good Subjects to Sedition;—they have,
in their late seditious Libel, signed *Brutus*, expressed the
most villainous Falshoods against the Soldiers: But as ungrateful as they are counted, it is well known, since their
Arrival in New-York, they have watched Night and Day, for the
Safety and Protection of the City and its Inhabitants. . . . It
is well known by the Officers of the 16th Regiment, as well as
by several others, that the Soldiers of the 16th, always gained
the Esteem and Good-will of the Inhabitants, in whatever Quarters they lay, and were never counted either insolent or ungrateful, except in this City. And likewise the Royal Regiment
of Artillery, who always behaved with Gratitude and Respect to
every one. But the Means of making your famous City, which you
so much boast of, an impoverished one, is your acting in Violation to the Laws of the British Government; but take Heed, lest
you reprent too late.—For if you boast so mightily of your
famous Exploits, as you have heretofore done (witness the late
Stamp-Act) we may allow you to be all *Alexanders*, and lie under
your Feet, to be trodden upon with Contempt and Disdain; but
before we so tamely submit, be assured that we will stand in
Defence of the Rights and Privileges due to a Soldier, and no
farther; but we hope, while we have Officers of Conduct to act
for us, they will do so, as we shall leave it to their Discretion, to act impartially for us, in Hopes they, and every honest Heart, will support the Soldiers Wives and Children, and
not Whores and Bastards, as has been so maliciously, falsly,
and audaciously inserted in their impertinent Libel, addressed
to the Public; for which, may the Shame they mean to brand our
Names with, stick on theirs.

15

LIEUTENANT GOVERNOR CADWALLADER COLDEN TO THE EARL OF HILLSBOROUGH

New York, February 21, 1770

My Lord, it is my duty to inform Your Lord[p] that a violent party, continue their assiduous endeavours to disturb the Govern[t], by working on the passions of the populace, and exciting riots, who in every attempt they have hitherto been unsuccessful, The last, might have been of fatal consequence, if not prevented by the prudent conduct of the Magistrates and Officers of the Army. An ill humour had been artfully worked up between the Towns people and Soldiers, which produced several affrays, and daily, by means of wicked incendiaries, grew more serious. At last some Towns people began to arm, and the Soldiers rushed from their Barracks to support their fellow Soldiers. Had it not been for the interpositon of the Magistrates, and of the most respectab[l]e Inhabitants, and of the Officers of the Army, it had become a very dangerous affair— as it was, only a few wounds and bruises were received on both sides. A very respectable number of the principal Citizens publicly met together, and sent 42 of their number to the Mayor, to assure the Magistrates of their assistance, in preserving the peace of the Town; and the Officers of the Army were no less assiduous in quieting the minds of the Soldiers, and in guarding against every accident, which might renew any dispute with the Towns people—since which, the place has remained quiet. It is not doubted here, that these disturbances were promoted by the Enemy of Gover[t], in order to raise an indignation against the Assembly (then sitting) for granting money to the Soldiers, who were represented as ready to cut the throats of the Citizens.

New York Colonial Documents, 8: 208. Few Colonials could match the variegated career of Cadwallader Colden, which spanned the entire provincial period (1688-1776). Colden achieved distinction as a politician, land speculator, scientist, historian, and philosopher. Appointed surveyor-general in 1720, councillor in 1721, and lieutenant governor in 1761, he held those posts until his death in September 1776.

The persons who appear on these occasions are of inferior
rank, but it is not doubted they are directed by some persons
of distinction in this place. It is likewise thought, they are
encouraged by some persons of note in England. They consist
chiefly of Dissenters, who are very numerous, especially in
the Country, and have a great influence over the Country Members of Assembly. The most Active among them are independents
from New England, or educated there, and of Republican principles. The friends of the administration, are of the Church
of England, the Lutherans, and the old Dutch congregation, with
several presbyterians.

. . . . .

16

LIEUTENANT GOVERNOR CADWALLADER
COLDEN TO THE EARL OF HILLSBOROUGH New York, July 7, 1770

. . . . .

Soon after it was known that the Parliam[en]t had repealed
the duties on Paper, Glass etc. the Merchants in this place
sent to Philadelphia that they might unitedly agree to a general importation of every thing except Tea. They at first received a favourable answer, and their agreement to the proposal
was not doubted; but soon after a letter was received at Philadelphia, from a Gentleman in England, on whom the Quakers in
that place, repose the greatest confidence, advising them to
persist in non importation, till every internal Taxation was
taken off; this changed the measures of Philadelphia; but the
principal Inhabitants of this place continue resolved to shew
their gratitude, for the regard the Parliament has had in removing the grievances they complained of. As there still remains a restless Faction, who from popular arguments, rumours
and invectives, are endeavouring to excite riots and opposition
among the lower class of people, a number of Gentlemen went
round the Town to take the sentiments of Individuals. I am
told, that 1180, among which are the principal Inhabitants, declared for importation, about 300 were neutral or unwilling to
declare their sentiments, and a few of any distinction declared

in opposition to it. I am informed likewise that the Merchants of this place resolved to acquaint the Merchants of Boston and Philadelphia with their inclinations to import.

. . . . .

17

THE ASSOCIATION OF THE NEW YORK CITY SONS OF LIBERTY
November 29, 1773

It is essential to the freedom and security of a free people, that no taxes be imposed upon them but by their own consent, or their representatives. For "what property have they in that which another may, by right, taken when he pleases to himself?" The former is the undoubted right of Englishmen, to secure which they expended millions and sacrificed the lives of thousands. And yet, to the astonishment of all the world, and the grief of America, the commons of Great Britain, after the repeal of the memorable and detestable stamp-act, reassumed the power of imposing taxes on the American colonies; and, insisting on it as a necessary badge of parliamentary supremacy, passed a bill, in the seventh year of his present majesty's reign, imposing duties on all glass, painters' colors, paper and teas, that should, after the 20th of November, 1767, be "imported from Great Britain into any colony or plantation in America."—This bill, after the concurrence of the lords, obtained the royal assent. And thus they who, from time immemorial, have exercised the right of giving to, or withholding from the crown, their aids and subsidies, according to their *own free will and pleasure*, signified by their representatives in parliament, do, by the act in question, deny us, their

---

Hezekiah Niles, comp., *Principles and Acts of the Revolution in America* . . . (Baltimore: William Ogden Niles, 1822), pp. 188-89. The loosely organized, amorphous Sons of Liberty, who emerged as a political force during the Stamp Act crisis of 1765-66, specialized in extralegal mob activity. Isaac Sears, John Lamb, and Alexander McDougall emerged as the principal leaders of the group, but little is known of the rank and file other than that it consisted mainly of artisans, mechanics, and seamen.

brethren in America, the enjoyment of the same right. As this
denial, and the execution of that act, involves our slavery,
and would sap the foundation of our freedom, whereby we should
become slaves to our brethren and fellow subjects, born to no
greater stock of freedom than the Americans—the merchants and
inhabitants of this city, in conjunction with the merchants and
inhabitants of the ancient American colonies, entered into an
agreement to decline a part of their commerce with Great Britain, until the above mentioned act should be totally repealed.
This agreement operated so powerfully to the disadvantage of
the manufacturers of England that many of them were unemployed.
To appease their clamors, and to provide the subsistence for
them, which the non-importation had deprived them of, the parliament, in 1770, repealed so much of the revenue act as imposed a duty on glass, painter's colors, and paper, and left
the duty on tea, as *a test of the parliamentary right to tax
us*. The merchants of the cities of New York and Philadelphia,
having strictly adhered to the agreement, so far as it is
related to the importation of articles subject to an American
duty, have convinced the ministry, that some other measures
must be adopted to execute parliamentary supremacy over this
country, and to remove the distress brought on the East India
company, by the ill-policy of that act. Accordingly, to increase the temptation to the shippers of tea from England, an
act of parliament passed the last session, which gives the
whole duty on tea, the company were subject to pay, upon the
importation of it into England, to the purchasers and exporters;
and when the company have ten millions of pounds of tea, in
their ware-houses exclusive of the quantity they may want to
ship, they are allowed to export tea, discharged from the payment of that duty, with which they were before chargeable. In
hopes of aid in the execution of this project, by the influence
of the owners of the American ships, application was made by
the company to the captains of those ships to take the tea on
freight; but they virtuously rejected it. Still determined on
the scheme, they have chartered ships to bring the tea to this
country, which may be hourly expected, to make an important
trial of our virtue. If they succeed in the sale of that tea,
we shall have no property that we can call our own, and then
we may bid adieu to American liberty.—Therefore, to prevent
a calamity which, of all others, is the most to be dreaded—
slavery, and its terrible concomitants—we, the subscribers,
being influenced from a regard to liberty, and disposed to use
all lawful endeavors in our power, to defeat the pernicious
project, and to transmit to our posterity, those blessings of
freedom which our ancestors have handed down to us; and to contribute to the support of the common liberties of America,
which are in danger to be subverted, *do*, for those important
purposes, agree to associate together, under the name and style

of the *sons of liberty of New-York*, and engage our honor to, and with each other faithfully to observe and perform the following *resolutions, viz.*

1st. *Resolved*, That whoever shall aid, or abet, or in any manner assist, in the introduction of tea, from any place whatsoever, into this colony, while it is subject, by a British act of parliament, to the payment of a duty, for the purpose of raising a revenue in America, he shall be deemed an enemy to the liberties of America.

2d. *Resolved*, That whoever shall be aiding, or assisting, in the landing, or carting of such tea, from any ship, or vessel, or shall hire any house, store-house, or cellar or any place whatsoever, to deposit the tea, subject to a duty as aforesaid, he shall be deemed an enemy to the liberties of America.

3d. *Resolved*, That whoever shall sell, or buy, or in any manner contribute to the sale, or purchase of tea, subject to a duty as aforesaid, or shall aid, or abet, in transporting such tea, by land or water, from this city, until the 7th George III. chap. 46, commonly called the revenue act, shall be totally and clearly repealed, he shall be deemed an enemy to the liberties of America.

4th. *Resolved*, That whether the duties on tea, imposed by this act, be paid in Great Britain or in America, our liberties are equally affected.

5th. *Resolved*, That whoever shall transgress any of these resolutions, we will not deal with, or employ, or have any connection with him.

18

GOVERNOR WILLIAM TRYON TO THE EARL OF DARTMOUTH
New York, January 3, 1774

. . . . .

Until the arrival of the Account of the Tea being destroyed at Boston I had conceived very sanguine Hopes that

New York Colonial Documents, 8: 407. Related by marriage to the Earl of Hillsborough, Tryon (1725-88) served as governor of New York from July 1771 to the collapse of royal government in

Temperate measures might have been manifested in the Conduct of
the Body of the People of this Province on the arrival of the
Tea, The association paper inclosed, and which was universally
approved by all better sort of the Inhabitants, seemed to justify the opinion so far as to the protection of the Property,
but the Boston intelligence instantly gave a different turn to
affairs, and I am now entirely uncertain what may be the issue;
My best Endeavors, however will be constantly exerted for the
peace of Society, and the good order of this His Majesty's Government, now, if possible, since the Outrage at Boston, become
a more important object of my attention; From the general
Appearance of the united opposition to the principle of the
Monopoly, and the Importation Duty in America, I can form no
other Opinion than that the landing, storing, and safe keeping
of the Tea, when stored, could be accomplished, but only under
the protection of the Point of the Bayonet, and Muzle of the
Canon, and even then I do not see how the consumption could be
effected.

. . . . .

19

AN ACCOUNT OF THE NEW YORK TEA PARTY

New York, April 22, 1774

On Monday . . . [April 18], advice was received from Philadelphia, that Captain Chambers, of the ship London, of this
port, had taken on board, at the port of London, 18 boxes of
fine tea. . . . The committee, and the inhabitants, were therefore determined to examine into the matter with great vigilance.
In the night, the long expected tea-ship, Nancey, Captain
Lockyer, arrived at Sandy-Hook. . . . Letters being delivered

---

(Cont'd.) 1775. He had previously been a lieutenant colonel in
the British army and governor of North Carolina (1765-71).
William Legge (1731-1801), the second Earl of Dartmouth, was
both first lord of trade and secretary of the American Department (1772-75). He was a relative and confidant of Frederick,
Lord North.

Rivington's New York Gazetteer, April 28, 1774. Author unknown.

to him by the pilot, from sundry gentlemen of this city, informing him of the determined resolution of the citizens not to
suffer the tea on board of his ship to be landed, he requested
the pilot to bring him up to procure necessaries, and make a
protest; but he would not do it till leave was obtained. Early
the next morning this was communicated to the committee; and it
appearing to them to be the sense of the city, that such leave
should be granted to him, the ship to remain at the Hook: the
pilot was immediately despatched to bring him up. This intelligence was immediately communicated to the public by a hand-
bill. At 6 P.M. the pilot-boat returned with Captain Lockyer
on board; and although the people had but a very short notice
of it, the wharf was crowded with the citizens, to see the man
whose arrival they long and impatiently wished, to give them an
opportunity to co-operate with the other colonies. The committee conducted him to the house of the Hon. Henry White, Esq;
one of the consignees, and there informed Captain Lockyer, that
it was the sense of the citizens that he should not presume to
go near the Custom-house, and to make the utmost despatch in
procuring the necessary articles he wanted for his voyage. To
this he answered, "That as the consignees would not receive his
cargo, he would not go to the Custom-house, and would make all
the despatch he could to leave the city." A committee of observation was appointed to go down in a sloop to the Hook, to
remain near the tea ship till she departs for London. And four
committees were appointed to watch the ship London, on her arrival, day and night, till she should be discharged.
     . . . . .
     Friday at noon, Captain Chambers came into the Hook; the
pilot asked him if he had any tea on board? He declared he had
none. Two of the committee of observation informed him of the
advices received of his having tea on board, and demanded a
sight of all his cockets, which was accordingly given them; nor
was the mark or number on his manifest.
     About 4 P.M. the ship came to the wharf, when she was
boarded by a number of the citizens. Capt. Chambers was inter-
rogated relative to his having the tea on board, but he still
denied it. He was then told that it was in vain to deny it,
for as there was good proof of its being on board, it would be
found, as there were committees appointed to open every package,
and that he had better be open and candid about it; and demanded the cocket for the tea; upon which he confessed it was
on board, and delivered the cocket. The owners and the committee immediately met at Mr. Francis's, [Fraunce's] where Captain
Chambers was ordered to attend. Upon examining him who was the
shipper and owner of the tea? he declared that he was the sole
owner of it. After the most mature deliberation, it was determined to communicate the whole state of the matter to the people, who were convened near the ship; which was accordingly

done. The Mohawks were prepared to do their duty at a proper
hour; but the body of the people were so impatient, that before
it arrived, a number of them entered the ship, about 8 P.M.
took out the tea, which was at hand, broke the cases, and
started their contents into the river, without doing any damage
to the ship or cargo. . . .

At 10 the people all dispersed in good order, but in great
wrath against the captain; and it was not without some risk of
his life that he escaped. Saturday in the morning the shipping
in the harbour displayed their colours, and a large flag was
hoisted on the Liberty Pole, and at 8 A.M. all the bells of the
city ran, pursuant to the notice published on Thursday. About
nine, the greatest number of people were collected at and near
the Coffee-House, that was ever known in this city. At a
quarter past nine the committee came out of the Coffee-House
with Captain Lockyer, upon which, the band of music attending,
played God save the King. . . . The committee, with the music,
conducted him through the multitude to the end of Murray's
wharf, where he was put on board the pilot-boat, and wished a
safe passage; upon which the multitude gave loud huzza's, and
many guns were fired, expressive of their joy at his departure.
The committee of observation at the Hook have cognizance of him
till a fair wind offers for his departure from thence. Thus to
the great mortification of the secret and open enemies of America, and the joy of all the friends of liberty and human nature,
the union of these colonies is maintained in a contest of the
utmost importance to their safety and felicity.

. . . . .

20

ALEXANDER McDOUGALL, "POLITICAL MEMORANDUMS"
New York, May 12-24, 1774

12 May. About noon Capt. Couper arrived in 26 days from
London & brought us the act of Parliament for shutting up the

Political memorandums relative to the Conduct of the Citizens
on the Boston Port Bill, McDougall Papers, Box I, The New-York
Historical Society. Printed with permission of the New-York
Historical Society. Merchant Alexander McDougall (1732-86) was

Port of Boston & that General Gage was appointed their Governor. . . . This intelligence was received with Great abhorence & indignation by the Sons of Freedom. The officers of Government indeavour to divide the People by intimating that nothing more was required by the act than the payment for the Tea, & that nothing was intended by Parliament against Newyork or any other of the Colonies. . . .

13 May. O[liver] Delancy declared that He would rather spend every shilling of his Fortune than that the Boston Port Bill should be complied with. This is to amuse & dupe the Sons of Liberty to get their confidence in order that they may be the more effectually deceived. . . .

14 May. This morning the Port act was published. . . . The City in General & Sons of Liberty in particular were warmer in their indignation to the Port Act. . . . The Sons of Liberty & a Number of the dry good[s] merchants think it necessary that a number of Merchants should be brought together to deliberate on the expediency of a non-importation agreement. For this purpose Capt. Sears spoke this day to a number of Merchants to meet next Monday evening at Francis's [i.e., Fraunces] Tavern, in order also to determine on a nomination of a Committee of Correspondence, to bring about a Congress. . . .

15 May. James Duane told in conversing . . . upon means to be taken to reli[e]ve Boston, & redress American Grievances that Ld North declared that if the non-importation agreement had continued 6 months longer the revenue act would have been totally repealed! A Number of the Merchants and the Sons of Liberty Judged it proper, as we had no advice from Boston of their receiving the act of Parliament against them, to dispatch an express with it to them, & to inform them of our Sympathising with them and our readiness to come into a non-importation agreement. . . . Sears & self wrote a Letter. . . . As no time was to be lost, we Judged it unnecessary to detain the express till the other members of our Committee signed it. . . .

May 16th 1774. To prevent any charge of design or chicane in calling the meeting of the Merchants I had two advertisements wrote & put up this day at 11 AM at the Coffee House. . . . The Friends of Liberty having no design in the Meeting but to deliberate on the expediency of a non-importation agreement, & to get an impartial spirited Committee of Correspondence appointed, used no arts to collect any persons to the meeting.

(Cont'd.) one of the most prominent radicals in New York City. He was a leader of the Sons of Liberty and a member of numerous extralegal committees. His radical activities and his imprisonment during 1770-71 for writing a libelous broadside, *To the Betrayed Inhabitants of . . . New York*, earned him the designation "the Wilkes of America."

But the Delancy Faction, altho the advertisments were to the
Merchants only, were at great Pains all the day to collect
every tool who was under their influence as well those in Trade
as out of it. No rooms of Francis's could contain the people
which obliged them to adjourn to the Exchange where at 8 PM
about 300 assembled. . . . Notwithstanding the fatal Conse-
quenses of the Port act were full[y] stated many were disposed
to impose on the meeting the belief that the payment of the
Tea would open the Port of Boston & they would come to no determination upon a non-importation agreement until the sense of
the other Colonies should be known which was only designed to
delay time. And others said Let us wait till we see what Boston requires of us. But this proceed[ed] from the same principle. When the Question was put whether a Committee of Correspondence should be appointed about 20 of them voted against
it. . . . The majority of the company were for a Committee of
15 or 21, but those who opposed the nominating a Committee saw
that it would be most favourable to their design, to nominate a
large Committee which would impede business and therefore
artefully got the Question put for the Committee to be 50, of
which 15 to make a board which induced many to imagine the Committee was to consist of 15 by this deception the Committee of
50 was carried. So intent were they on packing a Committee
that John DeLancy alone proposed five, & altho John Lamb was
voted by a great majority in the Nomination in the opinion
of . . . a vast number of impartial persons present, yet they
would not suffer his Name to be entered, on the List, nor did
they put Francis Lewis's on it who was unanimously Nominated
because they knew from a Conversation he had with Mr. Sherbrook
a little before the Question that He was in favour of a non-
importation agreement. And Mr. Jaunceys was put on the List
without a vote altho I objected to him, for his having told
Samuel Broome "that if the People of Boston opposed the Landing
the Tea by Force they would be guilty of Treason or Rebellion." . . . The whole of the Business of this meeting so far
as the Delancys had any agency in it, Evidenced a design to get
such a Committee nominated as would be under their direction,
with a view to gain credit with the people if any thing was
done to advance the Liberty cause or to prevent any thing being
done, in which case they would make a merit of it with administration to procure places for themsleves & their children. . . .
      May 17th 1774. . . . At 8 PM Mr Revere arrived express
from Boston & brought a Letter from Samuel Adams informing us
of the arrival of General Gage [and] inclosing a Vote of the
Town of Boston passed the 15th Instant and one from the Committee of Correspondence. These Letters as well as the Vote recommend a non-importation and non-exportation of Goods to Great
Britain & the West Indies as the only effectual means to open

their Port & redress American Grievances. At 9 PM the Letters
& Vote were read at the Coffee House.

May 18th. Ludlow the Marshal very impudently told me that
he was opposed to a non-importation and non-exportation agreement from Interest & that I should [not?] herd with those who
were for it. Mr. Young is much opposed to it & Mr Bache as
Equally so but assigns the disstress of the Poor as the reason.
The friends of Government & General Gage are industrious in the
Endeavours to divide the People. The Mechanicks published [an]
advertisment . . . to convene . . . in order to make choice of
a Committee of Correspondence of 25 Persons. They did accordingly meet at 6 o'Clock PM at Bardins . . . & unanimously approved the List . . . of 25 Nominated by a Number of Merchants
& others Friends to Liberty. At Noon Mr Revere the Boston express sett off for Philadelphia by whom the Committee wrote a
Letter to the Philadelphia Committee . . . and inclosed a Copy
of our Letter to the Boston Committee. . . . The Enemies of our
Common Liberties persist in their Endeavour to divide the people & to lull them into a state of Security. . . .

May 19th. Self sick. The meeting at Coffee House, was
not so full as might have been expected, Especially of the
Friends of Liberty, but its Enemies & those who were for the
Committee of 51 collected all their Force. Mr Isaac Low appeared without appointment of the Meeting as Moderator & wanted
to begin the business [on the] time appointed, but was prevented by Capt. Sears. When the Hour came Mr Sears wanted Him
to read the Letters from Boston & the resolutions . . . but he
would not do it . . . & then proposed the List of the Committee
of 51 to the meeting for their approbation. Mr. Sears then
said He would read the Letters & resolutions himself to the
People, but [was] interrupted by Mr. Low & the Waltons which
induced [him] to give it over. Mr. Low then proposed to the
people that those who were for the 51 should stand still &
those for the 25 to draw off. Mr. Sears then proposed that
those who were for 25 should stand still & those for 51 are to
draw off, but those who were for 51 artfully [threw?] the
meeting into such confusion that the Majority could not be well
known. Mr. Low was then called to by his Friends to come &
they would draw off with him. Capt. [Sears] replied that he
would go down & the People for the Committee of 25 would follow
him & it was added by some of his Friends, they would go up to
the City Hall & determine the majority by signing for the 25.
To this Mr Walton replied that none but the Freeholders & Freemen should sign. Mr. Sears replied that every man whose Liberties were concerned should sign but the Tradesmen who were for
the 25 said as they were working for others they would [lose]
their days work if they tarried any longer, which induced Mr.
Sears & Lamb to decline the design [of] determining the Majority [by] signing. . . .

May 20. At 6 this Evening the Mechanicks met at Hampden Hall being advised to do it in order to deliberate on acceding to the Committee of 51 to prevent a division in this alarming conjuncture. The result of which was that for the advancement of the common cause they would try the Committee of 51 & if they misbehaved that [they] would be removed.

May 21. The old Enemies to Liberty industrious in their Endeavours to persuade the people that they have no concern with the Bostonians. That Nothing is intended to us. But the People are too Zealous to be duped by such artifice. . . .

May 22. At 8 PM Mr Revere the Boston express returned from Philadelphia and brought a Letter from Charles Thomson enclosing the Copy of the Philadelphia Committee of Correspondence Letters & resolutions in answer to the Boston Letters. . . . Capt Sears and I advised the express to wait till next day for an answer from our Committee to the Letters he brought. . . .

May 23d. The Committee met at 10 AM at the Coffee House in pursuance of the Notice. Present upwards of 40 Members. . . . Mr Duane & self prevailed and Mr Jay & Mr Low with us were appointed a Committee to draw a draught of an Answer to the Boston Letter. . . . At 8 PM the Grand Committee met pursuant to adjournment. Before Mr. Duane came with the Draught Messrs. Evers, Bache, Shaw & others were disposed that the Congress should not be mentioned in the Letter that it was too soon to propose it but it was over ruled. When Mr. Duane came the Draught was immediately read to all. Shaw & others wanted it to be understood that the people of Boston were not suffering in the Cause of American Liberty & therefore objected to that part of the Letter where this is mentioned. But on this they were also over ruled. For Mr. Duane said "That if the Boston people were not suffering in the Cause of American Liberty we should cast them off and not write to them." But this was generally affirmed to be the case and the Draught was approved. . . . Mr. James Jauncy in the course of the Conversation upon the Boston Port Bill said "That he beleived on the payment of the Tea the Port would be opened.["] Upon the whole the Enemies of Liberty seemed to [be] discomfited that such a Letter has been wrote to Boston.

24th May. At 10 AM Mr Revere . . . departed for Boston with our Letter to their Committee. I urged upon him the expediency of their Committee's appointing time & place for the Congress as we did not do it in our Letter.

25 May. Mr. Sears informed me that Francis Lewis told him that John Watts endeavoured to convince him of the Ill policy of a non-importation agreement because "it would so distress the manufactures of Great Britain that they would come over here & the national revenues would be so affected with non-exporation that it would be ruined." To this Mr. Lewis replied

that rather than we should be Enslaved Let the King and
Navey . . . come here. His tampering shews that the Delancy
Junto are rising to prevent any thing being done for the relief
of Boston in order that they may make interest with Government
for places but their wicked designs will be defeated. Wrote
Chas. Thomson [of] Philadelphia. . . . Nothing material but the
Enemies & Lukewarm Friends to America are endeavouring to prej-
udice the people against a non-importation agreement.

21

GOUVERNEUR MORRIS TO MR.[JOHN?] PENN

New York, May 20, 1774

. . . . .

You have heard, and you will hear, a great deal about politics, and in the heap of chaff *you* may find some grains of
good sense. Believe me, Sir, freedom and religion are only
watchwords. We have appointed a Committee, or rather we have
nominated one. Let me give you the history of it. It is need-
less to premise, that the lower order of mankind are more easily led by specious appearances, than those of a more exalted
station. This, and many similar propositions you know better
than your humble servant.

The troubles in America, during Grenville's administration
put our gentry upon this finesse. They stimulated some daring
coxcombs to rouse the mob into an attack upon the bounds of

Jared Sparks, ed., *The Life of Gouverneur Morris, with Selec-*
tions from His Correspondence and Miscellaneous Papers . . . ,
3 vols. (Boston: Gray & Bowen, 1832), 1: 23-26. Morris (1752-
1816) was the son of Lewis Morris, second lord of the manor of
Morrisania in Westchester County. He graduated from King's
College in 1768 and was admitted to the bar in 1771. He maintained a conservative position on the imperial conflict until
opting strongly for independence after Lexington-Concord. His
unidentified correspondent is probably John Penn, governor of
Pennsylvania from 1763 to 1776.

order and decency. These fellows became the Jack Cades[1] of the
day, the leaders in all the riots, the belwethers of the flock.
The reason of the manoeuvre in those, who wished to keep fair
with the government, and at the same time to receive the in-
cense of popular applause, you will readily perceive. On the
whole, the shepherds were not much to blame in a politic point
of view. The belwethers jingled merrily, and roared out liberty, and property, and religion, and a multitude of cant terms,
which every one thought he understood, and was egregiously mistaken. For you must know the shepherds kept the dictionary of
the day, and, like the mysteries of the ancient mythology, it
was not for profane eyes or ears. This answered many purposes;
the simple flock put themselves entirely under the protection
of these most excellent shepherds. By and bye behold a great
metamorphosis, without the help of *Ovid* or his divinities, but
entirely effectuated by two modern genii, the god of ambition
and the goddess of faction. The first of these prompted the
shepherds to shear some of their flock, and then, in conjunction with the other, converted the belwethers into shepherds.
That we have been in hot water with the British Parliament ever
since, every body knows. Consequently these new shepherds had
their hands full of employment. The old ones kept themselves
least in sight, and a want of confidence in each other was not
the least evil which followed. The port of Boston has been
shut up. These sheep, simple as they are, cannot be gulled as
heretofore. In short, there is no ruling them; and now, to
leave the metaphor, the heads of the mobility grow dangerous
to the gentry, and how to keep them down is the question.
While they correspond with the other colonies, call and dismiss
popular assemblies, make resolves to bind the consciences of
the rest of mankind, bully poor printers, and exert with full
force all their other tribunitial powers, it is impossible to
curb them.

But art sometimes goes farther than force, and therefore
to trick them handsomely a committee of patricians was to be
nominated, and into their hands was to be committed the majesty
of the people, and the highest trust was to be reposed in them
by a mandate, that they should take care, *quod respublica non
capiat injuriam*. The tribunes, through the want of good leger-
demain in the senatorial order, perceived the finesse, and yesterday I was present at a grand division of the city, and there
I behold my fellow-citizens very accurately counting all their
chickens, not only before any of them were hatched, but before

---

[1]Leader of the "peasant revolt" of 1450 in Kent which enjoyed
the support of upper-middle-class elements and was aimed less
at landowners than at the opprobrious behavior of government
officials and at objectionable fiscal policies.

above one half of the eggs were laid. In short, they fairly
contended about the future forms of our government, whether it
should be founded upon Aristocratic or Democratic principles.
    I stood in the balcony, and on my right hand were ranged
all the people of property, with some few poor dependants, and
on the other all the tradesmen, &c., who thought it worth
their while to leave daily labour for the good of the country.
The spirit of the English Constitution has yet a little influence left, and but a little. The remains of it, however, will
give the wealthy people a superiority this time, but would they
secure it they must banish all schoolmasters and confine all
knowledge to themselves. This cannot be. The mob begin to
think and to reason. Poor reptiles! it is with them a vernal
morning; they are struggling to cast off their winter's slough,
they bask in the sunshine, and ere noon they will bite, depend
upon it. The gentry begin to fear this. Their committee will
be appointed, they will deceive the people, and again forfeit a
share of their confidence. And if these instances of what with
one side is policy, with the other perfidy, shall continue to
increase, and become more frequent, farewell aristocracy. I
see, and I see it with fear and trembling, that if the disputes
with Britain continue, we shall be under the worst of all possible dominions. We shall be under the domination of a riotous
mob.
    It is the interest of all men, therefore, to seek for re-
union with the parent State. A safe compact seems in my poor
opinion to be now tendered. Internal taxation is to be left
with ourselves. The right of regulating trade to be vested in
Britain, where alone is found the power of protecting it. I
trust you will agree with me, that this is the only possible
mode of union. Men by nature are free as air. When they enter into society, there is, there must be, an implied compact,
for there never yet was an express one, that a part of this
freedom shall be given up for the security of the remainder.
But what part? The answer is plain. The least possible, considering the circumstances of the society, which constitute
what may be called its political necessity. And what does this
political necessity require in the present instance? Not that
Britain should lay imposts upon us for the support of government, nor for its defence. Not that she should regulate our
internal police. These things affect us only. She can have no
right to interfere. To these things we ourselves are competent. But can it be said that we are competent to the regulating of trade? The position is absurd, for this affects every part of the British Empire, every part of the habitable
earth. If Great Britain, if Ireland, if America, if all of
them, are to make laws of trade, there must be a collision of
these different authorities, and then who is to decide the

vis major? To recur to this, if possible to be avoided, is the greatest of all great absurdities.

Political necessity therefore requires, that this power should be placed in the hands of one part of the empire. Is it a question which part? Let me answer by asking another. Pray which part of the empire protects trade? Which part of the empire receives almost immense sums to guard the rest? And what danger is in the trust? Some men object, that England will draw all the profits of our trade into her coffers. All that she can, undoubtedly. But unless a reasonable compensation for his trouble be left to the merchant here, she destroys the trade, and then she will receive no profit from it.

· · · · ·

22

DESCRIPTION OF ROYAL GOVERNMENT   New York, June 11, 1774

· · · · ·

By the Grants of this Province and other Territories to the Duke of York in 166¾ and 1674, the powers of Government were vested in him, and were accordingly exercised by his Governors until he ascended the Throne when his Rights as Proprietor merged in his Crown, and the Province ceased to be a charter Governm[en]t.

From that time it has been a Royal Government, and in its constitution nearly resembles that of Great Britain and the other Royal Governments in America. The Governor is appointed by the King during his Royal Will and pleasure by Letters pattent under the Great Seal of Great Britain with very ample Powers.—He has a Council in Imitation of His Majesty's Privy Council.—This Board when full consists of Twelve Members who

---

Report of Governor William Tryon to the Earl of Dartmouth, June 11, 1774, *New York Colonial Documents*, 8: 443-45. The instructions issued to each governor formed the "constitution" of the colony. It should be noted that suffrage was restricted to white adult males who were either freeholders (that is, owned property worth £40) or freemen (that is, shopkeepers and craftsmen licensed by the corporations of New York City and Albany). Moravians, Catholics, and Quakers were disfranchised.

are also appointed by the Crown during Will and Pleasure; any
three of whom make a Quorum.—The Province enjoys a Legislative
Body which consists of the Governor as the King's Representative; the Council in place of the House of Lords, and the Representatives of the People, who are chosen as in England: Of
these the City of New York sends four.— All the other Counties
(except the New Counties of Charlotte and Gloucester as yet not
represented send Two.—The Borough of Westchester, The Township
of Schenectady and the three manors of Renselaerswyck, Livingston and Cortlandt each send one; in the whole forming a Body
of Thirty one Representatives.

The Governor by his Commission is authorized to convene
them with the advice of the Council, and adjourn, prorogue or
dissolve the General Assembly as he shall judge necessary.

This Body has not power to make any Laws repugnant to the
Laws and Statutes of Great Britain. All Laws proposed to be
made by this Provincial Legislature, pass thro' each of the
Houses of Council and Assembly, as Bills do thro' the House of
Commons and House of Lords in England, and the Governor has a
Negative voice in the making and passing all such Laws. Every
law so passed is to be transmitted to His Majesty under the
Great Seal of the Province, within three Months or sooner after
the making thereof and a Duplicate by the next Conveyance, in
order to be approved or disallowed by His Majesty; And if His
Majesty shall disallow any such Law and the same is signified
to the Governor under the Royal Sign Manual or by Order of his
Majesty's Privy Council, from thenceforth such law becomes utterly void.—A law of the Province has limited the duration of
the Assembly to seven years.

The Common Law of England is considered as the Fundamental
law of the Province and it is the received Doctrine that all
the Statutes (not Local in their Nature, and which can be fitly
applied to the circumstances of the Colony) enacted before the
Province had a Legislature, are binding upon the Colony; but
that Statutes passed since do not affect the Colony, unless by
being specially named, such appears to be the Intention of the
British Legislature.

The Province has a Court of Chancery in which the Governor
or Commander in Chief sits as Chancellor, and the Practice of
the Court of Chancery in England is pursued as closely as possible. The Officers of this Court consist of a Master of the
Rolls newly created.—Two Masters.—Two Clerks in Court.—A
Register.—An Examiner, and a Serjeant at Arms.

Of the Courts of Common Law the Chief is called the Supreme Court.—The Judges of which have all the Powers of the
King's Bench, Common Pleas & Exchequer in England. This Court
sits once in every three months at the City of New York, and
the practice therein is modell'd upon that of the King's Bench
at Westminster.—Tho' the Judges have the powers of the Court

of Exchequer they never proceed upon the Equity side.—The
Court has no Officers but one Clerk, and is not organized or
supplied with any Officers in that Department of the Exchequer,
which in England has the care of the Revenue.—The Judges of
the Supreme Court hold their Offices during the King's Will &
Pleasure and are Judges of Nisi prius of Course by Act of Assembly, & annually perform a Circuit thro' the Counties.   The
Decisions of this Court in General are final unless where the
value exceeds £300 Sterling, in which case the subject may be
relieved from its errors *only* by an Application to the Govern-
or and Council, and where the value exceeds £500 Sterling an
appeal lies from the Judgment of the latter to His Majesty in
Privy Council.

By an Act of the Legislature of the Province suits are
prohibited to be brought in the Supreme Court where the value
demanded does not exceed £20 Currency.

The Clerk's Office of the Supreme Court, has always been
held as an appendage to that of Secretary of the Province.

There is also in each County an Inferior Court of Common
Pleas, which has the cognizance of all Actions real, personal
and mixed, where the matter in demand is above £5 in value.—
The practice of these Courts is a mixture between that of the
King's Bench and Common Pleas at Westminster.—Their errors are
corrected in the first Instance by Writ of Error brought into
the Supreme Court; and the Judges hold their Offices during
pleasure.—The Clerks of these Courts also hold their offices
during pleasure and are appointed by the Governor, except the
Clerk of Albany who is appointed under the King's mandate.

Besides these Courts the Justices of peace are by Act of
Assembly empowered to try all causes to the Amount of £5 currency, (except where the Crown is concerned, or where the Title
of Lands shall come into Question;—and Actions of Slander) but
the parties may either of them demand a Jury of Six Men.—If
wrong is done to either party, the person injured may have a
Certiorari from the Supreme Court, tho' the remedy is very in-
adequate.

The Courts of Criminal Jurisdiction are Correspondent to
those in England.—The Supreme Court exercises it in the City
of New York, as the King's Bench does at Westminster.—The
Judges when they go the Circuit have a Commission of Oyer and
Terminer and General Goal Delivery; and there are Courts of
Sessions held by the Justices of the Peace; the powers of which
and their proceeding correspond with the like Courts in England.—The Office of Clerk of the Sessions, is invariably connected with that of the Clerk of the Inferior Court of Common
Pleas in the respective Counties.

By Acts of the Provincial Legislature the Justices of the
Peace have an extraordinary Jurisdiction with respect to some
offences by which any three Justices, (one being of the Quorum)

where the Offender does not find Bail in 48 Hours after being
in the custody of the Constable, may try the party without any
or a Jury, for any Offence under the Degree of Grand Larceny;
and inflict any punishment for these small offences at their
Discretion, so that it exceeds not to Life or Limb.—And any
three Justices of the Peace (one being a Quorum) and Five Freeholders have power without a Grand or Petty Jury to proceed
against and try in a Summary Way, Slaves offending in certain
cases, and punish them even with Death.

The Duty of His Majesty's Attorney General of the Province,
is similar to the Duty of that Officer in England, and the Master of the Crown Office: He is appointed by the Crown during
pleasure, and His Majesty has no Sollicitor General nor Council
in the Province, to assist the Attorney General upon any Occasion.

There are two other Courts in the Province, The Court of
Admiralty which proceeds after the Course of the Civil Law in
matters within its Jurisdiction, which has been so enlarged by
divers statutes, as to include almost every breach of the Acts
of Trade.—From this Court an appeal lies to a Superior Court
of Admiralty, lately Established in North America by statute;
before this Establishment as appeal only lay to the High Court
of Admiralty of England.

The Prerogative Court concerns itself only in the Probate
of Wills and in matters relating to the Administration of the
Estates of Intestates and in granting Licences of Marriage.
The Governor is properly the Judge of this Court but it has
been usual for him to Act in general by a Deligate.

The Province is at present divided into fourteen Counties,
vizt The City and County of New York—The County of Albany—
Richmond (which comprehends the whole of Staten Island) King's,
Queen's and Suffolk (which include the whole of Nassau or Long
Island.) Westchester, Dutchess, Ulster, Orange, Cumberland,
Gloucester, Charlotte and Tryon.—For each of these Counties a
Sheriff and one or more Coroners are appointed by the Governor,
who hold their offices during pleasure.

As to the Military power of the Province, the Governor for
the time being is the Captain General and Commander in Chief
and appoints all the Provincial Military Officers during pleasure.

. . . . .

23

LIEUTENANT GOVERNOR CADWALLADER COLDEN TO THE EARL OF DARTMOUTH   New York, July 6, 1774

. . . . .
In my letter of June the 1st I inform'd your Lordship that
the People of this City had chosen a Committee of 51 Persons,
to correspond with the Sister Colonies on the present political
Affairs that many of this Committee were of the most considerable Merchants, and Men of Cool Tempers, who would endeavour to
avoid all extravagant and dangerous Measures. They have had a
continual struggle with those of a different Disposition: and
having for several Weeks succeeded in suspending any Resolutions, I was in hopes they would have maintained the only Conduct which can excuse them. But accounts repeatedly coming to
hand, from different Parts of the Continent, of the Appointment
of Deputies to meet in general Congress, this Measure was so
strenuously push'd that it was carried in the Committee of 51;
on Monday last; and five Persons were named for the Deputies
from this Province. . . . It is said the People are to be invited to meet on Thursday, to approve of the Deputies named by
the Committee. These Transactions are dangerous, my Lord, and
illegal; but by what means shall Government prevent them? An
Attempt by the Power of the Civil Magistrate, would only shew
their weakness, and it is not easy to say upon what foundation
a Military Aid should be called in. Such a Measure would involve us in Troubles, which it is thought much more prudent to
avoid; and to shun all Extreams, while it is yet possible.
Things may take a favourable turn. . . .
The present Political zeal and frenzy is almost entirely
confined to the City of New York. The People in the Counties
are no ways disposed to become active, or to bear any Part in
what is proposed by the Citizens. I am told all the Counties,
but one, have declined an Invitation, sent to them from New
York, to appoint Committees of Correspondence. This Province
is every where, my Lord, except in the City of New York, perfectly quiet and in good Order: and in New York a much greater
freedom of Speech prevails now, than has done heretofore.
. . . . .

New York Colonial Documents, 8: 469-70.

24

ENDORSEMENT OF A CONTINENTAL CONGRESS
New York City, July 7, 1774

At a numerous meeting of the inhabitants of the city of New-York, convened in the fields, by public advertisement, on Wednesday the 6th of July, 1774. . . .

The business of the meeting being fully explained by the chairman, and the dangerous tendency of the numerous and vile arts used by the enemies of America, to divide and distract her councils, as well as the misrepresentations of the virtuous intentions of the citizens of this metropolis, in this interesting and alarming state of the liberties of America, the following resolutions were twice read, and the question being separately put on each of them, they were passed without one dissentient.

1st. *Resolved, nem. con.* That the statute commonly called the Boston port act, is oppressive to the inhabitants of that town, unconstitutional in its principles, and dangerous to the liberties of British America; and that, therefore, we consider our brethren at Boston, as now suffering in the common cause of these colonies.

2d. *Resolved,* . . . That any attack or attempt to abridge the liberties, or invade the constitution of any of our sister colonies, is immediately an attack upon the liberties and constitution of all the British colonies.

3d. *Resolved,* . . . That the shutting up of any of the ports in America, with intent to exact from Americans, a submission to parliamentary taxations, or extort a reparation of private injuries, is highly unconstitutional, and subversive of the commercial rights of the inhabitants of this continent.

4th. *Resolved,* . . . That it is the opinion of this meeting, that if the principal colonies on this continent, shall come into a joint resolution, to stop all importation from, and exportation to Great Britain, till the act of parliament for blocking up the harbor of Boston be repealed, the same will prove the salvation of North America and her liberties, and that, on the other hand, if they continue their exports and imports, there is great reason to fear that fraud, power, and the most odious oppression, will rise triumphant over right, justice, social happiness, and freedom:—Therefore,

5th. *Resolved*, . . . That the deputies who shall represent this colony in the congress of American deputies, to be held at Philadelphia, about the first of September next, are hereby instructed, empowered, and directed to engage with a majority of the principal colonies, to agree, for this city, upon a non-importation from Great Britian, of all goods, wares and merchandizes, until the act for blocking up the harbor of Boston be repealed, and American grievances be redressed; and also to agree to all such other measures as the congress shall, in their wisdom, judge advansive of these great objects, and a general security of the rights and privileges of America.

6th. *Resolved*, . . . That this meeting will abide by, obey, and observe all such resolutions, determinations, and measures, which the congress aforesaid shall come into, and direct or recommend to be done, for obtaining and securing the important ends mentioned in the foregoing resolutions. And that an engagement to this effect be immediately entered into and sent to the congress, to evince to them, our readiness and determination to co-operate with our sister colonies, for the relief of our distressed brethren of Boston, as well as for the security of our common rights and privileges.

7th. *Resolved*, . . . That it is the opinion of this meeting, that it would be proper for every county in the colony, without delay, to send two deputies, chosen by the people, or from the committee, chosen by them in each county, to hold, in conjunction with deputies for this city and county, a convention for the colony (on a day to be appointed) in order to elect a proper number of deputies, to represent the colony in the general congress: but that, if the counties shall conceive this mode impracticable, or inexpedient, they be requested to give their approbation to the deputies who shall be chosen for this city and county, to represent the colony in congress.

8th. *Resolved*, . . . That a subscription should immediately be set on foot, for the relief of such poor inhabitants of Boston as are, or may be deprived of the means of subsistence, by the operation of the act of parliament for stopping up the port of Boston. The money which shall arise from such subscription, to be laid out as the city committee of correspondence shall think will best answer the end proposed.

9th. *Resolved*, . . . That the city committee of correspondence be, and they are hereby instructed to use their utmost endeavors to carry these resolutions into execution.

Ordered, That these resolutions be printed in the public newspapers of this city, and transmitted to the different counties in this colony, and to the committees of correspondence, for the neighboring colonies.

25

POUGHKEEPSIE RESOLUTIONS
Poughkeepsie, Dutchess County, August 10, 1774

At a Meeting of the Freeholders and Inhabitants of *Pough-keepsie* Precinct, in *Dutchess* County, in consequence of an ad-vertisement of the Supervisor of said Precinct, on the 10th of *August*, 1774. . . .

The question was put, "Whether we will choose a Committee agreeable to a request contained in a Letter from Mr. *Isaac Low*, Chairman of the Committee of Correspondence in *New-York*?" Which was carried in the Negative.

The following Resolves were then unanimously entered into:

1st. *Resolved*, That although the members of this meeting (and they are persuaded the inhabitants of *America* in general) are firm and unshaken in their allegiance to his Majesty King *George*, and are entirely averse to breaking their connection with the mother country, yet they think it necessary to declare, that they agree fully in opinion with the many respectable bodies who have already published their sentiments, in declar-ing that the unlimited right claimed by the *British* Parliament, in which we neither are, or can be represented, of making laws of every kind to be binding on the Colonies, particularly of imposing taxes, whatever may be the name or form under which they are attempted to be introduced, is contrary to the spirit of the *British* Constitution, and consequently inconsistent with that liberty which we, as *British* subjects, have a right to claim, and, therefore,

2d. *Resolved*, That it is the opinion of this meeting that letters of Instruction be directed to the Members of the Gener-al Assembly for the County of *Dutchess*, desiring that at the next meeting of the General Assembly for the Province of *New-York*, they will lay before that honourable House the dangerous consequences flowing from several late Acts of the *British* Par-liament imposing duties and taxes on the *British* Colonies in *America*, for the sole purpose of raising a revenue, and that they use their influence in the said House, and with the sever-al branches of the Legislature, to lay before his Majesty an humble Petition and Remonstrance, setting forth the state of

---

Peter Force, comp., *American Archives* . . . , 9 vols. (Washing-ton, D.C.: M. St. Clair and Peter Force, 1837-53), 4th ser., 1: 702.

our several grievances, and praying his Royal interposition for a repeal of the said Acts.

3d. *Resolved*, That it is the opinion of this meeting, that they ought, and are willing to bear and pay such part and proportion of the national expenses as their circumstances will admit of, in such manner and form as the General Assembly of this Province shall think proper; and that like sentiments, adopted by the Legislatures of the other Colonies, will have a tendency to conciliate the affections of the mother country and the Colonies, upon which their mutual happiness, we conceive, principally depends.

26

LIEUTENANT GOVERNOR CADWALLADER
COLDEN TO THE EARL OF DARTMOUTH New York, December 7, 1774

. . . . .

The first thing done here in consequence of the resolutions of the Congress, was the dissolution of the Committee of 51 in order to choose a new Committee to carry the measures of the Congress into effect. A day was appointed by advertisem[en]t for choosing sixty persons to form this new Committee. About thirty or forty citizens appeared at the election, and chose the sixty persons who had been previously named by the former Committee. I can, no otherwise, my Lord, account for the very small number of people who appeared on this occasion than by supposing that the measures of the Congress are generally disrelished. . . .

In the present Committee of this Place there are several gentlemen of property and who are esteemed to favor moderate and conciliatory [measures]. I was surprised to find such men joining with the Committee whose design is to execute the plan of the Congress. I have at length discovered that they act with a view to protect the City from the ravages of the Mob. For this purpose, they say they are obliged at present to support the measures of the Congress. That if they did not, the most dangerous men among us would take the Lead; and, under pretence of executing the dictates of the Congress would imme-

New York Colonial Documents, 8: 512-13.

diately throw the City into the most perilous situation. That
however considerable the numbers may be, who disapprove of violent riotous measures, yet the Spirit of Mobing is so much
abroad, it is in the Power of a few People at any time to raise
a Mob; and that the Gentlemen, and men of Property, will not
turn out to suppress them. I fear, my Lord, there is too much
truth in this representation. It is a dreadful situation. If
we are not rescued from it, by the wisdom and firmness of Parliament, the Colonies must soon fall into distraction and every
Calamity annexed to a total annihilation of Government.

. . . . .

27

ALEXANDER HAMILTON, *A FULL VINDICATION*
. . . *OF THE CONGRESS*   New York, December 15, 1774

. . . . .
    It was hardly to be expected that any man could be so pre-
sumptuous, as openly to controvert the equity, wisdom, and authority of the measures, adopted by the congress: an assembly
truly respectable on every account! Whether we consider the
characters of the men, who composed it; the number, and dignity
of their constituents, or the important ends for which they
were appointed. But, however improbable such a degree of presumption might have seemed, we find there are some, in whom it
exists. Attempts are daily making to diminish the influence of
their decisions, and prevent the salutary effects, intended by
them. The impotence of such insidious efforts is evident from
the general indignation they are treated with; so that no mate-

---

*A Full Vindication of the Measures of the Congress, from the
Calumnies of their Enemies; In Answer to A Letter, Under the
Signature of A. W. Farmer* . . . (New York: James Rivington,
1774), pp. 3-4, 6-8, 33. Born in Nevis, British West Indies,
in 1755 (or 1757), Hamilton immigrated to New York City in
1772. He was a student in King's College (Columbia University)
at the time of the First Continental Congress and under the
pseudonym "A Friend to America" wrote several pamphlets de-
fending the actions of the congress from the animadversions of
the "Westchester Farmer" (see document no. 30).

rial ill-consequences can be dreaded from them. But lest they
should have a tendency to mislead, and prejudice the minds of a
few; it cannot be deemed altogether useless to bestow some notice upon them.

And first, let me ask these restless spirits, whence
arises that violent antipathy they seem to entertain, not only
to the natural rights of mankind; but to common sense and common modesty. That they are enemies to the natural rights of
mankind is manifest, because they wish to see one part of their
species enslaved by another. That they have an invincible aversion to common sense is apparent in many respects: They endeavour to persuade us, that the absolute sovereignty of parliament
does not imply our absolute slavery; that it is a Christian
duty to submit to be plundered of all we have, merely because
some of our fellow-subjects are wicked enough to require it of
us, that slavery, so far from being a great evil, is a great
blessing; and even, that our contest with Britain is founded
entirely upon the petty duty of 3 pence per pound on East India
tea; whereas the whole world knows, it is built upon this interesting question, whether the inhabitants of Great-Britain
have a right to dispose of the lives and properties of the
inhabitants of America, or not? And lastly, that these men
have discarded all pretension to common modesty, is clear from
hence, first, because they, in the plainest terms, call an august body of men, famed for their patriotism and abilities,
fools or knaves, and of course the people whom they represented
cannot be exempt from the same opprobrious appellations; and
secondly, because they set themselves up as standards of wisdom
and probity, by contradicting and censuring the public voice in
favour of those men.

A little consideration will convince us, that the congress
instead of having "ignorantly misunderstood, carelessly neglected, or basely betrayed the interests of the colonies," have,
on the contrary, devised and recommended the only effectual
means to secure the freedom, and establish the future prosperity of America upon a solid basis. If we are not free and
happy hereafter, it must proceed from the want of integrity and
resolution, in executing what they have concerted; not from the
temerity or impolicy of their determinations.

. . . . .

The design of electing members to represent us in general
congress, was, that the wisdom of America might be collected in
devising the most proper and expedient means to repel this
atrocious invasion of our rights. It has been accordingly done.
Their decrees are binding upon all, and demand a religious observance.

We did not, especially in this province, circumscribe them
by any fixed boundary, and therefore as they cannot be said to
have exceeded the limits of their authority, their act must be

esteemed the act of their constituents. If it should be objected, that they have not answered the end of their election; but have fallen upon an improper and ruinous mode of proceeding: I reply, by asking, Who shall be the judge? Shall any individual oppose his private sentiment to the united counsels of men, in whom America has reposed so high a confidence? The attempt must argue no small degree of arrogance and self-sufficiency.

. . . . .

The only scheme of opposition, suggested by those, who have been, and are averse from a non-importation and non-exportation agreement, is, by REMONSTRANCE and PETITION. The authors and abettors of this scheme, have never been able to *invent* a single argument to prove the likelihood of its succeeding. On the other hand, there are many standing facts, and valid considerations against it.

In the infancy of the present dispute, we had recourse to this method only. We addressed the throne in the most loyal and respectful manner, in a legislative capacity; but what was the consequence? Our address was treated with contempt and neglect. The first American congress did the same, and met with similar treatment. The total repeal of the stamp act, and the partial repeal of the revenue acts took place, not because the complaints of America were deemed just and reasonable; but because these acts were found to militate against the commercial interests of Great Britain: This was the declared motive of the repeal.

. . . . .

There is less reason now than ever to expect deliverance, in this way, from the hand of oppression. The system of slavery, fabricated against America, cannot at this time be considered as the effect of inconsideration and rashness. It is the offspring of mature deliberation. It has been fostered by time, and strengthened by every artifice human subtilty is capable of. After the claims of parliament had lain dormant for awhile, they are again resumed and prosecuted with more than common ardour. The Premier has advanced too far to recede with safety: He is deeply interested to execute his purpose, if possible: we know he has declared, that he will never desist, till he has brought America to his feet; and we may conclude, nothing but necessity will induce him to abandon his aims. In common life, to retract an error even in the beginning, is no easy task. Perseverance confirms us in it, and rivets the difficulty; but in a public station, to have been in an error, and to have persisted in it, when it is detected, ruins both reputation and fortune. To this we may add, that disappointment and opposition inflame the minds of men, and attach them, still more, to their mistakes.

What can we represent which has not already been represented? what petitions can we offer, that have not already been offered? The rights of America, and the injustice of parliamentary pretensions have been clearly and repeatedly stated, both in and out of parliament. No new arguments can be framed to operate in our favour. Should we even resolve the errors of the ministry and parliament into the falibility of human understanding, if they have not yet been convinced, we have no prospect of being able to do it by any thing further we can say. But if we impute their conduct to a wicked thirst of domination and disregard to justice, we have no hope of prevailing with them to alter it, by expatiating on our rights, and suing to their compassion for relief; especially since we have found, by various experiments, the inefficacy of such methods.

Upon the whole, it is morally certain, this mode of opposition would be fruitless and defective. The exigency of the times requires vigorous and probable remedies; not weak and improbable. It would therefore be the extreme of folly to place any confidence in, much less, confine ourselves wholly to it.

This being the case, we can have no resource but in a restriction of our trade, or in a resistance *vi & armis*. It is impossible to conceive any other alternative. Our congress, therefore, have imposed what restraint they thought necessary. Those, who condemn or clamour against it, do nothing more, nor less, than advise us to be slaves.

. . . . .

The Farmer[1] cries, "tell me not of delegates, congresses committees, mobs, riots, insurrections, associations; a plague on them all. Give me the steady, uniform, unbiassed influence of the courts of justice. I have been happy under their protection, and I trust in God, I shall be so again."

I say, tell me not of the British Commons, Lords, ministry, ministerial tools, placemen, pensioners, parasites. I scorn to let my life and property depend upon the pleasure of any of them. Give me the steady, uniform, unshaken security of constitutional freedom; give me the right to be tried by a jury of my own neighbours, and to be taxed by my own representatives only. What will become of the law and courts of justice without this? The shadow may remain, but the substance will be gone. I would die to preserve the law upon a solid foundation; but take away liberty, and the foundation is destroyed.

. . . . .

---

[1]"A. W. Farmer" [Samuel Seabury].

28

EXTRACT OF A GENUINE LETTER TO A GENTLEMAN
FROM HIS FRIEND AT NEW YORK   New York, December 28, 1774

I know you conceive America hardly treated, and will think perhaps the change in my sentiments, owing to my private interest being hurt by their proceedings; I grant you this is too often the case, but not in the present instance. I came to this place highly prepossessed in their favour, but find their behavior so mad, so inconsistent with that gratitude they owe Great Britain, that I have entirely changed my opinion of them, tho' at the same time I do not entirely side with Government in all their measures, yet by what I can understand of the matter, which (though little) is, I believe, as much as most people do, who make the greatest noise here, should the liberty side get the better, it will end in the destruction of the colonies, as New England only wants to grind the other provinces. Most sensible people here, people of property, whom I should suppose interested as much as any in the matter, are of this opinion, and say that one master is better than a thousand, and that they would rather be oppressed by a King than by a rascally mob. 'Tis not only reducing everybody to a level, but it is entirely reversing the matter, and making the mob their masters. This province, as it is less violent, is looked upon with an evil eye by the rest, and with contempt called a Tory province; for in America, the distinction between Whigs and Tories prevail as much at present as ever it did in England. Every man who will not drink "destruction to his King," is a Tory, and liable to tar and feathers. In the east and southern provinces they are in actual rebellion, raising troops, and seizing ammunition in the most daring manner; the common people are mad, they only hear one side of the question, and believe they are oppressed because they are told so, which is all they know of the matter. As the fever is very high, a little bleeding is absolutely necessary. General Gage is by far too lenient in his measures, and had a few been killed at first, the rest would have been quiet; now multitudes must unavoidably suffer. Was the royal standard hoisted, thousands would flock to it,

---

Margaret W. Willard, ed., *Letters on the American Revolution, 1774-1776* (Boston: Houghton Mifflin Co., 1925), pp. 45-46. The identity of neither of the correspondents is known. The extract appeared in the *London Morning Chronicle and Daily Advertiser*, February 2, 1775.

that are as yet afraid to declare their sentiments. It is expected in a little time, and should it happen before we quit
the continent, I would not be the last to repair to it. If I
must light a match, it shall be for King George. I do not wish
it but I think I would not shun it.

29

RESOLUTIONS OF THE NEWTOWN TOWNSHIP COMMITTEE
Newtown, December 29, 1774

THAT this Committee, having taken into most serious and
deliberate consideration, the consequences that must evidently
flow from the several acts of the British parliament, being
established and carried into execution in order to raise a revenue in America; likewise that of having power to bind the people of the colonies, by statute, in all cases whatsoever; that
of extending the limits of the Admiralty courts, whereby the
judges of said courts are empowered to receive their salaries
and fees, from effects to be condemned by themselves, and his
Majesty's American subjects deprived of their right of trial by
jury; that of requiring oppressive security from the claimants
of ships or goods seized, before they shall be allowed to defend their property; that of empowering commissioners of the
customs, to break and enter houses without the authority of any
civil magistrate; that of stopping the port of Boston and chang-
ing the form of government in Massachusetts-Bay, and the Quebec
Bill; all of which as appears to us, are intended absolutely to
deprive his Majesty's most dutiful and loyal subjects, inhabitants of the American colonies, of their most inestimable rights
and privileges, by subjugating them to the British parliament,

---

"Resolves of the Committee chosen by the Freeholders of Newtown
Township, Queens County," *New York Journal*, January 5, 1775.
The number of persons who endorsed the resolutions is not known.
However, in the January 12, 1775, issue of James Rivington's
New York Gazetteer there appears a notice signed by fifty-six
residents of Newtown stating that they were "no way concerned
in those resolves" and that they do not "acknowledge any other
representatives but the Members of the General Assembly of the
province of NEW-YORK."

and driving them to the dire necessity of submitting to have their property taken from them without their consent; which we conceive as one of the most deplorable situations to which a free people can be reduced, and absolutely repugnant to the constitution of Great Britain, Therefore,

RESOLVED, First, that we consider it as our greatest happiness and glory, to be governed by the illustrious house of Hanover, and that we acknowledge and bear true and faithful allegiance to king George the third, as our rightful Sovereign, and under his protection, have a right to enjoy the privileges of the constitution of Great Britain, as founded on the revolution principles,[1] in as full and ample a manner as our fellow subjects residing there; that we consider ourselves as one people, connected by the strongest ties of interest and affection, and that we lament as our greatest misfortune, any occurrence which shall have a tendency to destroy that mutual confidence which the mother country and her colonies should repose in each other.

RESOLVED, Second, That we conceive it to be a fundamental part of the British constitution, that a man shall have the disposal of his own property, either by himself or representative; and as we are not, and from our local circumstances, cannot be represented in parliament, we consider all acts by them, imposing taxes on the colonies, as subversive of one of the most valuable privileges of the English constitution, and having a direct tendency to alienate the affections of the colonists from their parent state.

RESOLVED, Thirdly, That it is our indispensable duty, to transmit unimpaired to posterity, all our most valuable rights and privileges as we received them from our ancestors, particularly that most inestimable right, of disposing of our own property, either by ourselves or representatives.

RESOLVED, Fourthly, That as some mode of opposition to acts of parliament, imposing taxes in America, has been, by the inhabitants of the different colonies on this continent thought necessary, to secure their invaded rights and properties; which mode has been left to the determination of the delegates, sent by each colony, and met in congress, at Philadelphia in September last; they having, among other articles of their association, recommended, that a committee be chosen in every county, city, and town, whose business it should be to observe the conduct of all persons touching said association, and as we are willing to establish harmony and union, we will, so far as our influence extends, endeavour that the measures adopted and recommended by said Congress, be strictly adhered to in this town.

RESOLVED, Fifthly, As we highly approve of the wise, prudent, and constitutional mode of opposition, adopted by our

---

[1]The Glorious Revolution of 1688–89.

worthy Delegates in General Congress, to the several late tyrannical and oppressive acts of the British Parliament; We
therefore render our most sincere and hearty thanks to those
gentlemen, for their patriotic spirit, in so cheerfully under-
taking the difficult and arduous task, for their faithfullness
in council, and great wisdom, in drawing conclusions, which
through the influence of divine providence, we trust, will be
the means of securing us, our liberties and privileges, as free
born Englishmen, and again restore harmony and confidence
throughout the British empire, which is the hearty wish of all
the friends to Liberty, and foes to Oppression.

30

SAMUEL SEABURY, *AN ALARM TO THE LEGISLATURE*
New York, January 17, 1775

When you reflect upon the present confused and distressed
state of this, and the other colonies, I am persuaded, that you
will think no apology necessary for the liberty I have taken,
of addressing you on that subject. The unhappy contention we
have entered into with our parent state, would inevitably be
attended with many disagreeable circumstances, with many and
great inconveniences to us, even were it conducted on our part,
with *propriety* and *moderation*. What then must be the case,
when all proper and moderate measures are *rejected*? When not
even the *appearance* of decency is regarded? When nothing seems
to be consulted, but how to perplex, irritate, and affront, the
British Ministry, Parliament, Nation and *King*? When every
scheme that tends to *peace*, is branded with *ignominy*; as being

Clarence H. Vance, ed., *Letters of a Westchester Farmer (1774-*
1775) by the Reverend Samuel Seabury (1729-1796). Westchester
Historical Society Publications 8 (1930): pp. 151-55, 160-62.
The son of an Anglican minister, Seabury became rector of the
church at Westchester in 1767. An ardent pamphleteer, he cam-
paigned tirelessly for an American bishop and confuted the
measures of the Continental Congress in a series of publications under the pseudonym "A. W. Farmer." Despite his loyalism
he remained in the United States, and in 1784 he became the
first bishop of the Episcopal church in America.

the machination of slavery! When nothing is called FREEDOM but SEDITION! Nothing LIBERTY but REBELLION!

I will not presume to encroach so far upon your time, as to attempt to point out the *causes* of our unnatural contention with *Great Britain*. *You* are well acquainted with them.—Nor will I attempt to trace out the *progress* of that *infatuation*, which hath so deeply, so miserably, infected the *Colonies*. *You* must have observed its rise, and noted its rapid growth. But I intreat your patience and candour, while I make some *observations* on the *conduct* of the Colonies in *general*, and of *this* Colony in *particular*, in the present dispute with our *mother country:* By which it will appear, that *most*, if not *all* the measures that have been adopted, have been *illegal* in their *beginning*, *tyrannical* in their *operation*,—and that they *must* be *ineffectual* in the *event*.

It is the happiness of the *British Government*, and of all the *British Colonies*, that the people have a right to share in the legislature. This right they exercise by choosing *representatives*; and thereby constituting one branch of the legislative authority. But when they have chosen their representatives, that right, which was before diffused through the whole people, centers in their *Representatives alone*; and can legally be exercised by *none but them*. *They* become the guardians of the lives, the liberties, the rights and properties, of the people: And as *they* are under the most sacred obligations to discharge their trust with *prudence* and *fidelity*, so the *people* are under the strongest obligations to treat them with *honour* and *respect*; and to look to *them* for redress of all those grievances that they can justly complain of.

But in the present dispute with Great Britain, the *representatives of the people* have not only been *utterly disregarded*, but their *dignity* has been *trampled upon*, and their *authority contravened*.

A COMMITTEE, chosen in a *tumultuous, illegal* manner, usurped the most *depotic authority* over the *province*. They entered into contracts, compacts, combinations, treaties of alliance, with the other colonies, without *any* power from the *legislature of the province*. They agreed with the other Colonies to send Delegates to meet in convention at Philadelphia, to determine upon the *rights and liberties of the good people of this province*, unsupported by any Law. They issued notifications to the several supervisors through the colony, desiring them to *assemble the people*, in order to choose committees, to choose Delegates to represent them in the Congress. . . . They had the *insolence* to direct the manner in which the Delegates should be chosen in the *counties:* And the *greater* insolence, to count all the *friends to order and good government*,—those namely, who did not choose to obey their seditious mandate,—as being of *their party*, and as acquiescing in the *New-York choice*.

When the Delegates had met at Philadelphia, instead of
settling a reasonable plan of accommodation with the parent
country, they employed themselves in censuring acts of the
British parliament, which were principally intended to prevent
smuggling, and all *illicit trade*;—in writing addresses to the
people of *Great-Britain*, to the inhabitants of the *colonies* in
general, and to those of the *province of Quebec*, in *particular*;
with the *evident design* of making them *dissatisfied with their
present government*; and of *exciting clamours*, and raising *sedi-
tions* and *rebellions* against the *state*;—and in exercising a
legislative authority over all the colonies. They had the insolence to proclaim themselves "A FULL AND FREE REPRESENTATION
OF"—"HIS MAJESTY'S FAITHFUL SUBJECTS IN ALL THE COLONIES "FROM
NOVA-SCOTIA TO GEORGIA;" and, as such, have laid a *tax* on all
those colonies, viz. the *profits* arising from the *sales of all
goods* imported from Great-Britain, Ireland, &c. during the
months of December and January: Which *tax* is to be employed for
the *relief* of the *Boston poor*. They adopted a *mad set of resolves*, framed by an *arch rebel*, who hath since *fled his country*, for fear of being apprehended, and imposed afterwards upon
the deluded people of the county of *Suffolk* in the province of
Massachusetts-Bay; approving their wisdom and fortitude, and
recommending "a perseverance in the same "firm and *temperate*
conduct, as expressed in the" said resolves,—notwithstanding
those resolves entirely unhinged the *civil government* of that
province, fomented a *spirit of dissatisfaction to Great-Britain,
and of rebellion* against the *state*; and declared that the people of that county would not act always on the *defensive*,
against the King's troops.

. . . . .

By the first of these schemes, we are in danger of being
deprived of *many* of the *comforts*, and of *some* of the *necessaries* of life. We lie at the mercy of the merchants, who may
strip us of *every farthing*, by demanding what *they* shall think
only a reasonable profit on their goods. By the second, our
very mode of living is made subject to their inspection; and we
shall probably soon see these lordly Committee-men condescend
to go pimping, and peeping, and peering, into tea-canisters and
molasses jugs. By the third scheme, an *embargo* is to take
place, after the tenth of September next, on all *the farmers
produce* of EVERY KIND. So that should their whole plan be carried fully into execution, the laborious, necessary and numerous *body of* FARMERS would soon be reduced to distress and beg-
gary.

The state to which the GRAND CONGRESS, and the *subordinate
Committees*, have reduced the colonies, is *really deplorable*.
They have introduced a *system* of the most *oppressive tyranny*
that can possibly be imagined;—a *tyranny*, not only over the *actions*, but over the *words, thoughts, and wills*, of the *good*

people of this province. People have been threatened with the *vengeance of a mob*, for speaking in support of *order* and *good government.* Every method has been used to intimidate the *printers* from publishing any thing, which tended to *peace*, or seem'd in favour of government; while the most *detestable libels* against the *King*, the *British parliament*, and *ministry*, have been *eagerly read*, and *extravagantly commended*, as the *matchless productions* of some *heaven-born genius*, glowing with the *pure flame* of civil liberty. They not only oblige people to *pay* the tax assessed on their goods for the benefit of the Boston poor, but they also oblige them to say, that they are *willing* to do it; when it is notorious that many, if not most of them would refuse if they *dared.*

. . . . .

Be assured, Gentlemen, that a very great majority of your constituents disapprove of the late violent proceedings, and will support you in the pursuit of more *moderate measures*, as soon as You have *delivered* Them from the *tyranny of Committees*, from the *fear of violence*, and the *dread of mobs.* Recur boldly to your good, old, legal and successful way of proceeding, by *petition* and *remonstrance.*

Address yourselves to the *King* and the *two Houses of Parliament.* Let your representations be *decent* and *firm*, and principally directed to obtain a *solid American Constitution;* such as *we* can *accept* with *safety*, and *Great-Britain* can *grant* with *dignity.* Try the experiment, and you will assuredly find that our most gracious Sovereign and both Houses of Parliament will readily *meet* you in the *paths of peace.* Only shew your *willingness* towards an accommodation, by *acknowledging the supreme legislative authority of Great-Britian*, and I dare confidently pronounce the attainment of whatever YOU with *propriety*, can *ask*, and the LEGISLATURE OF GREAT-BRITAIN with *honour concede.*

Chapter three:

From Colony to State, 1775-77

By the early months of 1775 the protest movement exhibited many attributes of an independence movement. During the course of the preceding decade the rationale behind the popular front had been drastically altered (at stake was the fundamental issue of sovereignty rather than the efficacy of an act of Parliament), and the nascent extralegal political organization which first appeared in 1765 had evolved into a full-blown revolutionary apparatus. The actions of the First Continental Congress were pivotal. Promulgation of the Association in October 1774, with the appointment of committees of observation and inspection to enforce its provisions prohibiting trade with England, created a crisis of allegiance: the populace was forced to obey either the dictates of the extralegal committees or the established government. Moreover, the proliferation of committees—in New York there were approximately 150 by 1776—forged an unprecedented degree of political integration. With the formation of the First Provincial Congress in April 1775 New York boasted an extralegal political structure at the town, city, precinct, district, county, and colony level, which first paralleled and then replaced the duly constituted organs of government and ultimately coordinated the transition from a revolutionary to a republican regime.

The sparks from the muskets discharged at Lexington and Concord on April 19, 1775, ignited the highly combustible atmosphere. To Englishmen on both sides of the Atlantic the imperial conflict had escalated to the point at which it had to be resolved with swords, not olive branches. Although by the end of the year British and American soldiers had fought numerous engagements and virtually every colony was ruled by a de facto independent regime (Governor Tryon fled New York in October), the colonials did not face squarely the issue of de jure secession from the empire until the spring of 1776. On May 10 the Continental Congress instructed colonies which had not already done so to establish state governments. The Third

New York Provincial Congress, meeting in May, endorsed the veritable declaration of independence but entertained doubts about its authority to act on the matter. The county committees were therefore requested to elect delegates to the Fourth Provincial Congress to meet on July 9 to erect an independent state government. On July 10 the congress, having issued a declaration of independence the day before, transformed itself into the Convention of the Representatives of the State of New York, and on August 1 it appointed a committee to fashion a state constitution. The committee's draft, presented to the Convention in mid-March 1777, was adopted after important amendments on April 20. In June George Clinton commenced his eighteen years as governor and prepared to meet the legislature of the independent state of New York for the first time in September.

31

DECLARATION OF JAMAICA LOYALISTS
Jamaica, Long Island, January 27, 1775

WHEREAS a few people in the town of Jamaica, in Queen's County, on Long-Island, have taken upon themselves the name of a Committee, said to be chosen by a majority of the inhabitants of the said township: We the subscribers, freeholders and inhabitants of the said township of Jamaica, do think it our duty to declare, that we never gave our consent towards chusing that Committee, or making any resolves: As we utterly disapprove of all unlawful meetings and all tyrannical proceedings whatsoever; and as we have always been so, it is our firm resolution to continue peaceable and faithful subjects to his present Majesty King George the Third, our most gracious Sovereign; and we do further declare, that we do not acknowledge any other representatives but the General Assembly of this province, by whose wisdom and interposition we hope to obtain the wished redress of our grievances, in a constitutional way.
[138 signatures affixed]
N.B. Ninety-one of the above subscribers are freeholders, and the others very respectable inhabitants, wit in the township of Jamaica. . . .

Rivington's New York Gazetteer, February 2, 1775

N.B. There are not above 150 or 160 freeholders at most in this township.

32

NEW YORK CITY COMMITTEE CALL
FOR A PROVINCIAL CONGRESS   April 28, 1775

The distressed and alarming situation of our Country, occasioned by the sanguinary measures adopted by the British Ministry, (to enforce which, the Sword has been actually drawn against our brethren in the Massachusetts), threatening to involve this Continent in all the horrors of a civil War, obliges us to call for the united aid and council of the Colony, at this dangerous crisis.

Most of the Deputies who composed the late Provincial Congress, held in this City, were only vested with powers to chose Delegates to represent the Province at the next Continental Congress, and the Convention having executed that trust dissolved themselves: It is therefore thought adviseable by this Committee, that a Provincial Congress be immediately summoned to deliberate upon, and from time to time to direct such measures as may be expedient for our common safety.

We persuade ourselves, that no arguments can now be wanting to evince the necessity of a perfect union; and we know of no method in which the united sense of the people of the province can be collected, but the one now proposed. We therefore entreat your County heartily to unite in the choice of proper persons to represent them at a Provincial Congress to be held in this City on the 22d of May next.—Twenty Deputies are proposed for this City, and in order to give the greater weight and influence to the councils of the Congress, we could wish the number of Deputies from the counties, may be considerable.

We can assure you, that the appointment of a Provincial Congress, approved of by the inhabitants of this city in general, is the most proper and salutary measure that can be adopted in the present melancholy state of this Continent;

Calendar of Historical Manuscripts Relating to the War of the Revolution . . . , 2 vols. (Albany, N.Y.: Weed, Parsons and Co., 1865-66), 1: 4.

and we shall be happy to find, that our brethren in the different Counties concur with us in opinion.

33

THE GENERAL ASSOCIATION   Orange County, April 29, 1775

Persuaded that the salvation of the Rights and Liberties of America, depends under God, on the firm union of its inhabitants, in a vigorous prosecution of the measures necessary for its safety, and convinced of the necessity of preventing the anarchy and confusion which attend a disolution of the powers of Government, WE the Freemen, Freeholders, and Inhabitants of the County of Orange being greatly alarmed at the avowed design of the Ministry, to raise a revenue in America, and shocked by the bloody scene now acting in the Massachusetts-Bay, DO in the most solemn manner resolve never to become Slaves, and do associate under all the ties of Religion, Honour and Love to our Country, to adopt and endeavour to carry into execution whatever measures may be recommended by the Continental Congress or resolved upon by this Provincial Congress for the purpose of preserving our Constitution, and opposing the execution of the several arbitrary and oppressive acts of the British Parliament, until a reconciliation between Great-Britain and America, on constitutional principles, (which we most ardently desire,) can be obtained; and that we will in all things, follow the advice of our respective Committees, respecting the purposes aforesaid, the preservation of Peace, and good order, and the safety of individuals and private Property.

Calendar of Historical Manuscripts Relating to the War of the Revolution, 1: 5. Nothing is known of the identity of author(s) of the Association or of the meeting that adopted it.

34

LIEUTENANT GOVERNOR CADWALLADER COLDEN TO THE EARL OF DARTMOUTH

New York, May 3, 1775

. . . . .
The disunion of the Colonies being held up in America and
by many in Britain likewise as the only thing which could defeat the measures of the congress, the moment that the legislative Body of this Province, deviated from the General Association of the Colonies, and pointed out a different conduct, a
design was evidently formed in the other Colonies, to drive the
people from acquiescing in the measures of their Assembly, and
to force them into the General Plan of Association and Resistance. This design was heartily seconded by many among ourselves. Every species of public and private Resentment was
threatened to terrify the Inhabitants of this Province if they
continued disunited from the others. The certainty of losing
all the Debts due from the other Colonies, which are very considerable and every other argument of private Interest that
could influence the Merchants, or any one was industriously
circulated The minds of the people in the city were kept in
constant agitation, by Riots and attempts to prevent the Trans-
ports from loading here, with stores, Provisions &c for the
army. The want of any degree of Resolution in the Magistrates
to support the authority of Government in opposition to popular
measures, rendered the leaders of the People insolently bold
and daring—The friends of order and Government saw no power
either in the exertion of the Magistrates, or the feeble aid
that could be afforded by the very small body of Troops quartered in the city to protect their persons and property from
violence and destruction. Several Incidents combined to de-
press all legal Authority; and to increase the Terror of the
Inhabitants, which seemed to vanquish every thought of Resistance to popular Rage. In this unfortunate situation of the
City, the first accounts of an action between the Kings Troops
and People, near Boston, was published with horrid and aggra-
vating circumstances. The moment of consternation and anxiety
was seized. The people were assembled, and that scene of disorder and violence begun, which has entirely prostrated the
Powers of Government, and produced an association by which this

---

New York Colonial Documents, 8: 571.

Province has solemnly united with the others in resisting the
Acts of Parliament.

. . . . .

35

NEW YORK ASSOCIATION, ADDRESS TO
LIEUTENANT GOVERNOR CADWALLADER COLDEN

New York, May 11, 1775

It frequently happens under every Form of Government, that
the measures of administration excite the just jealousies of
the People, and that the same measures pursued divest them of
all confidence in those, in whose Hands the ordinary executive
Powers are lodged. In such a state of things it is natural for
the people to cast their eyes upon these of their fellow sufferers, on whose abilities and integrity they can rely; and to
ask their advice and direction for the Preservation of all that
is dear and valuable to them.

That such is the Frame & Temper of our Inhabitants; you
have had the fullest opportunity to know, in the course of that
Residence with which you have lately honored us

This City and County, as well as the rest of the Colony
have exercised the greatest Patience in waiting tho' in vain,
for a redress of the many unconstitutional Burdens under which
this whole Continent has groan'd for several years past. To
their inexpressible greif they have found, that the most duti-
full applications for Redress have not only been rejected but
have been answered by reiterated violations of their Rights

You cannot therefore wonder, Sir, that at this most interesting crisis, when their all is at stake, and when under the
authority of administration the Sword has been drawn, tho' un-
successfully against their Brethren of Massachusetts for as-
serting those invaluable Rights which are the common inheritance of Britons and Americans, that the City and County of New
York have proceeded to associate in the Common cause, and to
the election of a Committee and Delegates in Congress to represent them in their claims, and to direct their Councils and
conduct for the preservation of those inestimable priviledges,

to which the Great Creator the Order of their being as rational
creatures, & our happy constitution, have given them an undoubted title.

To this important end they have unanimously invested us
their Committee with a Trust which we are determined, with the
best of our abilities, and most faithfully to discharge; and in
the execution of which we think it our indispensible duty to
declare

That our Constituents, while they chearfully yield that
the legislative of the Parent State may make Provisions in
their Nature merely calculated to regulate the Trade of the empire, yet they claim as their indefeazable Birthright a Total
exemption from all Taxes internal and external by Authority of
Parliament; and from every Aid to the Crown, but on Royal Requisition to their Representatives in Assembly, constitutionally
convened and freely deliberating & determining upon every such
requisition

That they never can, nor will submit to the establishment
of unconstitutional Admiralty Jurisdictions; but will ever regard them, as Engines that may be employed for the most Tyrannical Purposes

That they are determined never to part with their precious
and lately invaded Right of Trial by Peers of their Vicinage in
any case whatsoever

That they look with the utmost dread on every expedient by
Authority of Parliament or otherwise, that may tend to secure
from condign punishm^t Offenders against the most essential
Rights of human Nature, by removing them for their trial to
places distant from the Scene of Perpetration at the discretion
of a Governor or Commander in Cheif

That they esteem and therefore will be every lawfull means
oppose the late oppressive restraints upon Commerce as subversive in their Nature of the liberties of America.

That they regard the hostile blockade of the Port of Boston, the attack upon the venerable Charter Rights of Massachusetts, the extension of the Bounds of Quebec, the establishment
of Popery, and an arbitrary form of Government in that Province,
and the exclusive Priviledges virtually given to it in the Indian Trade; as so many Steps of an ill judging administration
that most eminently endanger the liberty and prosperity of the
whole Empire.

That they view with inexpressible horror the bloody Standard erected in the Eastern Part of the confederated Colonies;
and feel as in their own bodies every stroke which their brave
compatriotes have received from the hands of their fellow subjects; cruelly & unnaturally armed against them by mistaken
ministerial severity

In short that they are determined to equip themselves for
maintaining with successfull bravery & resolution, the unques-
tionable Rights of Englishmen

Permit us at the same time, Sir, to assure you in their
behalf that tho' they are arming with the greatest Diligence
and industry; it is not with design to oppose, but to strength-
en Government in the due exercise of constitutional Authority,
it is to be in a state of readiness to repel every lawless attack by our Superiors, and to prevent anarchy and confusion to
which ministerial misconduct has evidently paved the way. It
is to defend the liberties of the subject, and to enable your
Honor and those in office under you efficaciously to administer
the just Government of this Colony

Your Honor cannot but see the sudden Transition of the Inhabitants of this Capital, from a state of Tumult occasioned by
the Hostilities committed against their Brethren; to Tranquillity and good order, as the consequence of our appointment. It
is our ardent wish, Sir, that the same Tranquillity and good
order may be permanent.

We look forward therefore with deep concern at the expected arrival of Troops from Great Britain. An event that
will probably be attended with innumerable mischeifs. Their
Presence will doubtless revive the Resentment of our Inhabitants at the repeatedly avowed design of subjugating the Colonies by military Force. Mutual jealousies may break out into
reciprocal violence. Thousands will in that case be poured in
upon us from our other Counties, and the neighbouring Colonies,
who we are well assured have resolved to prevent this city from
being reduced to the present situation of Boston. Thus, instead, of being a secure Garrison Town and Place of Arms, as is
vainly expected by some, the streets of New York may be deluged
with Blood, Such a destructive evil we are well assured your
Honor will do every thing in your Power to prevent, Permit us
then, sir, to beseech you to apply to General Gage for orders
that such Troops as may arrive from Great Britain or Ireland,
do not land or encamp in this City and County, and in case of
their arrival before your honor shall receive the Generals answer to solicit the command^g officer to the same purpose

Give us leave, Sir, to conclude by assuring you, that we
are determined to improve that confidence with which the People
have honored us, in strengthen^g the hand of the civil Majis-
trate in every lawfull measure calculated to promote the Peace
and just Rule of this Metropolis; and consistent with that
jealous attention which above all things we are bound to pay to
the violated Rights of America

36

LIEUTENANT GOVERNOR CADWALLADER COLDEN, ANSWER TO THE NEW YORK ASSOCIATION New York, May 13, 1775

I have the best authority to assure you, that our most gracious Sovereign and both Houses of Parliam^t have declared their Readiness to afford every just and reasonable Indulgence to the Colonies, whenever they should make a proper Application, on the Ground of any real Greivances they may have to complain of. This Declaration has been followed by a Resolution of the House of Commons, which it was expected would have manifested the Justice & moderation of Parliament, and a disposition to comply with every wish of the Subjects in America. They offer to forbear every kind of Taxation or Assessment on America; except such as are necessary for the Regulation of Commerce; and only require that the Colonies should make Provision by such ways and means as are best suited to their respective circumstances, for contributing a proportion to the Common defence of the Empire, for the support of their own civil Government and the administration of Justice. His Majestys Ministers did not doubt this Temper in Parliament would meet with such a Return on the part of the Colonies, as would lead to a happy issue of the present disputes, and to a re-establishment of the public Tranquillity on Grounds of equity, justice & moderation. Is it not then to be lamented as a most unfortunate event, that the Patience of the People was exhausted at the moment of this prospect of a peaceable and happy accomplishment of all their wishes. Will not those in whom they now confide yet endeavour to obtain it? must this Country, till now happy and flourishing beyond Paralell be involved in the dreadful Calamities ever attendant on civil Wars, while there remains one possible means untried, by which so great so cruel an evil might be averted?—You tell me, Gentlemen, that the people have lost all confidence in the ordinary officers of Government and that they have cast their eyes upon you for advice and direction. I can not divest myself of the most affectionate concern for the welfare, the Peace, and prosperity of the people over whom I have so long presided as the immediate Representative of their August Sovereign; with whom I have lived the Term of a long life & among whom I leave all that is dear and valuable to me. I am impelled by my duty, and a most zealous attachment to the Interest and safety of this People, to exhort you not to irritate

---

New York Colonial Documents, 8: 586-87.

the present enraged state of their minds, nor suffer them to plunge into Labrynths from whence they can neither advance nor retreat, but through Blood and Desolation

His Majestys ministers have, in the Strongest Terms expressed the satisfaction with which the King received the Assurances of the loyalty & affection of his faithful subjects in this Governm^t, and of their ardent desire for a permanent Reconciliation with the Mother Country I can not then conceive upon what grounds a suspicion is entertained, that the City of New York is to be reduced to the present State of Boston, I have not had the least intimation that any Regular Troops were destined for this Province. It is proper that General Gage should know your sentiments on this subject, and I shall embrace the first opportunity of communicating your request to him. At the same time I think there is reason to suspect, that this report has been invented to facilitate the introduction of an arm'd Force from Connecticut, which I am told is meditated. Will not the Apprehension of such a design rouse, you, Gentlemen, & every virtuous cityzen to avert, by every means in your power, a Measure so degrading, so dangerous to the Honor, safety, and freedom of this Colony

I have beheld with inexpressible anxiety, the state of Tumult and disorder which raged in the Metropolis of this Province; and I am sorry that a recent instance, since your appointment, revives the threatening prospect of Insecurity, to which the inhabitants are reduced. I exhort you to carry into effect the assurances you give me, that you are determined to improve that confidence with which the people have honored you, in strengthening the hands of the civil Majistrates. Let this be done immediately, and with impartial Firmness on every occasion; that the Houses, Persons, & Property of your fellow citzens may not be attacked and insulted with impunity, and every Degree of domestic security and Happiness sapped to the foundation.

37

TRYON COUNTY COMMITTEE RESOLUTIONS
Conajohary District, May 24, 1775

Resolved unanimously by this Committee, that it be Recommended to the Inhabitants of this District, and it is expected
that no person or persons, or any other for or in their Behalf
do or shall from this Day have any Dealings or other Connections in the Way of trade with any person or persons whatsoever,
who have not signed the Association entered into by this District. Also Resolved, that every owner of Slaves and Servants
do not permit them to absent themselves from home either by
Night or Day, unless they be upon their Masters or Mistresses
Lawful Business and with a Certificate specifying such Business;
And Such persons, as do infringe or break through these two
Resolutions will be dealt with as Enemies to the District and
to their Country: And it is Requested of every Friend to this
Country to take up and secure every Servant or Slave not having
such Certificate—
Ordered therefore that these Resolutions be published by
the Clerk of the Committee at all the publick places in the
District.

38

PROVINCIAL CONGRESS IMPOSITION OF THE ASSOCIATION
May 29, 1775

Resolved, That it be recommended, and it is hereby accordingly recommended to all the counties in this Colony, (who have

Samuel L. Frey, ed., _The Minute Book of the Committee of Safety
of Tryon County_ . . . (New York: Dodd, Mead and Co., 1905), pp.
16-17.

Journals of the Provincial Congress . . . _1775-1777_, 2 vols.
(Albany, N.Y., 1842), 1: 18.

not already done it,) to appoint county committees, and also sub-committees for their respective townships, precincts and districts, without delay, in order to carry into execution the resolutions of the Continental and this Provincial Congress.

And that it is also recommended to every inhabitant of this Colony, who has hitherto neglected to subscribe the general Association, to do it with all convenient speed. And for these purposes that the committees in the respective counties in which committees have been formed, to tender the said Association to every inhabitant within the several districts in each county. And that such persons in those counties or districts, who have not appointed committees as shall be appointed by the members of this Congress, representing such counties and districts respectively, do make such tender as aforesaid in such counties and districts respectively; and that the said committees and persons respectively do return the said Association and the names of those who shall neglect or refuse to sign the same, to this Congress, by the fifteenth day of July next, or sooner, if possible.

39

JAMES DUANE TO ROBERT R. LIVINGSTON, JR.

Philadelphia, June 7, 1775

. . . . .

Our publick Affairs are at length arrived at the most dangerous Extremity. The ministry with inflexible Obstinacy persevere in that inhuman System of despotism which was contrived to rob us of our Liberties, and because we cannot submit to so

---

Livingston Family Papers (Franklin D. Roosevelt Library, Hyde Park). Printed with permission of the F.D.R. Library. Duane (1733-97), a prominent New York City lawyer and proprietor of Duanesburg, a 40,000 acre estate near Albany, moved from a conservative to a moderate political stance during the course of the protest-independence movement. He served on numerous prerevolutionary committees and in the Continental Congress almost continuously until 1783; he was mayor of New York from 1784 to 1789. Robert R. Livingston, Jr. (1746-1813), the son of Judge Robert R. Livingston, was eventually appointed to the

humiliating a Condition they have drawn the Sword against our suffering Friends as Traitors and Rebels, and the Authority of Parliament is called in to starve the Southern as well as the Eastern Colonies into base Submission. To stand forth at such a Juncture in the Situation in which I am placed is indeed an arduous and difficult Task, requiring an uncommon Exertion both of Wisdom and Fortitude. In the best View we must expect numberless Inconveniencies from this Conflict. We must be exposed to Danger and be loaded with heavy Expences: but if we can thereby secure our Liberties on a Just and solid foundation, the End is worthy of the means, and we ought not to repine. We contend in a good Cause, and if we continue firm & united among ourselves—If by wise and temperate Conduct we manifest to the World a desire of Reconciliation and reunion with the parent State, on terms consistent with our Safety and the Interest and Happiness of the whole Empire—We may hope with the Blessings of Heaven that our virtuous Struggle will be rewarded with Success. Many of the measures we are pursuing must from their nature unfold themselves to publick View: but I am not at present at Liberty to communicate them. The Massachusett's is reduced to such an unhappy Crisis that it is more than probible that a general Engagement between the Country and the Ministerial Troops is at no great distance. Much will depend on this Event. Despair may supply the place of discipline and disappoint ministerial Vengeance. We cannot however where so much is at Stake contemplate this approaching Scene without the most painful apprehensions.

. . . . .

I am much pleased that young Mr. Livingston is raising a company in the Manor. I wish he may extend his Views further, in the only plan, which, independent of the grand Contest, will render landed property Secure. We must think in Time of the means of assuring the Reins of Government when these Commotions shall subside. Licenciousness is the natural Object of a civil [*war* crossed out] discord and it can only be guarded against by placing the Command of the Troops in the hands of Men of property and Rank who, by that means, will preserve the same Authority over the Minds of the people which they enjoyed in the time of Tranquillity.

. . . . .

(Cont'd.) post of chancellor of New York (1777-1801) and played an active role in the drama of the Revolution at both the local and national levels.

40

JOHN JONES TO JAMES DUANE   New York, July 13, 1775

I have had the pleasure of receiving your last favor of
the 6th. instant by Mr. Rutledge & Mr. Middleton,[1] whose short
stay here I have endeavoured to render as agreeable as I cou'd
by every attention in my power. I wish I cou'd have made it
more so; but alas!, with with an equal mixture of shame, grief
& indignation I speak it, the wretched, contemptible policy of
this Province in general, & of our friends in particular relative to the present interesting dispute, renders it almost impossible for a stranger of liberal spirit and genuine patriotism to pass his time agreeably among us. Such of our friends
as were particularly concerned in the late erroneous measures
of our Assembly,[2] though convinced in the most mortifying manner of the impropriety of their conduct, yet have too much
pride to make a generous acknowledgment of it,—by their future
conduct atone in some measure for their past errors. Instead
of this, they are watching with the little Jealous & envious
eye of party spirit, every false step & imprudent maneuvre of
their paltry Provincial rivals, who are by no means sparing of
opportunities for censure.
    In the disposal of offices, particularly in the military
department the most shameful partiality prevails, all or most
of the inferior commissioned officers being selected from the
creatures & absolute dependents of the governing party. Indeed
the conduct of our gentry & principal people has rendered this
vile arrangement almost inevitable. Wou'd to Heaven I cou'd
throw a veil over this nakedness of my countrymen, but their

"The Duane Letters," *Southern History Association Publications*
(July 1903) 7: 248-50. Jones was a prominent New York City
physician; Duane was then in Philadelphia attending the Continental Congress.

[1]Congressmen from South Carolina.

[2]The "late erroneous measures" of the Assembly undoubtedly
refer to the adoption by that body in January 1775 of a petition to the king, a memorial to the House of Lords, and a remonstrance to the House of Commons—action interpreted by some
as a defeat for the radicals and non-compliance with the efforts of the Continental Congress to effect a united front of
colonial protest.

shame is already gone forth among the nations, & those who visit us are scandalized at the disgraceful sight. . . .

The conduct of our Governor has been very unexceptionable ever since his arrival,[3] having wisely adopted the prudent line of calm acquiescence, contented to act as a mere passenger, while other pilots guide the helm of our political ship amidst the dreadful storm. Nor has this pacific resolution been disturbed, except in one instance by a foolish address of our wise corporation, who were subjected to a shameful mortifying acknowledgment of their own impotence by a solemn Provincial veto, which I suppose will keep them wise, i. e. silent, during the present reign.

The Governor assured me he had no commission of a particular nature to execute here, either jointly or separately . . . He showed me copies of several letters to Lord Dartmouth, in which he gave a true & faithful description of the situation of these Colonies, & pointed out as plainly as the delicacy of his office wou'd permit him, the absurdity & impracticability of the present ministerial measures, & for this candor & integrity I think he merits the esteem & regard of every man in America.

. . . . .

41

ROBERT R. LIVINGSTON, JR., TO JOHN JAY
Livingston Manor, July 17, 1775

. . . . .

I told you some time before I left you that many of our Tenants here refused to sign the association, & resolved to stand by the King as they called it, in hopes that if he succeeded they should have their Lands. Since troops have been

---

[3]Governor Tryon had returned to New York early in June after a fourteen-month sojourn in England.

John Jay Papers, Columbia University. Printed with permission of the Columbia University Libraries. Jay (1745-1829), the son of wealthy New York City merchant Peter Jay, graduated from King's College (Columbia University) and emerged after 1768 as one of the ranking members of the New York bar. He was a

raised in the province & two of my Brothers have got commissions they have been frightened & changed their battery. In
order to excuse themselves they assert that they can not engage
in the controversy since as their leases are for lives their
families must want when they are killed. Tho this is common to
them & every other man whose family is supported by his labour;
yet to deprive them of all excuse, my father has declared to
them that a new lease shall be given to the family of every man
who is killed in the service & Mrs. Livingston has come to the
same resolution. Notwithstanding which the scoundrels have as
we are informed sent in a petition to the congress replete with
falsehoods & charges injurious to the memory of my Grandfather
& Mrs. Livingston. I sh[oul]d be glad to hear the particulars.
My father has made them a general offer of that if any man of
reputation appointed by the congress or any other way can shew
a single instance of injustice that he will repay at threefold.
You who know the lenity of his disposition & the extream low
rents (not equal to one per Cent on the value) of the Lands
will take care to set this matter right if such petition should
be presented you, & at the same time use some prety [*sic*]
strong language to intimidate fellows who act on no principle
but fear & will if they meet with the least encouragement throw
the whole country into confusion.

. . . . .

42

THE MONITOR, NO. VIII   December 28, 1775

. . . . .

The conduct of far the greatest part of my countrymen,
amid the fiery trial in which we are now engaged, affords abun-
dant matter for panegyrick, and, if persisted in with steady

(Cont'd.) member of several revolutionary committees, a delegate to the Continental Congress (president for the year 1778-
79), and chief justice of the New York supreme court from 1776
to 1779.

New York Journal, December 28, 1775. The author of *The Monitor*
essays has not been identified.

uniformity, will be a bright example for the imitation, and a
prolifick theme for the praises of future ages. I wish, for
the honour of humanity, the same encomium could be extended
without exception; but it is a melancholy truth that the behavior of many among us might serve as the severest satire upon
the species. It has been a compound of inconsistency, false-
hood, cowardice, selfishness, and dissimulation. *Proteus* like,
they have been in continual change; have borrowed what shapes
and assumed what forms they found convenient to promote their
sinister purposes. The most charitable construction to be put
upon their conduct is, that they have had no system, and have
been at perpetual variance with themselves; the most natural is,
that they have been consistent only in a hypocritical conceal-
ment of their real principles and intentions. There is no alternative but to suppose that, while they have been exclaiming
against anarchy in the state, they have been the unhappy vic-
tims of an intellectual chaos, a total confusion of understanding, which has obstructed the operations of common sense, and
tossed them at random upon the waves of caprice, liable to be
driven about by every gust of ministerial intrigue; or that
they have only artfully diversified the means to one great
end—the ruin of their Country; making the service of the Ministry their supreme good, and resolving to conform all their
actions to the most perfect standard of submission.
. . . . .
     The very men who have now luckily fallen into such a
pleasant dream of loyalty and obedience, in the time of the
Stamp Act, were most of them "patriots of distinguished note;"
the most vociferous clamorers for liberty and property; the
life and soul of mobs; the leaders in all the valorous exploits
of plebeian phrensy, such as parading the streets with effigies,
pulling down houses, tarring and feathering, and the like. In
a word, they did not scruple in those days to run headlong into
practices much more wanton and disorderly than any that have
happened in the course of our present struggle, which has been
managed with singular decency, regularity, and prudence.
     They then thought it no treason, no mortal sin, no Repub-
lican or Presbyterian contrivance, to form a Continental Congress; to petition and remonstrate with spirit and freedom; to
deny the right of taxation claimed and exercised by the Parliament; to enter into agreements for the restriction of commerce;
to act in every respect with suitable vigour and resolution.
They did not tremble at the sound of Ministerial vengeance;
neither were they afraid to adopt any decisive measure, because
it might tend to irritate, to widen the breach, to throw an
obstacle in the way of peace and reconciliation, and the rest
of the trite nonsense, the product of these exuberant times.
The contracted views of party, the sordid motives of ambition
and avarice, had not then taken such firm hold on their minds

as they have since. They felt the force of reason, listened to
its dictates, and co-operated in the necessary means of bringing speedy relief to their Country.

What a miserable reverse do we now behold! These mighty
champions for the liberty of their Country have dwindled into
a puny tribe of voluntary slaves. They have meanly abandoned
the lofty ground they formerly stood upon, and are contented to
become obsequious dependants on the bounteous indulgence of a
despotick Ministry and venal Parliament for all they possess.
While Administration, in pursuance of an open claim of unbound-
ed authority over us, are driving us, as far as lies in their
power, to the brink of perdition; while they are practising all
the violences, as well as the refinements of destruction,
against us, with an avowed intention to compel us to contribute
as much as they think proper to the expenses of the Empire, or
rather to the maintenance of parasites and minions, these
shameless apostates are not simply inactive in the defence of
their Country: they are industrious in promoting the views of
its enemies; they are continually using all the arts of cunning
and deceit to propagate the contagion of disaffection, to damp
the zeal and ardour of their countrymen, and to discredit every
method which is devised for the preservation of our common,
essential rights; they have condemned those very principles and
measures for which themselves were once the foremost advocates. . . .

Not to dwell longer upon so disgustful a theme, I will observe, in fine, that this party has, from time to time, fluctu-
ated between the most opposite and contradictory opinions. It
has held that the Parliament intended to enslave us, and that
it did not intend to enslave us: That the duty upon tea was a
tax, and that it was not a tax: That the Parliament has no
right of taxation over us, and that it has a right of taxation;
but, at the same time, no right to exercise that right: That
the appointment of a Congress was a wise and necessary expedient, and that is was an unwise and destructive one: That the
Association ought to be supported, and that it ought not to be
supported. In a word, that the Colonies have been much injured
and oppressed, and that they have not been injured nor oppressed, but are so many nurseries of ingratitude, treason, and
rebellion!

I fear they have at length fatally settled upon this sandy
and dishonourable foundation: that, wherever right may be, power is on the side of the Parliament; and that, by enlisting under their banners, they at least espouse the strongest and safest party—disregarding, like true men of the world, the
inferior considerations of justice and integrity.

The dread of losing their property by confiscation is a
principal motive of their persevering attachment to the minis-

terial cause; and is a mean of making new proselytes to their party. . . .

43

PETER VAN SCHAACK, THOUGHTS
ON EMPIRE AND INDEPENDENCE   Kinderhook, January 1776

The only foundation of all legitimate governments, is certainly a compact between the rulers and the people, containing mutual conditions, and equally obligatory on both the contracting parties. No question can therefore exist, at this enlightened day, about the lawfulness of resistance, in cases of gross and palable infractions on the part of the governing power. It is impossible, however, clearly to ascertain every case which shall effect a dissolution of this contract; for these, though always tacitly implied, are never expressly declared, in any form of government.

As a man is bound by the sacred ties of conscience, to yield obedience to every act of the legislature so long as the government exists, so, on the other hand, he owes it to the cause of liberty, to resist the invasion of those rights, which, being inherent and unalienable, could not be surrendered at the institution of the civil society of which he is a member. In times of civil commotions, therefore, an investigation of those rights, which will necessarily infer an inquiry into the nature of government, becomes the indispensable duty of every man.

There are perhaps few questions relating to government of more difficulty, than that at present subsisting between Great Britain and the Colonies. It originated about the *degree* of subordination we owe to the British Parliament, but by a rapid progress, it seems now to be whether we are members of the empire or not. In this view, the principles of Mr. Locke and other advocates for the rights of mankind, are little to the purpose. His treatise throughout presupposes rulers and subjects of the *same state*, and upon a supposition that we are members

From the journal of Peter Van Schaack, in Henry C. Van Schaack, *The Life of Peter Van Schaack, LL.D., Embracing Selections from his Correspondence and Other Writings* . . . (New York: D. Appleton & Co., 1842), pp. 54-58.

of the empire, his reasonings, if not inapplicable, will be
found rather to militate against our claims; for he holds the
necessity of a *supreme power*, and the necessary existence of
one legislature only in every society, in the strongest terms.

Here arises the doubt: if we are parts of the same state,
we cannot complain of a *usurpation*, unless in a qualified
sense, but we must found our resistance upon an *undue and oppressive* exercise of a power we recognize. In short, our reasonings must resolve into one or the other of the following
three grounds, and our right of resistance must be founded upon
either the first or third of them; for either, first, we owe no
obedience to any acts of Parliament; or, secondly, we are bound
by all acts to which British subjects in Great Britain would,
if passed with respect to them, owe obedience; or, thirdly, we
are subordinate in a certain degree, or, in other words, certain acts may be valid in Britain which are not so here.

Upon the first point I am exceedingly clear in my mind,
for I consider the Colonies as members of the British empire,
and subordinate to the Parliament. But, with regard to the
second and third, I am not so clear. The necessity of a supreme power in every state, strikes me very forcibly; at the
same time, I foresee the destructive consequences of a right in
Parliament to bind us in all cases whatsoever. To obviate the
ill effects of either extreme, some middle way should be found
out, by which the benefits to the empire should be secured arising from the doctrine of a supreme power, while the abuses of
that power to the prejudice of the colonists should be guarded
against; and this, I hope, will be the happy effect of the
present struggle.

The basis of such a compact must be, the securing to the
Americans, the essential rights of Britons, but so modified as
shall best consist with the general benefit of the *whole*. If
upon such a compact, we cannot possess the specific privileges
of the inhabitants of Great Britain, (as for instance a representation in Parliament we cannot,) this must not be an obstacle; for there is certainly a point in which the general good
of the whole, with the least possible disadvantage to every
part, does centre, though it may be difficult to discern it,
and every *individual* part must give way to the *general good*.
. . . . .
It may be said, that these principles terminate in passive
obedience: far from it. I perceive that several of the acts exceed those bounds, which, of right, ought to circumscribe the
Parliament. But, my difficulty arises from this, that, taking
the whole of the acts complained of together, they do not, I
think, manifest a system of slavery, but may fairly be imputed
to human frailty, and the difficulty of the subject. Most of
them seem to have sprung out of particular occasions, and are
unconnected with each other, and some of them are precisely of

the nature of other acts made before the commencement of his present Majesty's reign, which is the era when the supposed design of subjugating the colonies began. If these acts have exceeded what is and *ought to be declared* to be the line of right, and thus we have been sufferers in *some respects* by the undefined state of the subject, it will also, I think, appear from such a union, when established, if past transactions are to be measured by the standard hereafter to be fixed, that *we* have hitherto been deficient in other respects, and derived *benefit* from the same unsettled state.

In short, I think those acts may have been passed without a preconcerted plan of enslaving us, and it appears to me that the more favorable construction ought ever to be put on the conduct of our rulers. I cannot therefore think the government *dissolved*; and as long as the society lasts, the power that every individual gave the society when he entered into it, can never revert to the individuals again, but will always remain in the community.

If it be asked how we come to be subject to the authority of the British Parliament, I answer, by the same compact which entitles us to the benefits of the British constitution, and its laws; and that we derive advantage even from some kind of subordination, whatever the degree of it should be, is evident, because, without such a controlling common umpire, the colonies must become independent states, which would be introductive of anarchy and confusion among ourselves.

Some kind of dependence being then, in my idea, necessary for our own happiness, I would choose to see a claim made of a constitution which shall concede this point, as before that is done by us, and rejected by the mother country, I cannot see any principle of regard for my country, which will authorize me in taking up arms, as absolute *dependence* and *independence* are two extremes which I would avoid; for, should we succeed in the latter, we shall still be in a sea of uncertainty, and have to fight among ourselves for that constitution we aim at.

. . . . .

I am fully convinced, that men of the greatest abilities, and the soundest integrity, have taken parts in this war with America, and their measures should have a fair trial. But this is too serious a matter, implicitly to yield to the authority of any characters, however, respectable. Every man must exercise his own reason, and judge for himself; "for he that appeals to Heaven must be sure that he has right on his side," according to Mr. Locke. It is a question of morality and religion, in which a man cannot conscientiously take an active part, without being convinced in his own mind of the justice of the cause; for obedience while government exists being clear on the one hand, the dissolution of the government must be equally so, to justify an appeal to arms; and whatever disagreeable

consequences may follow from dissenting from the general voice,
yet I cannot but remember that I am to render an account of my
conduct before a more awful tribunal, where no man can be justified, who stands accused by his own conscience of taking part
in measures, which, through the distress and bloodshed of his
fellow-creatures, may precipitate his country into ruin.

44

PROVINCIAL CONGRESS CALL FOR THE
ESTABLISHMENT OF STATE GOVERNMENT   May 27, 1776

The order of the day being read, Congress proceeded to
hear the report of the committee on the resolution of Continental Congress of the (15th May,) relating to a new form of government; the same was read, and being again read by paragraphs,
[was adopted] in the words following, to wit:
That your committee are of opinion that the right of framing, creating, or new modeling civil government, is, and ought
to be, in the people.
2dly. That as the present form of government, by Congress
and Committees in this Colony, originated from, so it depends
on, the free and uncontrolled choice of the inhabitants thereof.
3dly. That the said form of government was instituted
while the old form of government still subsisted, and therefore
is necessarily subject to many defects which could not then be
remedied by any new institutions.
4thly. That by the voluntary abdication of the late Governor Tryon, the dissolution of our Assembly for want of due
prorogation, and the open and unwarrantable hostilities committed against the persons and property of the inhabitants of all
the United Colonies in North America by the British fleets and
armies, under the authority and by the express direction and
appointment of the King, Lords and Commons of Great Britain,
the said old form of government is become, *ipso facto*, dissolved; whereby it hath become absolutely necessary for the
good people of this Colony to institute a new and regular form
of internal government and police. The supreme legislative and
executive power in which should, for the present, wholly reside

Journals of the Provincial Congress, 1: 462-63.

and be within this Colony, in exclusion of all foreign and external power, authority, dominion, jurisdiction and preeminence whatsoever.

5thly. That doubts have arisen, whether this Congress are invested with sufficient authority to frame and institute such new form of internal government and police.

6thly. That those doubts can and of right ought to be removed by the good people of this Colony only.

7thly. That until such new form of internal police and government be constitutionally established, or until the expiration of the term for which this Congress was elected, this Congress ought to continue in the full exercise of their present authority, and in the meantime ought to give the good people of each several and respective county in this Colony, full opportunity to remove the said doubts, either by declaring their respective representatives in this Congress, in conjunction with the representatives of the other counties respectively, competent for the purpose of establishing such new form of internal police and government, and adding to their number, if they shall think proper, or by electing others in the stead of the present members, or any or either of them, and increasing (if they should deem it necessary) the number of deputies from each county, with the like powers as are now vested in this Congress, and with express authority to institute and establish such new and internal form of government and police as aforesaid.

8thly. That, therefore, this House takes some order to be publicly notified throughout the several counties in this Colony, whereby the inhabitants of each county respectively, on a given day to be appointed in each of them respectively by this Congress for the purpose, may, by plurality of voices, either confirm their present representatives respectively in this Congress in their present powers, and with express authority, in conjunction with the representatives in this Congress for the other counties, to institute a new internal form of government and police for this Colony, suited to the present critical emergency, and to continue in full force and effect until a future peace with Great Britain shall render the same unnecessary, or elect new members for that purpose, to take seats in Congress in the place of those members respectively who shall not be so confirmed. The whole number to be capable of such addition or increase in each respective county, as aforesaid.

45

PROVINCIAL CONGRESS TO THE
CONTINENTAL CONGRESS DELEGATION
Poughkeepsie, June 10, 1776

. . . . .

They [i.e., the members of the Provincial Congress] are unanimously of opinion that you are not authorized by your Instructions to give the sense of this Colony on the Question of declaring it to be & continue an independent State nor does this Congress incline to instruct you on that point, it being a matter of doubt whether their Constituents intended to vest them with a Power to deliberate and determine on that Question. Indeed the majority of this Congress are clearly of opinion that they have not such authority.

As measures have lately been taken and are now pursuing for obtaining the consent and authority of the People for establishing a new and regular form of Government the necessity of which seems generally to be acknowledged—This Congress think it would be imprudent to require the sentiments of the People relative to the Question of Independence lest it sh[oul]d create Divisions and have an unhappy Influence on the other.

The earliest opportunity will however be embraced for ascertaining the sentiments of the inhabitants of this Colony on that important Question, and of obtaining their consent to vest the Congress of the Colony for the time being with authority to deliberate and determine on that and every other Matter

---

Calendar of Historical Manuscripts Relating to the War of the Revolution, 1: 320. On June 8 the delegates dispatched an urgent appeal for explicit advise from the Provincial Congress because of uncertainty as to whether their instructions precluded voting on the impending question of independence. This response proved unsatisfactory, and on July 2 they reiterated their plea for directions "whether we are to consider our Colony bound by the Vote of the Majority in Favor of Independency and vote at large on such Questions as may arise in Consequence thereof or only concur in such Measures as may be absolutely necessary for the Common safety and defence of America exclusive of the Idea of Indepen[den]cy." Edmund C. Burnett, ed., *Letters of Members of the Continental Congress*, 8 vols. (Washington, D.C.: Carnegie Institution of Washington, 1921-36), 1: 524.

of General Concern, and to instruct their delegates in Continental Congress thereupon.

46

NEW YORK CITY MECHANICKS UNION,
ADDRESS TO THE PROVINCIAL CONGRESS   June 14, 1776

With due confidence in the declaration which you lately made to the Chairman of our General Committee that you are, at all times, ready and willing to attend to every request of your "constituents or any part of them;" we, the Mechanicks in Union . . . beg leave to represent that one of the clauses in your Resolve, respecting the establishment of a new form of Government is erroneously construed, and for that reason may serve the most dangerous purposes. . . . We could not, we never can, believe you intended that the future delegates or yourselves should be vested with the power of framing a new Constitution for this Colony, and that its inhabitants at large should not exercise the right which *God* has given them, in common with all men, to judge whether it be consistent with their interest to accept or reject a Constitution framed for that State of which they are members. This is the birthright of every man, to whatever state he may belong. There he is, or ought to be, by inalienable right, a co-legislator with all the other members of that community. Conscious of our own want of abilities, we are, alas! but too sensible that every individual is not qualified for assisting in the framing of a Constitution. But that share of common sense which the Almighty has bountifully distributed amongst mankind in general, is sufficient to quicken every one's feeling, and enable him to judge rightly what degree of safety and what advantages he is likely to enjoy, or be deprived of, under any Constitution proposed to him. For this reason, should a preposterous confidence in the abilities and integrity of our future Delegates delude us into measures which might imply a renunciation of our inalienable right to ratify our laws, we believe that your wisdom, your patriotism, your own interest, nay, your ambition itself, would urge you to exert all the powers of persuasion you possess, and try every

---

Force, comp., *American Archives*, 4th ser., 6: 895-96.

method which, in your opinion, would deter us from perpetrating that impious and frantick act of self-destruction; for as it would precipitate us into a state of absolute slavery, the lawful power which till now you have received from your constituents to be exercised over a free people, would be annihilated by that unnatural act. It might probably accelerate our political death; but it must immediately cause your own.

. . . . .

47

PROVINCIAL CONGRESS DECLARATION OF INDEPENDENCE
July 9, 1776

Resolved, unanimously, That the reasons assigned by the Continental Congress for declaring the *United Colonies* free and independent States, are cogent and conclusive; and that while we lament the cruel necessity which has rendered that measure unavoidable, we approve the same, and will, at the risk of our lives and fortunes, join with the other colonies in supporting it.

. . . . .

Resolved, That the Delegates of this State in Continental Congress, be, and they are hereby, authorized to consent to and adopt all such measures as they may deem conducive to the happiness and welfare of the *United States of America.*

48

JOHN ALSOP TO THE NEW YORK CONVENTION
Philadelphia, July 16, 1776

Yesterday our President read in Congress a resolve of your
honourable body, dated the 9th instant, in which you declare
New York a free and independent State. I can't help saying
that I was much surprised to find it come through that channel.
The usual method hitherto practised has been for the Convention
of each Colony to give their Delegates instructions to act and
vote upon all and any important questions. And from the last
letter we were favoured with from your body, you told us that
you were not competent or authorized to give us instructions on
that grand question; nor have you been pleased to answer our
letter of the 2d instant, any otherwise than by your said resolve transmitted to the President. I think we were entitled
to an answer.

I am compelled, therefore, to declare, that it is against
my judgment and inclination. As long as a door was left open
for a reconciliation with Great Britain upon honourable and
just terms, I was willing and ready to render my country all
the service in my power, and for which purpose I was appointed
and sent to this Congress; but as you have, I presume, by that
declaration, closed the door of reconciliation, I must beg
leave to resign my seat as a Delegate from New York, and that I
may be favoured with an answer and my dismission.

Burnett, ed., *Letters of Members of the Continental Congress*,
2: 12-13. Alsop, a prominent New York City merchant, was a
conspicuous figure in the extralegal activities of the prerevolutionary era. He was a member of virtually every important
revolutionary committee, the Provincial Congress, and the Continental Congress. Alsop was one of the "whig-loyalist" who
countenanced firm opposition to certain aspects of British colonial policy but repudiated secession from the Empire.

49

PROVINCIAL CONGRESS PACIFICATION RESOLUTION
August 10, 1776

WHEREAS, this Convention has received information that the inhabitants of Kings county have determined not to oppose the enemy,

Resolved unanimously, That a committee be appointed to repair forthwith to the said county, and inquire concerning the authenticity of such report; and in case they find it well founded, that they be empowered to disarm and secure the disaffected inhabitants; to remove or destroy the stock of grain; and if they judge it necessary, to lay the whole county waste. And for the execution of these purposes, they be directed to apply to Genl. [Nathanael] Greene, or the commander of the Continental troops in that county, for such assistance as they shall want.

50

THE REVEREND CHARLES INGLIS TO THE
REVEREND DR. RICHARD HIND   New York, October 31, 1776

. . . . .

. . . Although civil liberty was the ostensible object, the bait that was flung out to catch the populace at large and engage them in the rebellion, yet it is now past all doubt that

---

Journals of the Provincial Congress, 1: 567-68.

E. B. O'Callaghan, ed., *Documentary History of the State of New York*, 4 vols. (Albany, N.Y.: Weed, Parsons and Co., 1849-51), 3: 1050-53, 1055, 1060, 1064-65. Inglis (1734-1816) was the assistant of the Reverend Samuel Auchmuty, rector of Trinity Church in New York City. He was active in the efforts to obtain an American bishop for the Anglican church and wrote *The True Interest of America Impartially Stated* (1776, a rebuttal

an abolition of the Church of England was one of the principal
springs of the dissenting leaders' conduct; and hence the una-
nimity of the dissenters in this business. Their universal
defection from government, emancipating themselves from the
jurisdiction of Great Britain, and becoming independent, was a
necessary step towards this grand object. I have it from good
authority that the Presbyterian ministers, at a synod where
most of them in the middle colonies were collected, passed a
resolve to support the continental congress in all their measures. This and this only can account for the uniformity of
their conduct; for I do not know one of them, nor have I been
able, after strict inquiry, to hear of any, who did not, by
preaching and every effort in their power, promote all the
measures of the congress, however extravagant.

The Clergy amidst this scene of tumult and disorder, went
on steadily with their duty; in their sermons, confining themselves to the doctrines of the Gospel, without touching on
politics; using their influence to allay our heats and cherish
a spirit of loyalty among their people. This conduct, however
harmless, gave great offence to our flaming patriots, who laid
it down as a maxim, "That those who were not for them were
against them." The Clergy were everywhere threatened, often
reviled with the most opprobious language, sometimes treated
with brutal violence. Some have been carried prisoners by
armed mobs into distant provinces, where they were detained in
close confinement for several weeks, and much insulted, without
any crime being even alleged against them. Some have been
flung into jails by committees for frivolous suspicions of
plots, of which even their persecutors afterwards acquitted
them. Some who were obliged to fly their own province to save
their lives have been taken prisoners, sent back, and are
threatened to be tried for their lives because they fled from
danger. Some have been pulled out of the reading desk because
they prayed for the king, and that before independency was declared. Others have been warned to appear at militia musters
with their arms, have been fined for not appearing, and
threatened with imprisonment for not paying those fines. Others have had their houses plundered, and their desks broken
open under pretence of their containing treasonable papers.

. . . . .

The present rebellion is certainly one of the most cause-
less, unprovoked, and unnatural that ever disgraced any country;

(Cont'd.) to Thomas Paine's *Common Sense*. After the war he emigrated to Canada, where he became bishop of Nova Scotia. The
Reverend Dr. Hind was secretary of the Society for the Propaga-
tion of the Gospel in Foreign Parts, the missionary agency of
the Anglican church.

a rebellion marked with peculiarly aggravated circumstances of guilt and ingratitude; yet amidst this general defection, there are very many who have exhibited instances of fortitude and adherence to their duty which do honour to human nature and Christianity; many who, for the sake of a good conscience, have incurred insults, persecution, and loss of property, when a compliance with the spirit of the times had insured them applause, profit, and that eminence of which the human heart is naturally so fond. . . . It is but justice to say that those instances were exhibited by the members of our Church: there is not one of the clergy in the provinces I have specified, of whom this may not be affirmed; and very few of the laity who were respectable or men of property, have joined in the rebellion.

Thus matters continued; the clergy proceeding regularly in the discharge of their duty where the hand of violence did not interfere, until the beginning of last July, when the congress thought proper to make an explicit declaration of independency, by which all connexion with Great Britain was to be broken off, and the Americans released from any allegiance to our gracious sovereign. For my part, I had long expected this event: it was what the measures of the congress from the beginning uniformly and necessarily led to.

This declaration increased the embarrassments of the clergy. To officiate publicly, and not pray for the king and royal family according to the liturgy, was against their duty and oath, as well as dictates of their conscience; and yet to use the prayers for the king and royal family would have drawn inevitable destruction on them. The only course which they could pursue, to avoid both evils, was to suspend the public exercise of their function, and shut up their churches.

. . . . .

About the middle of April, Mr. Washington, commander in Chief of the rebel forces, came to town with a large reinforcement. Animated by his presence, and I suppose, encouraged by him, the rebel committees very much harrassed the loyal inhabitants here and on Long Island. They were summoned before those committees, and upon refusing to give up their arms, and take the oaths that were tendered, they were imprisoned or sent into banishment. An army was sent to Long Island to disarm the inhabitants who were distinguished for their loyalty. Many had their property destroyed, and more were carried off prisoners. It should be observed, that members of the Church of England were the only sufferers on this occasion. The members of the Dutch Church are very numerous there, and many of them joined in opposing the rebellion; yet no notice was taken of them, nor the least injury done to them.

. . . . .

On Sunday, the 15th of September, General Howe, with the King's forces, landed on New York Island, . . . upon which the rebels abandoned the city, and retired toward King's Bridge, which joins this island to the continent. Early on Monday morning, the 16th, I returned to the city, which exhibited a most melancholy appearance, being deserted and pillaged. My house was plundered of everything by the rebels. My loss amounts to near 200£. this currency, or upwards of 100£. sterling. The rebels carried off all the bells in the city, partly to convert them into cannon, partly to prevent notice being given speedily of the destruction they meditated against the city by fire, when it began. On Wednesday, I opened one of the churches, and solemnized Divine service, when all the inhabitants gladly attended, and joy was lighted up in every countenance on the restoration of our public worship; for very few remained but such as were members of our Church.

. . . Upon the whole, the Church of England has lost none of its members by the rebellion as yet—none, I mean, whose departure from it can be deemed a loss; on the contrary, its own members are more firmly attached to it than ever. And even the sober and more rational among dissenters—for they are not all equally violent and frantic—look with reverence and esteem on the part which Church people here have acted. I have not a doubt but, with the blessing of Providence, his Majesty's arms will be successful, and finally crush this unnatural rebellion. . . . Then will be the time to make that provision for the American Church, which is necessary, and place it on at least an equal footing with other denominations by granting it an episcopate, and thereby allowing it a full toleration. . . . And I may appeal to all judicious persons, whether it is not as contrary to sound policy, as it certainly is to right reason and justice, that the King's loyal subjects here, members of the national Church, should be denied a privilege the want of which will discourage and diminish their numbers, and that merely to gratify the clamours of dissenters, who have now discovered such enmity to the constitution, and who will ever clamour against anything that will tend to benefit or increase the Church here. The time indeed, is not yet full come to move in this affair; but I apprehend it is not very distant, and, therefore, it should be thought of. . . .

51

THE CONSTITUTION OF THE STATE OF NEW YORK   April 20, 1777

AND WHEREAS this Convention having taken this declaration into their most serious consideration, did on the ninth day of July last past, unanimously resolve, that the reasons assigned by the Continental Congress for declaring the United Colonies free and independent States, are cogent and conclusive: and that while we lament the cruel necessity which has rendered that measure unavoidable, we approve the same, and will, at the risk of our lives and fortunes, join the other Colonies in supporting it.

By virtue of which several acts, declarations and proceedings mentioned and contained in the afore recited resolves or resolutions of the General Congress of the United American States, and of the Congresses or Conventions of this State, all power whatever therein hath reverted to the people thereof, and this Convention hath by their suffrages and free choice been appointed, and among other things, authorized to institute and establish such a government as they shall deem best calculated to secure the rights and liberties of the good people of this State, most conducive of the happiness and safety of their constituents in particular, and of America in general.

I. This Convention, therefore, in the name and by the authority of the good people of this State, doth ordain, determine and declare, that no authority shall, on any pretence whatever, be exercised over the people or members of this State, but such as shall be derived from and granted by them.

II. This Convention doth further, in the name and by the authority of the good people of this State, ordain, determine and declare, that the supreme Legislative power, within this State, shall be vested into two separate and distinct bodies of men; the one to be called the Assembly of the State of New York; the other to be called the Senate of the State of New York; who together shall form the Legislature, and meet once at least in every year for the despatch of business.

III. AND WHEREAS laws inconsistent with the spirit of this constitution or with the public good, may be hastily and unadvisedly passed:

Be it Ordained. That the Governor for the time being, the Chancellor, and the Judges of the Supreme Court, or any two of

---

Journals of the Provincial Congress, 1: 894-98. The Constitution was not submitted to the citizenry for ratification.

them, together with the Governor, shall be, and hereby are, constituted a Council to revise all bills about to be passed into laws by the Legislature; and for that purpose shall assemble themselves from time to time, when the Legislature shall be convened; for which nevertheless they shall not receive any salary or consideration, under any pretence whatever. And that all bills, which have passed the Senate and Assembly, shall, before they become laws, be presented to the said Council for their revisal and consideration; and if, upon such revision and consideration, it should appear improper to the said Council, or a majority of them, that the said bill should become a law of this State, that they return the same, together with their objections thereto in writing, to the Senate, or House of Assembly, in whichsoever the same shall have originated, who shall enter the objections sent down by the Council at large on their minutes, and proceed to reconsider the said bill. But if after such reconsideration two-thirds of the said Senate, or House of Assembly, shall, notwithstanding the said objections, agree to pass the same, it shall, together with the objections, be sent to the other branch of the Legislature, where it shall also be reconsidered, and if approved by two-thirds of the members present, it shall be a law.

And in order to prevent any unnecessary delays,

Be it further Ordained, That if any bill shall not be returned by the Council within ten days after it shall have been presented, the same shall be a law, unless the Legislature shall, by their adjournment, render a return of the said bill within ten days impracticable; in which case the bill shall be returned on the first day of the meeting of the Legislature, after the expiration of the said ten days.

IV. That the Assembly shall consist of a least seventy members, to be annually chosen in the several counties in the proportions following, viz:

For the city and county of New York	*nine*
the city and county of Albany	*ten*
the county of Dutchess	*seven*
the county of Westchester	*six*
the county of Ulster	*six*
the county of Suffolk	*five*
the county of Queens	*four*
the county of Orange	*four*
the county of Kings	*two*
the county of Richmond	*two*
the county of Tryon	*six*
the county of Charlotte	*four*
the county of Cumberland	*three*
the county of Gloucester	*two*

V. That as soon after the expiration of seven years, subsequent to the termination of the present war, as may be, a
census of the electors and inhabitants in this State be taken,
under the direction of the Legislature. And if on such census,
it shall appear that the number of Representatives in Assembly,
from the said counties, is not justly proportioned to the number of electors in the said counties respectively, that the
Legislature do adjust and apportion the same by that rule. And
further, that once in every seven years, after the taking of
the said first census, a just account of the electors resident
in each county shall be taken; and if it shall thereupon appear
that the number of electors in any county, shall have increased
or diminished one or more seventieth parts of the whole number
of electors, which on the said first census shall be found in
this State, the number of Representatives for such county shall
be increased or diminished accordingly, that is to say, one
Representative for every seventieth part as aforesaid.

VI. AND WHEREAS an opinion hath long prevailed, among divers of the good people of this State, that voting at elections
by ballot, would tend more to preserve the liberty and equal
freedom of the people, then voting *viva voce*; to the end therefore, that a fair experiment be made which of those two methods
of voting is to be preferred:

Be it Ordained, That as soon as may be, after the termination of the present war between the United States of America
and Great Britain, an act or acts be passed by the Legislature
of this State, for causing all elections, thereafter to be held
in this State, for Senators and Representatives in Assembly, to
be by ballot, and directing the manner in which the same shall
be conducted: *And Whereas* it is possible, that after all the
care of the Legislature in framing the said act or acts, certain inconveniences and mischiefs, unforeseen at this day, may
be found to attend the said mode of electing by ballot:

It is further Ordained, That if after a full and fair experiment shall be made of voting by ballot aforesaid, the same
shall be found less conducive to the safety or interest of the
State than the method of voting *viva voce*, it shall be lawful
and constitutional for the Legislature to abolish the same;
provided two-thirds of the members present in each House respectively shall concur therein; and further, that during the
continuance of the present war, and until the Legislature of
this State shall provide for the election of Senators and Representatives in Assembly by ballot, the said elections shall be
made *viva voce*.

VII. That every male inhabitant, of full age, who shall
have personally resided within one of the counties of this
State for six months immediately preceding the day of election,
shall, at such election, be entitled to vote for Representative
of the said county in Assembly; if, during the time aforesaid,

he shall have been a freeholder, possessing a freehold of the
value of twenty pounds, within the said county, or have rented
a tenement therein of the yearly value of forty shillings, and
been rated, and actually paid taxes to this State: provided
always, that every person who now is a freeman of the city of
Albany, or who was made a freeman of the city of New York, on
or before the fourteenth day of October, in the year of our
Lord one thousand seven hundred and seventy-five, and shall be
actually and usually resident in the said cities respectively,
shall be entitled to vote for Representatives in Assembly
within his said place of residence.

VIII. That every elector, before he is admitted to vote,
shall, if required by the returning officer, or either of the
inspectors, take an oath, or if of the people called Quakers,
an affirmation, of allegiance to the State.

IX. That the Assembly thus constituted, shall choose their
own Speaker, be judges of their own members, and enjoy the same
privileges, and proceed in doing business in like manner as the
Assemblies of the Colony of New York of right formerly did; and
that a majority of the said members shall, from time to time,
constitute a House to proceed upon business.

X. And this Convention doth further, in the name, and by
the authority of the good people of this State, ordain, determine and declare, that the Senate of the State of New York
shall consist of twenty-four freeholders, to be chosen out of
the body of the freeholders, and that they be chosen by freeholders of this State, possessed of freeholds of the value of
one hundred pounds, over and above all debts charged thereon.

XI. That the members of the Senate be elected for four
years, and immediately after the first election, they be divided by lot into four classes, six in each class, and numbered
one, two three and four; that the seats of the members of the
first class shall be vacated at the expiration of the first
year; the second class the second year; and so on continually,
to the end, that the fourth part of the Senate, as nearly as
possible, may be annually chosen.

XII. That the election of Senators shall be after this
manner: that so much of this State as is now parcelled into
counties, be divided into four great districts; the southern
district to comprehend the city and county of New York, Suffolk,
Westchester, Kings, Queens and Richmond counties; the middle
district to comprehend the counties of Dutchess, Ulster and Orange; the western district the city and county of Albany, and
Tryon county; and the eastern district, the counties of Charlotte, Cumberland and Gloucester. That the Senators shall be
elected by the freeholders of the said districts, qualified as
aforesaid in the proportions following, to wit: in the southern
district nine; in the middle district six; in the western district six; and in the eastern district three.

And be it Ordained, That a census shall be taken as soon
as may be, after the expiration of seven years from the termination of the present war, under the direction of the Legislature; and if on such census it shall appear, that the number of
Senators is not justly proportioned to the several districts,
that the Legislature adjust the proportion as near as may be,
to the number of freeholders qualified as aforesaid in each
district.   That when the number of electors, within any of the
said districts, shall have increased one-twenty-fourth part of
the whole number of electors, which by the said census, shall
be found to be in this State, an additional Senator shall be
chosen by the electors of such district.   That a majority of
the number of Senators to be chosen as aforesaid, shall be necessary to constitute a Senate sufficient to proceed upon business; and that the Senate shall in like manner with the Assembly, be the judges of its own members.

And be it Ordained, That it shall be in the power of the
future Legislatures of this State, for the convenience and advantage of the good people thereof, to divide the same into
such further and other counties and districts as shall to them
appear necessary.

XIII. And this Convention doth further, in the name and by
the authority of the good people of this State, ordain, determine and declare, that no member of this State shall be disfranchised or deprived of any of the rights or privileges secured to the subjects of this State, by this Constitution,
unless by the law of the land, or the judgment of his peers.

XIV. That neither the Assembly nor the Senate shall have
power to adjourn themselves for any longer time than two days,
without the mutual consent of both.

XV. That whenever the Assembly and Senate disagree, a conference shall be held in the presence of both, and be managed
by committees to be by them respectively chosen by ballot.
That the doors, both of the Senate and Assembly shall at all
times be kept open to all persons, except when the welfare of
the State shall require their debates to be kept secret.   And
the journals of all their proceedings shall be kept in the manner heretofore accustomed by the General Assembly of the Colony
of New York, and except such parts as they shall as aforesaid
respectively determine not to make public, be from day to day
(if the business of the Legislature will permit) published.

XVI. It is nevertheless provided, that the number of Senators shall never exceed one hundred, nor the number of Assembly
three hundred; but that whenever the number of Senators shall
amount to one hundred, or of the Assembly to three hundred,
then and in such case, the Legislature shall from time to time
thereafter, by laws for that purpose, apportion and distribute
the said one hundred Senators and three hundred Representatives,
among the great districts and counties of this State in propor-

tion to the number of their respective electors; so that the representation of the good people of this State, both in the Senate and Assembly, shall forever remain proportionate and adequate.

XVII. And this Convention doth further, in the name and by the authority of the good people of this State, ordain, determine and declare, that the supreme executive power and authority of this State, shall be vested in a Governor; and that statedly once in every three years, and as often as the seat of government shall become vacant, a wise and discreet freeholder of this State shall be by ballot elected Governor by the freeholders of this State, qualified as before described to elect Senators; which elections shall be always held at the times and places of choosing Representatives in Assembly for each respective county, and that the person who hath the greatest number of votes within the said State shall be Governor thereof.

XVIII. That the Governor shall continue in office three years, and shall by virtue of this office be General and Commander-in-Chief of all the militia, and Admiral of the navy of this State; that he shall have power to convene the Assembly and Senate on extraordinary occasions; to prorogue them from time to time, provided such prorogations shall not exceed sixty days in the space of any one year; and, at his discretion, to grant reprieves and pardons to persons convicted of crime, other than treason or murder, in which he may suspend the execution of the sentence until it shall be reported to the Legislature at their subsequent meeting; and they shall either pardon or direct the execution of the criminal, or grant a further reprieve.

XIX. That it shall be the duty of the Governor to inform the Legislature, at every session, of the condition of the State, so far as may respect his department; to recommend such matters to their consideration as shall appear to him to concern its good government, welfare and prosperity; to correspond with the Continental Congress, and other States; to transact all necessary business with the officers of government, civil and military; to take care that the laws are faithfully executed, to the best of his ability, and to expedite all such measures as may be resolved upon by the Legislature.

XX. That a Lieutenant-Governor shall at every election of a Governor, and as often as the Lieutenant-Governor shall die, resign, or be removed from office, be elected in the same manner with the Governor, to continue in office until the next election of a Governor; and such Lieutenant Governor shall, by virtue of his office, be President of the Senate, and, upon an equal division, have a casting voice in their decisions, but not vote on any other occasion.

And in case of the impeachment of the Governor, or his removal from office, death, resignation, or absence from the

State, the Lieutenant-Governor shall exercise all the power and
authority appertaining to the office of Governor, until another
be chosen, or the Governor absent or impeached, shall return or
be acquitted: provided, that when the Governor shall, with the
consent of the Legislature, be out of the State, in time of war,
at the head of a military force thereof, he shall still continue in his command of all the military force of this State,
both by sea and land.

XXI. That whenever the government shall be administered by
the Lieutenant-Governor, or he shall be unable to attend as
President of the Senate, the Senators shall have power to elect
one of their own members to the office of President of the Senate, which he shall exercise *pro hac vice*; and if during such
vacancy of the office of Governor, the Lieutenant-Governor
shall be impeached, displaced, resign, die, or be absent from
the State, the President of the Senate shall in like manner as
the Lieutenant-Governor administer the government, until others
shall be elected by the suffrage of the people at the succeeding election.

XXII. And this Convention doth further, in the name and by
the authority of the good people of this State, ordain, determine and declare, that the Treasurer of this State shall be appointed by act of the Legislature, to originate with the Assembly; provided, that he shall not be elected out of either
branch of the Legislature.

XXIII. That all officers, other than those, who by this
Constitution are directed to be otherwise appointed, shall be
appointed in the manner following, to wit: The Assembly shall,
once in every year, openly nominate and appoint one of the Senators from each great district, which Senators shall form a
Council for the appointment of the said officers, of which the
Governor, for the time being, or the Lieutenant-Governor, or
the President of the Senate, when they shall respectively administer the government, shall be president, and have a casting
voice, but no other vote; and with the advice and consent of
the said Council, shall appoint all the said officers; and that
a majority of the said council be a quorum; and further, the
said Senators shall not be eligible to the said Council for two
years successively.

XXIV. That all military officers be appointed during
pleasure; that all commissioned officers, civil and military,
be commissioned by the Governor, and that the chancellor, judges of the supreme court, and first judge of the county court,
in every county, hold their offices during good behaviour, or
until they shall have respectively attained the age of sixty
years.

XXV. That the chancellor and judges of the supreme court
shall not at the same time hold any other office, excepting
that of Delegate to the General Congress upon special occasions;

and that the first judges of the county courts in the several
counties, shall not at the same time hold any other office, excepting that of Senator or Delegate to the General Congress.
But if the chancellor, or either of the said judges, be elected
or appointed to any other office, excepting as is before excepted, it shall be at his option in which to serve.

XXVI. That sheriffs and coroners be annually appointed,
and that no person shall be capable of holding either of the
said offices more than four years successively, nor the sheriff,
of holding any other office at the same time.

XXVII. *And be it further Ordained*, That the register and
clerks in chancery be appointed by the chancellor; the clerks
of the supreme court by the judges of the said court; the clerk
of the court of probates by the judge of the said court; and
the register and marshal of the court of admiralty, by the
judge of the admiralty. The said marshal, registers and clerks
to continue in office during the pleasure of those by whom
they are to be appointed as aforesaid.

And that all attorneys, solicitors and counsellors at law,
hereafter to be appointed, be appointed by the court, and licensed by the first judge of the court in which they shall respectively plead or practise, and be regulated by the rules and
orders of the said courts.

XXVIII. *And be it further Ordained*, That where, by this
Convention, the duration of any office shall not be ascertained,
such office shall be construed to be held during the pleasure
of the council of appointment: provided that new commissions
shall be issued to the judges of the county courts, (other than
to the first judge,) and to justices of the peace, once at
least in every three years.

XXIX. That town clerks, supervisors, assessors, constables
and collectors, and all other officers heretofore eligible by
the people, shall always continue to be so eligible, in the
manner directed by the present or future acts of the Legislature.

XXX. That Delegates to represent this State in the General
Congress of the United States of America, be annually appointed
as follows, to wit: The Senate and Assembly shall each openly
nominate as many persons as shall be equal to the whole number
of Delegates to be appointed; after which nomination they shall
meet together, and those persons named in both lists shall be
Delegates. And out of those persons whose names are not in
both lists, one-half shall be chosen by the joint ballot of the
Senators and Members of Assembly, so met together as aforesaid.

XXXI. That the style of all laws shall be as follows, to
wit: "Be it enacted by the People of the State of New York, represented in Senate and Assembly." And that all writs and other proceedings shall run in the name of "the People of the

State of New York," and be tested in the name of the chancellor, or chief judge of the court from whence they shall issue.

XXXII. And this Convention doth further in the name and by the authority of the good people of this State, ordain, determine and declare, that a court shall be instituted for the trial of impeachments and correction of errors, under the regulations which shall be established by the Legislature; and to consist of the President of the Senate, for the time being, and the Senators, chancellor and judges of the supreme court, or the major part of them; except that when an impeachment shall be prosecuted against the chancellor, or either of the judges of the supreme court, the person so impeached, shall be suspended from exercising his office until his acquittal. And, in like manner, when an appeal from a decree in equity shall be heard, the chancellor shall inform the court of the reasons of his decree, but shall not have a voice in the final sentence. And if the cause to be determined shall be brought up by a writ of error on a question of law, on a judgment in the supreme court, the judges of that court shall assign the reasons of such their judgment, but shall not have a voice for its affirmance or reversal.

XXXIII. That the power of impeaching all officers of the State, for mal and corrupt conduct in their respective offices, be vested in the Representatives of the people in Assembly; but that it shall always be necessary that two-third parts of the members present shall consent to, and agree in, such impeachment. That previous to the trial of every impeachment, the members of the said court shall respectively be sworn, truly and impartially, to try and determine the charge in question according to evidence; and that no judgment of the said court shall be valid, unless it shall be assented to by two-third parts of the members then present; nor shall it extend farther than to removal from office, and disqualification to hold or enjoy any place of honour, trust or profit, under this State. But the party so accused, shall be, nevertheless, liable and subject to indictment, trial, judgment and punishment, according to the laws of the land.

XXXIV. *And it is further Ordained*, That in every trial on impeachment or indictment for crimes or misdemeanors, the party impeached or indicted shall be allowed counsel, as in civil actions.

XXXV. And this Convention doth further, in the name, and by the authority of the good people of this State, ordain, determine, and declare, that such parts of the common law of England, and of the statute law of England and Great Britain, and of the acts of the Legislature of the Colony of New York, as together did form the law of the said Colony on the nineteenth day of April, in the year of our Lord one thousand seven hundred and seventy-five, shall be and continue the law

of this State; subject to such alterations and provisions as
the Legislature of this State shall, from time to time, make
concerning the same. That such of the said acts as are temporary, shall expire at the times limited for their duration respectively.

That all such parts of the common law, and all such of the
said statutes and acts aforesaid, or parts thereof, as may be
construed to establish or maintain any particular denomination
of Christians or their ministers, or concern the allegiance
heretofore yielded to, and the supremacy, sovereignty, government or prerogatives, claimed or exercised by the King of Great
Britain and his predecessors, over the Colony of New York and
its inhabitants, or are repugnant to this Constitution, be, and
they hereby are, abrogated and rejected.

And this Convention doth further ordain, that the resolves
or resolutions of the Congresses of the Colony of New York, and
of the Convention of the State of New York, now in force, and
not repugnant to the government established by this Constitution, shall be considered as making part of the laws of this
State; subject, nevertheless, to such alterations and provisions as the Legislature of this State may, from time to time,
make concerning the same.

XXXVI. *And be it further Ordained,* That all grants within
this State, made by the King of Great Britain, or persons acting under his authority, after the fourteenth day of October,
one thousand seven hundred and seventy-five, shall be null and
void. But that nothing in this Constitution contained, shall
be construed to affect any grants of land within this State,
made by the authority of the said King or his predecessors, or
to annul any charters to bodies politic, by him or them, or any
of them, made prior to that day. And that none of the said
charters shall be adjudged to be void by reason of any non-user
or misuser of any of their respective rights or privileges,
between the nineteenth day of April, in the year of our Lord
one thousand seven hundred and seventy-five, and the publication of this Constitution. And further, that all such of the
officers described in the said charters respectively, as by the
terms of the said charters were to be appointed by the Governor
of the Colony of New York, with or without the advice and consent of the Council of the said King in the said Colony, shall
henceforth be appointed by the Council established by this Constitution for the appointment of officers in this State, until
otherwise directed by the Legislature.

XXXVII. AND WHEREAS it is of great importance to the safety of this State, that peace and amity with the Indians within
the same, be at all times supported and maintained: AND WHEREAS
the frauds too often practised towards the said Indians in contracts made for their lands, have in divers instances been productive of dangerous discontents and animosities:

Be it Ordained, That no purchases or contracts for the sale of lands made since the fourteenth day of October, in the year of our Lord one thousand seven hundred and seventy-five, or which may hereafter be made with or of the said Indians, within the limits of this State, shall be binding on the said Indians, or deemed valid, unless made under the authority and with the consent of the Legislature of this State.

XXXVIII. AND WHEREAS we are required by the benevolent principles of rational liberty, not only to expel civil tyranny, but also to guard against that spiritual oppression and intolerance wherewith the bigotry and ambition of weak and wicked priests and princes have scourged mankind: This Convention doth further, in the name and by the authority of the good people of this State, ordain, determine and declare, that the free exercise and enjoyment of religious profession and worship, without discrimination or preference, shall forever hereafter be allowed within this State to all mankind; provided that the liberty of conscience hereby granted shall not be so construed as to excuse acts of licentiousness or justify practices inconsistent with the peace or safety of this State.

XXXIX. AND WHEREAS the ministers of the gospel are by their profession, dedicated to the service of God and the cure of souls, and ought not to be diverted from the great duties of their function: Therefore, no minister of gospel, or priest of any denomination whatsoever, shall at any time hereafter, under any pretence or description whatever, be eligible to, or capable of holding, any civil or military office or place within this State.

XL. AND WHEREAS it is of the utmost importance to the safety of every State, that it should always be in a condition of defence; and it is the duty of every man who enjoys the protection of society, to be prepared and willing to defend it: This Convention therefore in the name and by the authority of the good people of this State, doth ordain, determine and declare, that the militia of this State at all times hereafter, as well in peace as in war, shall be armed and disciplined and in readiness for service. That all such of the inhabitants of this State, being of the people called Quakers, as from scruples of conscience may be averse to the bearing of arms, be therefrom excused by the Legislature, and do pay to the State such sums of money in lieu of their personal service, as the same may, in the judgment of the Legislature, be worth; and that a proper magazine of warlike stores, proportionate to the number of inhabitants, be forever hereafter at the expense of this State; and by acts of the Legislature, established, maintained and continued in every county in this State.

XLI. And this Convention doth further ordain determine and declare in the name and by the authority of the good people of this State, that trial by jury in all cases in which it hath heretofore been used in the colony of New York, shall be established and remain inviolate forever. And that no acts of attainder shall be passed by the Legislature of this State, for crimes other than those committed before the termination of the present war; and that such acts shall not work a corruption of blood. And further, that the Legislature of this State shall, at no time hereafter, institute any new court or courts but such as shall proceed according to the course of the common law.

    XLII. And this Convention doth further, in the name and by the authority of the good people of this State, ordain, determine and declare, that it shall be in the discretion of the Legislature to naturalize all such persons, and in such manner as they shall think proper, provided all such of the persons so to be by them naturalized, as being born in parts beyond sea, and out of the United States of America, shall come to settle in, and become subjects of this State, shall take an oath of allegiance to this State, and abjure and renounce all allegiance and subjection to all and every foreign king, prince, potentate and State, in all matters ecclesiatical as well as civil.

Chapter four:

Experiment in Independence, 1778-86

By the end of 1777 New York had undergone the transformation from colony to state, but whether the metamorphosis was transitory or permanent was a question still to be determined. The radicals had carried the day during the prerevolutionary decade with surprising ease, but with independence the numerous loyalists took to the field en masse to assist the redcoats in suppressing the rebellion. Thus independence turned on the ability of the Americans to effect a political as well as a military victory, to withstand internal as well as external pressures. British occupation of New York City from September 1776 to November 1783 complicated both tasks; throughout the war the strategically located metropolis served as a haven for loyalists and a base for British military operations. New York State was the scene of internecine warfare between rebel and royalist armies, between Indians and frontier settlers, and between loyalist guerrilla bands and provincial militia units. It is impossible to convey (or to calculate, for that matter) the extent of the damage and suffering wrought by the war, but the fact that nearly one-third of the engagements of the war occurred in the Empire State suggests the magnitude of the struggle.

The year of decision was 1781—the year the Americans achieved the requisite political and military victories to secure independence. With the assent of Maryland in February, the Articles of Confederation, adopted by the Continental Congress in November 1777, took effect as the first constitution of the United States on March 1, 1781. (New York ratified the Articles on February 6, 1778, the second state to agree to the charter.) Seven months later, on October 19, the surrender of the British army commanded by Charles, Lord Cornwallis, to a combined allied force under George Washington and the Marquis de Lafayette at Yorktown ended the military phase of the Revolution and set in motion a chain of political and diplomatic events that led to formal recognition of American independence.

By the terms of the treaty signed on September 3, 1783, the
United States of America officially became a member of the international community. On November 25, 1783, to the accompani-
ment of a thirteen-gun salute, the Stars and Stripes replaced
the Union Jack as the last British remnants left New York City.
For New Yorkers the colonial past lay behind; ahead loomed an
uncertain future as an independent state and nation.

Even before the conclusion of the Treaty of Paris ending
the War of Independence Americans began to turn their attention
from the battlefield to the domestic front. At no time during
the 1780s was the success of the experiment in republicanism
taken for granted. Although the new nation faced formidable
external problems (relating to diplomatic recognition, foreign
commerce, and encroachment by Britain and Spain), its future
depended on its ability to resolve imposing internal problems
stemming from both the War and the Revolution.

In New York, as elsewhere, there were pecuniary as well
as political dimensions to the transition from wartime to
peacetime. An artificial economic boom temporarily obscured
the serious dislocation and devastation wrought by seven years
of protracted war. But by 1785 inflation, personal and public
indebtedness, the disruption of interstate and international
commerce, and the physical destruction of land and property
posed a fundamental threat to the stability and well-being of
New York society. The resolution of fiscal problems and the
reconstruction of a viable economic order were the most pressing provincial tasks of the postrevolutionary era. However,
many people regarded the treatment of Tories as the paramount
issue: reconciliation or revenge—that was the question. The
termination of hostilities found loyalists under laws of pro-
scription, banishment, and confiscation; not until 1788 were
most of the restrictions removed and the rights of citizenship
restored to most remaining Tories.

The legacies of the Revolution itself constituted the most
perplexing problems confronting the revolutionary generation,
including translating the rhetoric of the Declaration of Independence into reality, framing a constitutional-legal environ-
ment and political system that emobdied the principles of republicanism, giving expression to the social forces unleashed by
the Revolution, and devising a mode of federalism that provided
for effective local and central government. The Spirit of
Seventy-six manifested itself in a variety of ways—democratization of officeholding, abolition of the vestiges of feudal
land tenure, separation of church and state, antislavery agitation, revision of the civil and criminal codes, proliferation
of public educational institutions, and a host of humanitarian
reform enterprises. But whatever progress was made at the
state level—and the record is mixed—defects in the Articles

of Confederation and state parochialism created major problems
at the national level.

52

ACT APPOINTING COMMISSIONERS
FOR DETECTING CONSPIRACIES

February 5, 1778

WHEREAS the late convention did appoint [September 21,
1776] a board of commissioners for the purpose of enquiring
into detecting and defeating all conspiracies which might be
formed in this State against the liberties of *America*

And whereas, by reason of the present invasion of this
State and of the disaffection of sundry of the inhabitants of
the same, it will be expedient to continue the said board which
experience hath shewn to be of great use and importance. To
the end therefore that the State and the peace of the same may
be efectually guarded and secured against the wicked machina-
tions and designs of the foreign and domestic foes thereof

Be it enacted . . . That the governor, lieutenant governor, or president of the senate who for the time being shall
administer the government of this State be and he hereby is authorized and empowered from time to time to appoint by commission by and with the advice and consent of the council of appointment so many persons not exceeding ten as he shall think
proper to be commissioners for the Purposes aforesaid and that
the said commissioners or any three of them be and they hereby
are authorized and empowered to do and perform the several acts
matters and things herein after mentioned viz: that the said
commissioners or any three of them shall be and they hereby are
authorized and impowered to send for persons and papers and administer oaths and to apprehend and confine or cause to be apprehended and confined in such manner and under such restrictions and limitations as to them shall appear necessary for the
public safety all persons whose going at large shall in the
judgment of the said commissioners or any three of them appear
dangerous to the safety of this State. To take bonds and

AN ACT appointing commissioners for detecting and defeating
conspiracies and declaring their powers. *Laws of the State of
New York* (Albany, N.Y.: J. B. Lyon Co., 1886), 1: 8-10.

and recognizances from time to time to the people of this State
for the good behaviour safe custody or appearance of such of
the said persons and of all others now confined for the like
cause as they may think proper in such sums and upon such conditions as unto them shall appear expedient; and the said bonds
and recognizances if forfeited to prosecute or to cancel and
release upon such terms and conditions and to discharge from
confinement any of the said persons absolutely and without any
terms or conditions as they may think proper *and also* from time
to time to make such provision for the safe custody and com-
fortable subsistence of all persons who may from time to time
be so confined as aforesaid in such manner as they may think
proper provided always that by reason or colour of any thing
herein contained the said commissioners or any of them shall
not be impowered to inflict any corporal punishment upon any or
either of the said persons confined as aforesaid.

And be it further enacted . . . that no judge or magistrate shall bail any of the persons who may be confined by authority of the said commissioners and that no court shall deliver any of the gaols within this State of any person or persons so confined as aforesaid unless such persons shall have
been indicted and tried for the offence or offences for which
he or she shall have been respectively committed. . . .

. . . . .

And be it further enacted . . . that this act shall continue in force, until the first day of *November*, in the year of
our Lord one thousand seven hundred and seventy-eight, and no
longer.

53

ACT AFFECTING NEUTRALS   June 30, 1778

WHEREAS certain of the inhabitants of this State have during the course of the present cruel war, waged by the king and

---

AN ACT more effectually to prevent the mischiefs arising from
the example and influence of persons of equivocal and suspected
characters in this State. *Laws of the State of New York*, 1:
87-88. This statute is a revision of an act passed on March 7,
1777.

and parliament of *Great-Britain* against the people of these
States, affected to maintain a neutrality which there is reason
to suspect was in many instances dictated by a poverty of spirit and an undue attachment to property. *And whereas* divers of
the said persons, some of whom advocated the *American* cause
till it became serious, have notwithstanding the forbearance of
their countrymen and contrary to the faith pledged by their
paroles, ungratefully and insiduously from time to time by artful misrepresentations and a subtle dissemination of doctrines
fears and apprehensions false in themselves and injurious to
the *American* cause, seduced certain weak minded persons from
the duties they owed their country. *And whereas* the welfare of
this State loudly demands that some decisive measures be taken
with respect to the said persons, and it being repugnant to
justice as well as good policy that men should be permitted to
shelter themselves under a government which they not only refused to assist in rearing, but which some of them daily endeavour to undermine and subvert. *And whereas* such few of the
said persons as may have been led to take a neutral part by
conscientious doubts and scruples, have had more than sufficient time to consider and determine the same

   Be it enacted . . . That the commissioners appointed for
inquiring into detecting and defeating all conspiracies which
may be formed in this State against the liberties of *America* or
any three of them be and they hereby are authorized and strictly charged and required to cause all such persons of neutral
and equivocal characters in this State whom they shall think
have influence sufficient to do mischief in it, to come before
them and to administer to the said persons respectively the
following oath (or if of the people called Quakers) affirmation
viz

   "I A B do solemnly and without any mental reservation or
equivocation whatever, swear and call God to witness (or if of
the people called Quakers) affirm that I do believe and acknowledge the State of *New York* to be of right a free and independent State. And that no authority or power can of right be exercised in or over the said State, but what is or shall be
granted by or derived from the people thereof. *And further*
that as a good subject of the said free and independent State
of *New York*, I will to the best of my knowledge and ability
faithfully do my duty. And as I shall keep or disregard this
oath, so help and deal with me Almighty God."

   And be it further enacted . . . That if on the said oath
or affirmation being so tendered, the said person or persons
shall refuse to take the same, the said commissioners do forthwith remove the said person or persons so refusing to any place
within the enemy's lines, and by writing under their hands and
seals certify the names of such person or persons to the sec-

retary of this State, who is hereby required to record and file the said certificates.

And be it further enacted . . . That if any of the said neutrals, shall abscond or absent himself with an apparent view to avoid the force of this act, the said commissioners shall by notice, published in one or more of the news-papers of this State, demand of the said person or persons, so absconding or absenting, to appear before them, at such place in this State, and at such time, not exceeding twenty one days from the time of such publication, as they shall assign. *And further*, That Default in such Appearance, shall be adjudged to amount to and is hereby declared to be a Refusal to take the said Oath or Affirmation.

And be it further enacted . . . That if any of the persons removed to places within the enemy's lines by the said commissioners, in pursuance of this act, or who having as aforesaid, absconded or absented, shall not on notice as aforesaid appear before the said commissioners, and take the oath or affirmation aforesaid, shall thereafter be found in any part of this State; such person or persons so found, shall on conviction thereof, be adjudged guilty of misprison of treason.

And to the end, That this State may be in some measure compensated for the injuries it has sustained, by the evil example or practices of the said neutrals, and that others may be detered on similar occasions, from acting a part so unmanly and ingnominious;

Be it further enacted . . . That all lands held in this State, on the twenty-sixth day of *June* instant, in fee simple or fee tail, or which may hereafter be acquired by, or devised, granted, or descend to any of the persons who shall refuse to take the aforesaid oath or affirmation, when called upon by the said commissioners, shall forever thereafter, be charged with double taxes, in whosoever hands the said lands may hereafter be.

And be it further enacted . . . That the said commissioners, previous to the removal of the said several persons within the enemy's lines, shall from time to time, notify the person administering the government of this State for the time being, of the several persons so to be removed, who is hereby authorised to detain and confine, such of the said persons as he shall think proper, for the purpose of exchanging them for any of the subjects of this State, in the power of the enemy.

. . . . .

54

Peter Van Schaack to John Jay Kinderhook, August 14, 1778

I owe it to the friendship which formerly subsisted between us, to explain myself on a very serious subject, before I
quit this country, perhaps forever. The charitable construction which every man would wish to be put upon his own conduct,
will, I hope, induce you to do justice to *my* principles; principles not formed without consideration; not dependent on un-
decisive events, and not to be deserted at the approach of danger.

I suffer, sir, as you must see, for a difference of
opinion merely, on a question wherein I am not only justifiable,
but under the most sacred obligation to exercise my own private
judgment. In a case like this, involving considerations of
moral duty, there can be no *choice*, and he who disobeys the
dictates of his own mind, stands convicted. Punishment by the
civil power for a difference of opinion in the abstract, will
be reprobated by every liberal man; but, in the present case,
its justice is derived from the dangerous tendency of those
opinion, in that they uphold a supremacy *foreign* to the government of the state. They are *but opinions*, nevertheless; and
that their evil tendency cannot be restrained, or prevented,
without so harsh a measure as the present, I believe will not,
when considered without passion, be believed: and if it *can*,
the government (which, too, is not exempt from obligation,) is
bound to adopt more lenient methods.

Whoever recurs to the origin of the present war, must admit, (unless he arrogates to himself infallibility, and sup-
poses, moreover, that no man can really differ from him and be
innocent,) that there were many men, who, from principle, dis-
sented from the public measures; and if there were others, who
were *not* actuated by principle, I believe this was not peculiar
to *one* side. All, however, had a right to take their part.
These men, according to the laws of nature and of nations,
should have been permitted, in the beginning of the war, to remove; or, if detained, it could only be as prisoners of war, or,
at most, a passive obedience to the laws, and not the active
services of subjects, ought to have been required of them. The
declaration of war from the crown of Great Britain, in 1756,[1]

Henry C. Van Schaack, *Life of Peter Van Schaack*, pp. 121-22.

[1]The Seven Years War, or the Great War for the Empire.

permitted all the subjects of the French king then in England
to remove with their effects, or promised them the protection
of the laws; and this, I believe, is the general practice in
Europe. A different policy, however, has here prevailed, the
particulars of which I need not enumerate, and the effects have
been just what might have been expected from *such* a system; but
the difficulties which have arisen from the attempts to compel
the consciences of men, ought not surely to be imputed to *them*.

The harshness of the present act,[2] is aggravated by the
change of circumstances, and converts that which was a right,
into a punishment; and makes that severity in the government,
which was heretofore incumbent on them as an act of justice.
Consider, sir, you have derived aids from these people in the
prosecution of the war, and have detained them in the most perilous times; and now, when in the declared sense of the people
in power the danger subsides, by an inverted order the severity
increases. Is this answering the design of punishment? Is it
conformable to those reasons, upon the strength of which, the
few are raised above the many? Is it consistent with that justice due to individuals, from which rulers cannot divest themselves? or is it in the least agreeable to the spirit of the
law of Solon against neutrality, which I have heard you quote?

Let me entreat you to recur to first principles; your government, professed to be formed upon them, is too young to excuse inattention to them. Read with the same temper *you used*,
Locke, Montesquieu and Beccaria, upon the rights of individuals,
and the duties of those in power, and compare them with the
present practice, and I fancy *you* will think that Great Britain
has not alone trampled upon the rights of mankind.

. . . . .

----

[2]See document no. 53.

55

ALEXANDER HAMILTON TO JOHN HOLT
                                  Poughkeepsie, October 19, 1778

        While every method is taken to bring to justice those men
whose principles and practices have been hostile to the present
revolution, it is to be lamented that the conduct of another
class, equally criminal, and, if possible, more mischievous,
has hitherto passed with impunity, and almost without notice.
I mean that tribe who, taking advantage of the times, have carried the spirit of monopoly and extortion to an excess which
scarcely admits of a parallel. Emboldened by the success of
progressive impositions, it has extended to all the necessaries
of life. The exorbitant price of every article, and the depre-
ciation upon our currency, are evils derived essentially from
this source. When avarice takes the lead in a state, it is
commonly the forerunner of its fall. How shocking is it to
discover among ourselves, even at this early period, the
strongest symptoms of this fatal disease!
        . . . . .

56

"COUNTRY MAN," ON REPRISALS AND RESPONSIBILITY
                                            May 17, 1779

        . . . . .
        It is a matter of the highest regret to great numbers, I
might say to the people in general of this State . . . that the
confiscation bill was not passed into a law, the last session

---

New York Journal, October 19, 1778. Holt published the *Journal*.
Hamilton's communication was not private but rather a "letter
to the editor."

New York Journal, May 17, 1779. The identity of the author is
unknown.

of the Assembly. The public are impatient to know through whose means the completion of that most necessary and important bill was obstructed and put off, tho' they hope it will be one of the first works of the next session. We are also uneasy that the votes of the Legislature are not published, at least in time for us to know before every new election, by the votes of the old one, in what manner they have acquitted themselves, and how well they are entitled to our future choice, which surely no one can have the least pretension to who voted against the confiscation bill.

. . . . .

57

ACT FOR THE FORFEITURE AND
SALE OF LOYALIST ESTATES

October 22, 1779

WHEREAS during the present unjust and cruel war waged by the king of Great Britain against this State, and the other United States of America, divers persons holding or claiming property within this State have voluntarily been adherent to the said king his fleets and armies, enemies to this State and the said other United States, with intent to subvert the government and liberties of this State and the said other United States, and to bring the same in subjection to the crown of Great Britain by reason whereof the said persons have severally justly forfeited all right to the protection of this State and

---

AN ACT, for the forfeiture and sale of the estates of persons who have adhered to the enemies of this State, and for declaring the sovereignty of the people of this State in respect to all property within the same. *Laws of the State of New York*, 1: 173-84. It is impossible to calculate precisely either the extent of confiscation or its impact on New York society. However, two generalizations seem safe: (1) the amount of property confiscated was large, the sale of loyalist lands yielding approximately $3,000,000 in state revenue; and (2) confiscation was an impetus to the democratization of landholding, because most of the land was eventually sold to middling farmers or tenants exercising preemption rights.

to the benefit of the laws under which said property is held or claimed.

And whereas the public justice and safety of this State absolutely require that the most notorious offenders should be immediately hereby convicted and attainted of the offence aforesaid in order to work a forfeiture of their respective estates and vest the same in the people of this State. *And whereas* the Constitution of this State hath authorized the legislature to pass acts of attainder, for crimes committed before the termination of the present war.

I. *Be it therefore enacted* . . . That [60 names] are hereby severally declared to be *ipso facto* convicted and attainted of the offence aforesaid, and that all and singular the estate both real and personal held or claimed by them the said persons severally and respectively, whether in possession, reversion or remainder, within this State, on the day of the passing of this act, shall be and hereby is declared to be forfeited to, and vested in the people of this State.

II. *And be it further enacted* . . . That the said several persons hereinbefore particularly named shall be and hereby are declared to be forever banished from this State, and each and every of them who shall at any time hereafter be found in any part of this State, shall be and are hereby adjudged and declared guilty of felony, and shall suffer death as in cases of felony without benefit of clergy. . . .

III. *Be it further enacted* . . . That it shall and may be lawful for the grand jurors at any supreme court of judicature to be held for this State, or at any court of oyer and terminer and general gaol delivery or general or quarter sessions of the peace to be held in and for any county of this State, whenever it shall appear to such grand jurors by the oath of one or more credible witness or witnesses, that any person or persons, whether in full life or deceased, generally reputed, if in full life to hold or claim, or if deceased, to have held or claimed at the time of their death respectively, real or personal estate within this State, hath or have been guilty of the offence aforesaid, to prefer bills of indictment against such persons as shall then be in full life for such offence, and in relation to the offence committed by such persons in their lives time as shall then be deceased severally and respectively, notwithstanding that such offence may have been committed elsewhere than in the county for which such grand jurors shall be summoned. . . .

IV. *And be it further enacted* . . . That . . . the sherifs of the respective counties where such indictments shall be taken shall forthwith cause notices thereof agreeable to such form as is herein after mentioned to be published in one or more of the public news papers within this State, for at least four weeks.

V. *And be it further enacted* . . . That in every case of a neglect to appear and traverse agreeable to the sherif's notice, the several persons charged in such indictment whether in full life or deceased shall respectively be and hereby are declared to be and shall be adjudged guilty of the offences charged against them respectively. And the several persons who shall in pursuance of this act either by reason of such default in not appearing and traversing as aforesaid or upon trial be convicted of the offence aforesaid shall forfeit all and singular the estate both real and personal, whether in possession reversion or remainder, held or claimed by them respectively within this State to the people of this State. . . .

. . . . .

XIIII. *And be it further enacted* . . . That the absolute property of all messuages lands tenements and hereditaments and of all rents royalties, franchises, prerogatives, priviledges, escheats, forfeitures, debts, dues duties and services by whatsoever names respectively the same are called and known in the law, and all right and title to the same, which next and immediately before [July 9, 1776] did vest in, or belong, or was, or were due to the crown of Great Britain . . . shall be vested in the people of this State. . . .

XV. *And be it further enacted* . . . That the person administering the government of this State for the time being shall be . . . authorized and required by and with the advice and consent of the council of appointment to appoint, during the pleasure of the said council . . . three commissioners of forfeitures for each of the great districts of this State. That the said commissioners or a majority of them shall be . . . authorized and required from time to time, to sell and dispose of all real estate within their respective districts, forfeited or to be forfeited to the people of this State, at public vendue to the highest bidder or bidders, and in such parcels as they shall from time to time think proper first giving eight weeks notice of each sale in one or more of the public news papers in this State containing a description as to the quantity by estimation of the lands or tenements to be sold, the situation thereof and the name or names of the person or persons by the conviction and attainder of whom the said lands or tenements are deemed to have become forfeited, and to make seal and deliver to the purchaser or purchasers respectively good and sufficient deeds and conveyances in the law, to vest the same in them respectively and their respective heirs and assigns upon such purchaser or purchasers respectively producing such receipt from the treasurer as is herein after mentioned. That every such purchaser and purchasers shall by virtue of such deeds and conveyances respectively be so vested in title seizin and possession of the lands and tenements so purchased as to have and maintain in his, her or their name or names any action

for recovery thereof or damages relating thereto any actual
seizin or possession thereof in any other person or persons
notwithstanding. That every such deed and conveyance shall be
deemed to operate as a warranty from the people of this State,
to the purchaser or purchasers respectively and their respective heirs and assigns for the lands or tenements thereby respectively granted and conveyed against all claims titles and
incumbrances whatsoever and such purchaser or purchasers respectively and their respective heirs or assigns shall in case
of eviction have such remedy and relief upon such warranty in
such manner as shall be more particularly provided for in such
future act or acts of the legislature as are herein after mentioned

Provided that the said commissioners shall not be authorized to sell any lands in larger parcels than the quantity of
five hundred acres in each parcel, that no more than one farm
shall be included in one and the same sale, and that the sales
shall be made in the county where the lands or tenements to be
sold respectively lie.

. . . . .

XVII. . . . *And whereas* in many instances, lands, the
reversion or remainder whereof is or may become forfeited to
this State, are possessed by tenants who have at considerable
expence made or purchased the improvements on the same, and
which tenants have constantly, uniformly and zealously, since
the commencement of the present war, endeavored to defend and
maintain the freedom and independence of this United States.

XVIII. *Be it therefore further enacted* . . . That where
lands the reversion or remainder whereof is hereby or may become forfeited to the people of this State, shall be possessed
by any tenant of the character above described, and who, or
whose ancestor, testator or intestate, shall have made or purchased the improvements on the same, they shall continue in
possession at their former rents and be at liberty as heretofore to transfer their improvements untill the fee simple of
the said lands shall be sold, they paying their respective
rents and the present arearages thereof in money equal to the
current prices of the articles of produce in which their rents
were heretofore paid, into the treasury of this State, if such
rents were reserved in produce, or if reserved in money then in
so much money as will be equivalent to the price of wheat at
seven shillings per bushel. And that when the fee simple of
the said lands shall be sold by the commissioners to be appointed in pursuance of this act, they shall cause such lands
to be appraised by three appraisers, at what shall be deemed
the then present value thereof, exclusive of the improvements
thereon, at the time of appraising; That one of the said appraisers shall be elected by the commissioners, another by the

tenant claiming the benefit intended by this clause, and the third by the said other two appraisers. . . .

. . . . .

XXIII. *And be it further enacted* . . . That the said commissioners shall not be authorized to sell any lands which at the time of the sale thereof, shall be within the power of the enemy, any thing herein before mentioned notwithstanding. . . .

. . . . .

XXVI. *And be it further enacted* . . . That each and every person or persons claiming an estate or interest under any person deceased shall and may upon affidavit of such claim and of the death of the person under whom such claim shall be made to be read and filed in court, be admitted to traverse the indictments against the persons under whom they so respectively claim. . . .

58

PUBLIC ADDRESS OF THE STATE LEGISLATURE　　March 13, 1781

. . . . .

FRIENDS AND FELLOW-CITIZENS—While government is without corruption, the representatives of a free people cannot be inattentive to the opinions of their constituents: They will hear their complaints and examine into the causes of them; if they proceed from errors in government, they will endeavor to correct such errors; if they originate in evils which arise from their peculiar situation, they will explain the necessity which gives them birth—well satisfied that such evils will be borne with patience, by those virtuous citizens, who count temporary inconveniences as dust in the balance when weighed against their own freedom, and the happiness of posterity.

The weight of taxes, the rigorous measures that have been used to restrain the disaffected, exertions oppressive to individuals by which supplies have been obtained, the wants of the army, the calls upon the militia, and the destruction of our frontiers, are the principal sources from which the present

---

"An Address from the legislature of the state of New-York, to their Constituents" in Niles, comp., *Principles and Acts of the Revolution,* pp. 129-32.

discontents are supposed to flow. At first view, it will appear that most of these complaints militate against each other,
and that to diminish the cause of some evils, others must be
increased: Thus, to procure supplies without force, money must
be obtained and taxes rendered more burthensome; to relieve the
frontiers, great demands must be made upon the militia; to conduct military operations with sucess, vigor and energy must be
given to government, and temporary restraint be imposed upon
the liberty of the subject. Those who candidly admit these
truths, will judge of the embarrassments which perplex the legislature—will make proper allowances for them, and by aiding
and supporting government, enable their rulers to distinguish
between the manly representations of freemen and real patriots,
and the insidious murmurs of these grovelling souls, whom the
flesh pots of Egypt would lure back to the land of bondage.
   [There follows a detailed discussion of the above points.]
   . . . . .
   Thus, friends and fellow citizens, impelled by the lauda-
ble principle that the public weal only ought to influence the
conduct of its servants, have we admitted the justice of some
of your complaints, promised our endeavors to lessen the cause
of others, submitted to your candor our observations on those
which we cannot deem grievous, pointed at the embarrassments
which surround us, and the means we have pursued to remove
them; but while duty dictated this line of conduct on our part,
it becomes *us, the temporary representatives of the majesty of
the people*, to prosecute this address in a style which freemen
ought to use to their equals; and we therefore cannot hesitate
to assert, that is is incumbent on you candidly to distinguish
between errors in the general system of the laws themselves,
and the persons employed in the execution of them; between
those which your situation and circumstances render unavoidable.
Your representations have been useful in pointing out defects,
but in your fortitude, in a due obedience to the laws, and in a
determination to support the authority of government, can relief only be obtained against partial burthens, and although we
cannot suspect that you will be remiss in these great duties of
the good citizen, yet it behoves [*sic*] us to advise you, that a
criminal negligence has been lately too prevalent with some;
that it is your duty to interfere, especially whilst the British tyrant insults you with his unmeaning offers of peace and
pardon, and whilst his infamous emissaries industriously attempt to excite the honest, but credulous friend of his country,
to unwarrantable commotions, and induce him to mix with well
founded grievances, those that do not exist. We mention this
to sound the alarm to you, whose zeal and firmness have remained unshaken in every vicissitude of the present contest,
that the weak and unwary may, by your example, be led to the
better policy of removing the difficulties and embarrassments

which lay between us and *the great objects* we have in view, IN-DEPENDENCE, LIBERTY, and PEACE, and not, by throwing fresh difficulties in the way, remove to a more remote period the completion of your wish.

. . . . .

Your representatives feel themselves incapable of believing that any but the misguided, the weak and the unwary amongst our fellow-citizens, can be guilty of so foully staining the honor of the state, and wantonly becoming parricides of their own, and the peace and happiness of their posterity—Let us then all, for our interest is the same with one heart and one voice, mutually aid and support each other. Let us steadily, unanimously, and vigorously, prosecute the great business of establishing our independence. Thus shall we be free ourselves, and leave the blessings of freedom to millions yet unborn.

59

THE STATE LOYALTY OATH   March 26, 1781

Be it enacted . . . That each and every person who shall at any time hereafter be elected or appointed to any public place or office, shall instead of taking the oath of allegiance prescribed by the act [of March 17, 1778] take and subscribe the following oath or affirmation, to wit,
"I   do hereby solemnly without any mental reservation or equivocation whatsoever, swear and declare, and call God to witness (or if the people called Quakers, affirm) that I renounce and abjure all allegiance to the King of Great Britain; and that I will bear true faith and allegiance to the State of New York as a free and independent State and that I will in all things to the best of my knowledge and ability do my duty as a good and faithful subject of the said State ought to do, so help me God."
That the said oath or affirmation required by this act shall be taken and subscribed before the several persons, and

---

AN ACT for the better securing the independence of this State, and to that end requiring all public officers and electors within this State, to take the test oath therein contained. *Laws of the State of New York*, 1: 355-56.

in like manner as the oath of allegiance prescribed in and by
the said act, is required to be taken and subscribed.

And be it further enacted . . . That at every election
hereafter to be held within this State . . . the person or persons authorized by law or custom to preside at such election,
shall tender and administer the oath or affirmation aforesaid,
to each elector presenting himself to vote at such election, if
the person or persons presiding at such election shall have
reason to suspect that such elector hath not taken an active
and decisive part in favor of the United States in the present
war, against the king of Great Britain and his adherents; or if
such elector shall be challenged by any other elector who shall
have taken the said oath or affirmation, as not having taken an
active and decisive part in the present war as aforesaid; and
if the elector so suspected or challenged, shall refuse to take
the said oath or affirmation, when so tendered to him as aforesaid, he shall not be permitted to vote at such election—That
if at any such election the person or persons presiding shall
receive the vote or ballot of any elector so challenged as
aforesaid, and who upon being tendered the said oath or affirmation shall refuse to take the same, the said person or persons so presiding shall for each offence forfeit the sum of
five pounds, to any person who will sue for the same, and to be
recovered with costs—That it shall be lawful for the person or
persons presiding at any such election, and he or they are
hereby required to administer the said oath or affirmation to
any elector who shall voluntarily offer to take the same.

60

ALEXANDER HAMILTON, "THE CONTINENTALIST," NO. 1
New York, July 12, 1781

. . . . .

It would be the extreme of vanity in us not to be sensible,
that we began this revolution with very vague and confined no-
tions of the practical business of government. To the greater

---

The New-York Packet, and the American Advertiser, July 12, 1781.
Hamilton penned six installments of "The Continentalist" between July 12, 1781, and July 4, 1782, under the nom de plume

part of us it was a novelty: Of those, who under the former
constitution had had opportunities of acquiring experience, a
large proportion adhered to the opposite side, and the remainder can only be supposed to have possessed ideas adapted to the
narrow colonial sphere, in which they had been accustomed to
move, not of that enlarged kind suited to the government of an
INDEPENDENT NATION.

There were no doubt exceptions to these observations—men
in all respects qualified for conducting the public affairs,
with skill and advantage; but their number was small; they were
not always brought forward in our councils; and when they were,
their influence was too commonly borne down by the prevailing
torrent of ignorance and prejudice.

On a retrospect however, of our transactions, under the
disadvantages with which we commenced, it is perhaps more to be
wondered at, that we have done so well, than that we have not
done better. There are indeed some traits in our conduct, as
conspicuous for sound policy, as others for magnanimity. But,
on the other hand, it must also be confessed, there have been
many false steps, many chimerical projects and utopian specula-
tions, in the management of our civil as well as of our military affairs. A part of these were the natural effects of the
spirit of the times dictated by our situation. An extreme
jealousy of power is the attendant on all popular revolutions,
and has seldom been without its evils. It is to this source we
are to trace many of the fatal mistakes, which have so deeply
endangered the common cause; particularly that defect, which
will be the object of these remarks, A WANT OF POWER IN CON-
GRESS.

The present Congress, respectable for abilities and integrity, by experience convinced of the necessity of a change, are
preparing several important articles to be submitted to the respective states, for augmenting the powers of the Confederation.
But though there is hardly at this time a man of information in
America, who will not acknowledge, as a general proposition,
that in its present form, it is unequal, either to a vigorous
prosecution of the war, or to the preservation of the union in
peace; yet when the principle comes to be applied to practice,
there seems not to be the same agreement in the modes of reme-
dying the defect; and it is to be feared, from a disposition
which appeared in some of the states on a late occasion,[1] that
the salutary intentions of Congress may meet with more delay

_____

(Cont'd.) "A. B.," in which he set forth the necessity of an
augmented central authority.

[1]The reference is probably to the attempt by Congress to amend
the Articles to permit a 5 percent federal impost to liquidate

and opposition, than the critical posture of the states will
justify.

. . . . .

History is full of examples, where in contests for liberty,
a jealousy of power has either defeated the attempts to recover
or preserve it in the first instance, or has afterwards subverted it by clogging government with too great precautions for
its felicity, or by leaving too wide a door for sedition and
popular licenciousness. In a government framed for durable
liberty, not less regard must be paid to giving the magistrate
a proper degree of authority, to make and execute the laws with
vigour, than to guarding against encroachments upon the rights
of the community. As too much power leads to despotism, too
little leads to anarchy, and both eventually to the ruin of the
people. These are maxims well known, but never sufficiently
attended to, in adjusting the frames of governments. Some momentary interest or passion is sure to give a wrong bias, and
pervert the most favourable opportunities.

. . . . .

In comparison of our governments with those of the ancient
republics, we must, without hesitation, give the preference to
our own; because, every power with us is exercised by representation, not in tumultuary assemblies of the collective body of
the people, where the art or impudence of the ORATOR or TRIBUNE,
rather than the utility or justice of the measure could seldom
fail to govern. Yet whatever may be the advantage on our side,
in such a comparison, men who estimate the value of institutions, not from prejudices of the moment, but from experience
and reason, must be persuaded, that the same JEALOUSY of POWER
has prevented our reaping all the advantages, from the examples
of other nations, which we ought to have done, and has rendered
our constitutions in many respects feeble and imperfect.

Perhaps the evil is not very great in respect to our
[state] constitutions; for notwithstanding their imperfections,
they may, for some time, be made to operate in such a manner,
as to answer the purposes of the common defence and the maintenance of order; and they seem to have, in themselves, and in
the progress of society among us, the seeds of improvement.

But this is not the case with respect to the FEDERAL GOV-
ERNMENT; if it is too weak at first, it will continually grow
weaker. The ambition and local interests of the respective
members, will be constantly undermining and usurping upon its
prerogatives, till it comes to a dissolution; if a partial com-

---

(Cont'd.) the national debt. Rhode Island's recalcitrance
thwarted the attempt; two years later New York blocked a similar proposal.

bination of some of the more powerful ones does not bring it to a more SPEEDY and VIOLENT END.

61

ACT ABOLISHING ENTAILS   July 12, 1782

I. *Be it enacted* . . . That in all cases, wherein any person or persons would if this law had not been made, had been seized in fee-tail, of any lands tenements hereditaments, such person or persons shall, in future, be deemed to be seized of the same in fee-simple.

And further, That where any lands tenements or hereditaments, shall heretofore have been devised, granted, or otherwise conveyed, by a tenant in tail, and the person, to whom such devise, grant, or other conveyance shall have been made, his or her heirs or assigns, shall, from the time such devise took effect, or from the time such grant or other conveyance was made, to the day of the passing of this act, been in the uninterrupted possession of such lands, tenements or hereditaments, and claiming and holding the same under such devise, grant, or other conveyance, then such grant, devise, or other conveyance, shall be deemed as good legal and effectual to all intents, as if such tenant in tail had, at the time of the making of such devise, grant, or other conveyance, been seized of such lands, tenements or hereditaments in fee simple, any law to the contrary hereof notwithstanding.

AN ACT to abolish entails, to confirm conveyances by tenants in tail, to distribute estates real of intestates, to remedy defective conveyances to joint tenants, and directing the mode of such conveyances in future. *Laws of the State of New York,* 1: 501-2. A common mode of land transfer in colonial America, entailment was designed to keep family property holdings intact through restrictive inheritance: entailed estates could not be disposed of, in whole or in part, except to a specified succession of heirs. Most states abolished this remnant of feudal land tenure soon after independence.

62

LEGISLATIVE RESOLVE CALLING FOR A
REVISION OF THE ARTICLES OF CONFEDERATION
                      Poughkeepsie, July 20-21, 1782

.   .   .   .   .
    Resolved, That it appears to this Legislature; after full
and solemn Consideration of the several Matters communicated by
the Honorable the Committee of Congress, relative to the present Posture of our Affairs, foreign and domestic, and contained
in a Letter from the Secretary for foreign Affairs respecting
the Former, as well as of the Representations from Time to Time
made by the Superintendent of the Finances of the United States,
relative to his particular Department—That the Situation of
these States is in a peculiar Manner critical, and affords the
strongest Reason to apprehend from a Continuance of the present
Constitution of the Continental Government; a Subversion of
public Credit; and Consequences highly dangerous to the Safety
and Independence of these States.
.   .   .   .   .
    Resolved, That it is the Opinion of this Legislature, that
the present System of these States, exposes the common Cause to
a precarious Issue, and leaves us at the Mercy of Events over
which we have no Influence; a Conduct extremely unwise in any
Nation, and at all Times, and to a Change of which we are impelled at this Juncture, by Reasons of peculiar and irresist-
able Weight; and that it is the natural Tendency of the Weakness and Disorders in our national Measures, to spread
Diffidence and Distrust among the People, and prepare their
Minds to receive the Impressions the Enemy wish to make.
    Resolved, That the general State of European Affairs, as
far as they have come to the Knowledge of this Legislature, affords in their Opinion, reasonable Ground of Confidence, and
assures us, that with judicious vigorous Exertion on our Part,
we may rely on the final Attainment of our Object; but far
from justifying Indifference and Security, calls upon us by
every Motive of Honor, good Faith and Patriotism, without Delay,

Journal of the Senate of the State of New York [1782] (Poughkeepsie, N.Y.: John Holt, 1782), pp. 89-90. Probably written
by Alexander Hamilton, the resolution was forwarded to the Continental Congress, but no action was taken on it. The resolution passed in the Senate on the 20th; in the House, on the
21st.

to unite in some System more effectual, for producing Energy,
Harmony and Consistency of Measures, than that which now exists,
and more capable of putting the common Cause out of the Reach
of Contingencies.

Resolved, That in the Opinion of this Legislature, the
radical Source of most of our Embarrassments, is the Want of
sufficient Power in Congress, to effectuate that ready and perfect Co-operation of the different States, on which their immediate Safety and future Happiness depend—That Experience has
demonstrated the Confederation to be defective in several essential Points, particularly in not vesting the fœderal Government either with a Power of providing Revenue for itself, or
with ascertained and productive Funds, secured by a Saction so
solemn and general, as would inspire the fullest Confidence in
them, and make them a substantial Basis of Credit—That these
Defects ought to be without Loss of Time repaired, the Powers
of Congress extended, a solid Security established for the Payment of Debts already inured, and competent Means provided for
future Credit, and for supplying the current Demands of the
War.

. . . . .

Resolved, That it appears to this Legislature, that the
aforegoing important Ends, can never be attained by partial Deliberations of the States, separately; but that it is essential
to the common Welfare, that there should be as soon as possible
a Conference of the Whole on the Subject; and that it would be
adviseable for this Purpose, to propose to Congress to recommend, and to each State to adopt the Measure of assembling a
general Convention of the States, specially authorised to revise and amend the Confederation, reserving a Right to the respective Legislatures, to ratify their Determinations.

. . . . .

63

LIEUTENANT COLONEL BENJAMIN THOMPSON
TO LORD GEORGE GERMAIN   New York, August 6, 1782

. . . . .
    You cannot conceive, nor can any language describe, the
distress that all ranks of people here have been thrown into by
the intelligence of the Independence of America being acknowledged by Great Britain, and the loyalists being given up to the
mercy of their enemies. The Militia who for some weeks have
done the whole of the garrison duty in this city have peremp-to-
rily refused to serve any longer, and the General has been
obliged to relieve them by bringing regular troops into town.
The loyalists at Lloyds Neck and the other posts are in a state
of anarchy and confusion little short of actual rebellion.
Papers have been stuck up about town inviting Sir Guy Carleton
to take command of the army here and to oppose by force the
measures of the new administration, and promising thousands to
assist him. In short an universal despair and phrenzy prevails
within these lines, and I should not be surprised if very
alarming consequences were to follow from the temper people are
in. They seem to be as void of prudence as they are destitute
of hope, and a kind of language is now spoken publicly in the
streets that is enough to make one tremble for what is to follow from these convulsions. The Provincial Corps will disband
of themselves,—or what is infinitely more to be dreaded, they
will take arms in opposition to these measures. They feel
themselves deeply injured. For my own part I am at a loss what
opinion to form respecting the end of all these commotions. . . .
    . . . . .

Historical Manuscripts Commission. *Report on the Manuscripts
of Mrs. Stopford-Sackville* . . . , 49, pt. 2 (Hereford: His
Majesty's Stationery Office, 1910), pp. 252-53. Thompson,
later Count Rumford, served as an undersecretary of state for
the American Department from 1780 to 1782 and commanded a loyalist force, the King's American Dragoons, during the war.
Lord George Germain, Viscount Sackville, was secretary of state
of the American Department from 1775 to 1782.

64

ALEXANDER HAMILTON TO ROBERT MORRIS
                                Albany, August 13, 1782

I promised you in former letters to give you a full view of the situation and temper of this State. I now sit down to execute that task.

You have already in your possession a pretty just picture of the State, drawn by the Legislature, perhaps too highly-colored in some places, but just and, in the main, true.

It is the opinion of the most sensible men with whom I converse, who are best acquainted with the circumstances of the State, and who are least disposed to exaggerate its distress as an excuse for inactivity, that its faculties for revenue are diminished at least two thirds.

It will not be difficult to conceive this when we consider that five out of the fourteen counties of which the State is composed, including the capital, are in the hands of the enemy; that two and part of a third have revolted; two others have been desolated the greater part by the ravages of the enemy and of our own troops, and the remaining four have more or less suffered partial injuries from the same causes. Adding the fragments of some to repair the losses of others, the efficient property, strength, and force of the State will consist in little more than four counties.

In the distribution of taxes before the war, the city of New York used to be rated at one third of the whole; but this was too high, owing probably to the prevailing of the country influence. Its proper proportion I should judge to have been about one fourth, which serves further to illustrate the probable decrease of the State.

Manuscript Division, Library of Congress. Printed in Henry Cabot Lodge, ed., *The Works of Alexander Hamilton* (New York: G. P. Putnam's Sons, 1886), 8: 63-70, and Harold C. Syrett and Jacob E. Cooke, eds., *The Papers of Alexander Hamilton*, 16 vols. to date (New York: Columbia University Press, 1961-   ), 3: 132-43. A Philadelphia merchant with considerable financial experience derived from committee work in the Continental Congress from 1775 to 1778, Morris (1734-1806), the so-called financier of the American Revolution, was chosen superintendent of finance in February 1781 and was charged with solving the pecuniary problems plaguing the nation.

Our population, indeed, is not diminished in the same degree, as many of the inhabitants of the dismembered and ruined counties, who have left their habitations, are dispersed through those which remain; and it would seem that the labor of the additional hands ought to ensure the culture and value of these. But there are many deductions to be made from this apparent advantage: the numbers that have *recruited* the British army; those that have been furnished to ours; the emigrations to Vermont and to the neighboring States, less harassed by the war, and affording better encouragements to industry, both which have been considerable.

Besides these circumstances, many of the fugitive families are a burthen for their substance upon the State. The fact is, labor is much dearer than before the war.

This State has certainly made, in the course of the war, great exertions, and, upon many occasions, of the most exhausting kind. This has sometimes happened from want of judgment; at others, from necessity. When the army, as has too often been the case, has been threatened with some fatal calamity—for want of provisions, forage, the means of transportation, etc.,—in consequence of pressing applications from the Commander-in-Chief, the Legislature have been obliged to have recourse to extraordinary expedients to answer the pressing emergency, which have both distressed and disgusted the people. There is no doubt that, with a prudent and systematic administration, the State might have rendered more benefit to the common cause, with less inconvenience to itself, than by all its forced efforts; but there, as everywhere else, we have wanted experience and knowledge. And, indeed, had this not been the case, every thing everywhere has been so radically wrong, that it was difficult, if not impossible, for any one State to be right.

The exposed situation of the frontier, and the frequent calls upon the inhabitants for personal service on each extremity, by interfering with industry, have contributed to impoverish the State and fatigue the people.

Deprived of foreign trade, our internal traffic is carried on upon the most disadvantageous terms. It divides itself into three branches: with the city of New York, with Jersey and Pennsylvania, and with New England.

That with New York consists chiefly of luxuries on one part and returns of specie on the other. I imagine we have taken goods from that place to the amount of near £30,000. The Legislature passed a severe law to prevent this intercourse, but what will laws avail against the ingenuity and intrepidity of avarice?

From Jersey and Pennsylvania we take about £30,000 more, and we pay almost entirely in cash.

From Massachusetts and other parts of New England we purchase to the amout of about £50,000, principally in tea and
salt. (The articles of tea and salt alone cost this State the
annual sum of £60,000.) We sell to these States to the value
of about £30,000.

The immense land transportation, of which the chief part
is carried on by the subjects of other States, is a vast incum-
brance upon our trade.

The principal article we have to throw in the opposite
scale is the expenditures of the army. Mr. Sands informs me
that the contractors for the main army and West Point lay out
in this State at the rate of about $60,000 a year; Mr. Duer,
for these northern posts, about $30,000. If the Quartermaster-
General expends as much more in his department, the whole will
amount to about $180,000. I speak of what is paid for in spe-
cie, or such paper as answers the purpose of specie. These
calculations cannot absolutely be relied on, because the data
are necessarily uncertain, but they are the result of the best
information I can obtain, and, if near the truth, prove that
the general balance of trade is against us—a plain symptom of
which is *an extreme* and *universal* scarcity of money.

The situation of the State with respect to its internal
government is not more pleasing. Here we find the general disease which infects all our constitutions—an excess of popularity. There is no *order* that has a will of its own. The inquiry constantly is what will *please*, not what will *benefit*,
the people. In such a government there can be nothing but temporary expenditure, fickleness, and folly.

But the point of view in which this subject will be interesting to you is that which relates to our finances. I gave
you, in a former letter, a sketch of our plan of taxation, but
I will now be more particular.

The general principle of it is apparent, according to *circumstances and abilities collectively considered*. The ostensible reason for adopting this vague basis was a desire of equality. It was pretended that this could not be obtained so well
by any fixed tariff of taxable property, as by leaving it to
the discretion of persons chosen by the people themselves to
determine the ability of each citizen. But perhaps the true
reason was a desire to discriminate between the *Whigs* and *Tories*. This chimerical attempt at perfect equality has resulted
in total inequality, or rather this narrow disposition to over-
burthen a particular class of citizens (living under the protection of the government) has been retorted upon the contriv-
ers or their friends, wherever that class has been numerous
enough to preponderate in the election of the officers who were
to execute the law. The exterior figure a man makes, the decency and meanness of his manner of living, the personal
friendships or dislikes of the assessors, have much more share

in determining what individuals shall pay, than the proportion
of property.

. . . . .

The temper of the State, which I shall now describe, may
be considered under two heads—that to the rulers and that of
the people.

The rulers are generally zealous in the common cause,
though their zeal is oftentimes misdirected. They are jealous
of their own power; but yet, as this State is the immediate
theatre of the war, these apprehensions of danger, and an opinion that they are obliged to do more than their neighbors, make
them very willing to part with power in favor of the Federal
Government. This last opinion and an idea added to it, that
they have no credit for their past exertions, has put them out
of humor and indisposed many of them for future exertions. I
have heard several assert that in the present situation of this
State, nothing more ought to be expected than that it maintain
its own government and keep up its quota of troops.

This sentiment, however, is as yet confined to few, but it
is too palpable not to make proselytes.

. . . . .

As to the people, in the early periods of the war, near
one half of them were avowedly more attached to Great Britain
than to their liberty, but the energy of the government has
subdued all opposition. The State by different means has been
purged of a large part of its malcontents; but there still remains, I dare say, a third, whose secret wishes are on the side
of the ememy; the remainder sigh for peace, murmur at taxes,
clamor at their rulers, change one incapable man for another
more incapable, and, I fear, if left to themselves, would, too
many of them, be willing to purchase peace at any price—not
from inclination to Great Britain or disaffection to independence, but from mere supineness and avarice.

The speculation of evils from the claims of Great Britain
gives way to the pressure of inconveniences actually felt, and
we required the event which has lately happened—the recognition of our independence by the Dutch—to give a new spring to
the public hopes and the public passions. This has had a good
effect, and if the Legislature can be brought to adopt a wise
plan for its finances, we may put the people in better humor,
and give a more regular and durable movement to the machine.
The people of this State, as far as my observation goes, have
as much firmness in their make and as much submission to government as those of any part of the Union. It remains for me
to give you an explicit opinion of what is practicable for this
State to do.

Even with a judicious plan of taxation I do not think the
State can afford, or the people will bear, to pay more than
£70,000 or £80,000 a year. In its entire and flourishing state,

according to my mode of calculation it could not have exceeded £230,000 or £240,000; and reduced as it is, with the wheels of circulation so exceedingly clogged for want of commerce and a sufficient medium, more than I have said cannot be expected. Past experience will not authorize a more flattering conclusion. Out of this is to be deducted the expense of the interior administration and the money necessary for the levies of men. The first amounts to about £15,000, as you will perceive by the inclosed slate; but I suppose the Legislature would choose to retain £20,000. The money hitherto yearly expended in recruits has amounted to between £20,000 and £30,000; but on a proper plan £10,000 might suffice. There would then remain £40,000 for your department.

But this is on the supposition of a change of system; for with the present I doubt there being paid into the Continental treasury one third of that sum. I am endeavoring to collect materials for greater certainty upon this subject. But the business of supplies has been so diversified, lodged in such a variety of independent hands, and so carelessly transacted, that it is hardly possible to get any tolerable idea of the gross and net product.

. . . . .

You will perceive, sir, I have neither flattered the State nor encouraged high expectations. I thought it my duty to exhibit things as they are, not as they ought to be. I shall be sorry to give you an ill opinion of the State for want of equal candor in the representations of others; for, however disagreeable the reflection, I have too much reason to believe that the true picture of other States would be, in proportion to their circumstances, equally unpromising. All my inquiries and all that appears induce this opinion. I intend this letter in *confidence* to yourself, and therefore I endorse it *private*.

. . . . .

65

ALEXANDER HAMILTON, *PHOCION LETTERS*   January–April, 1784

[FIRST LETTER]

. . . . .

Nothing is more common than for a free people, in times of
heat and violence, to gratify momentary passions, by letting
into the government, principles and precedents which afterwards
prove fatal to themselves. Of this kind is the doctrine of
disqualification, disfranchisement and banishment by acts of
legislature. The dangerous consequences of this power are manifest. If the legislature can disfranchise any number of citizens at pleasure by general descriptions, it may soon confine
all the votes to a small number of partizans, and establish an
aristocracy or an oligarchy; if it may banish at discretion all
those whom particular circumstances render obnoxious, without
hearing or trial, no man can be safe, nor know when he may be
the innocent victim of a prevailing faction. The name of liberty applied to such a government would be a mockery of common
sense.

. . . . .

The men who are at the head of the party which contends
for disqualification and expulsion, endeavoured to inlist a
number of people on their side by holding out motives of private advantage to them. To the trader they say, you will be
overborne by the large capitals of the Tory merchants; to the
Mechanic, your business will be less profitable, your wages
less considerable by the interference of Tory workmen. A man,
the least acquainted with trade, will indeed laugh at such suggestion.

. . . . .

But say some, to suffer these wealthy disaffected men to
remain among us, will be dangerous to our liberties; enemies to
our government, they will be always endeavouring to undermine
it and bring us back to the subjection of Great-Britain. The

---

*A Letter from Phocion to the Considerate Citizens of New-York,
On the Politics of the Day*, 1st ed. (New York: Samuel Loudon,
[January] 1784), pp. 5–6, 16, 19–21. *A Second Letter from
Phocion* . . . (New York: Samuel Loudon, [April] 1784), pp. 6–8,
31, 41–42. Hamilton's *Second Letter* was written in response to
Mentor's Reply to Phocion's Letter . . . (New York: Shepard
Kollock, [February or March] 1784).

safest reliance of every government is on mens interests. This
is a principle of human nature, on which all political speculation to be just, must be founded. Make it the interest of
those citizens, who, during the revolution, were opposed to us
to be friends to the new government, by affording them not only
protection, but a participation in its privileges, and they
will undoubtedly become its friends. The apprehension of returning under the dominion of Great Britain is chimerical; if
there is any way to bring it about, the measures of those men,
against whose conduct these remarks are aimed, lead directly to
it. A disorderly or a violent government may disgust the best
citizens, and make the body of the people tired of their Independence.

. . . . .
The idea of suffering the Tories to live among us under
disqualifications, is equally mischievous and absurd. It is
necessitating a large body of citizens in the state to continue
enemies to the government, ready, at all times, in a moment of
commotion, to throw their weight into that scale which medi-
tates a change whether favourable or unfavourable to public
liberty.

Viewing the subject in every possible light, there is not
a single interest of the community but dictates moderation
rather than violence. That honesty is still the best policy;
that justice and moderation are the surest supports of every
government, are maxims, which however they may be called trite,
at all times true, though too seldom regarded, but rarely neglected with impunity. Were the people of America, with one
voice, to ask, What shall we do to perpetuate our liberties and
secure our happiness? The answer would be, "govern well" and
you have nothing to fear either from internal disaffection or
external hostility. Abuse not the power you possess, and you
need never apprehend its diminution or loss. But if you make
a wanton use of it, if you furnish another example, that despotism may debase the government of the many as well as the
few, you like all others that have acted the same part, will
experience that licentiousness is the fore-runner to slavery.

. . . . .

[SECOND LETTER]

. . . . .
The principles of all the arguments I have used or shall
use, lie within the compass of a few simple propositions, which,
to be assented to, need only to be stated.

First, That no man can forfeit or be justly deprived, without his consent, of any right, to which as a member of the com-

munity he is entitled, but for some crime incurring the forfeiture.

Secondly, That no man ought to be condemned unheard, or
punished for supposed offences, without having an opportunity
of making his defence.

Thirdly, That a crime is *an act* committed or omitted, in
violation of public law, either forbidding or commanding it.

Fourthly, That a prosecution is in its most precise signi-
fication, an *inquiry* or *mode of ascertaining*, whether a particular person has committed, or omitted such *act*.

Fifthly, That *duties* and *rights* as applied to subjects are
reciprocal; or in other words, that a man cannot be a *citizen*
for the purpose of punishment, and not a *citizen* for the purpose of privilege.

These propositions will hardly be controverted by any man
professing to be a friend to civil liberty. . . .

By the declaration of Independence on the 4th of July, in
the year 1776, acceded to by our Convention on the ninth, the
late colony of New-York became an independent state. All the
inhabitants, who were subjects under the former government, and
who did not withdraw themselves upon the change which took
place, were to be considered as citizens, owing allegiance to
the new government, This, at least, is the legal presumption;
and this was the principle, in fact, upon which all the measures of our public councils have been grounded. Duties have
been exacted, and punishments inflicted according to this rule.
If any exceptions to it were to be admitted, they could only
flow from the *indulgence* of the state to such individuals, as
from peculiar circumstances might desire to be permitted to
stand upon a different footing.

The inhabitants of the southern district, before they fell
under the power of the British army, were as much citizens of
the state as the inhabitants of other parts of it. They must,
therefore, continue to be such, unless they have been divested
of that character by some posterior circumstance. This circumstance must, either be—

Their having, by the fortune of war, fallen under the power of the British army.

Their having forfeited their claim by their own misconduct.

Their having been left out of the compact by some subsequent association of the body of the state, or

Their having been dismembered by treaty.

. . . . .

When the advocates for legislature discriminations are
driven from one subterfuge to another, their last resting place
is—that this is a new case, the case of a revolution. Your
principles are all right say they, in the ordinary course of
society, but they do not apply to a situation like ours. This
is opening a wilderness, through all the labyrinths of which,

it is impossible to pursue them: The answer to this must be,
that there are principles eternally true and which apply to all
situations; such as those that have been already enumerated—
that we are not now in the midst of a revolution but have happily brought it to a successful issue—that we have a constitution formed as a rule of conduct—that the frame of our government is determined and the general principle of it is settled—
that we have taken our station among nations have claimed the
benefit of the laws which regulate them, and must in our turn
be bound by the same laws—that those eternal principles of
social justice forbid the inflicting punishment upon citizens,
by an abridgement of rights, or in any other manner, without
conviction of some specific offence by regular trial and con-
demnation—that the constitution we have formed makes the trial
by jury the only proper mode of ascertaining the delinquences
of individuals—that legislative discriminations, to supersede
the necessity of inquiry and proof, would be an usurpation on
the judiciary powers of the government, and a renunciation of
all the maxims of civil liberty—that by the laws of nations
and the rules of justice, we are bound to observe the engagements entered into on our behalf, by that power which is invested with the constitutional prerogative of treaty—and that
the treaty we have made in its genuine sense, ties up the hands
of government from any species of future prosecution or punishment, on account of the part taken by individuals in the war.
. . . . .
  To ripen inquiry into action, it remains for us to justify
the revolution by its fruits.
  If the consequences prove, that we really have asserted
the cause of human happiness, what may not be expected from so
illustrious an example?—In a greater or less degree, the world
will bless and imitate!
  But if experience, in this instance, verifies the lesson
long taught by the enemies of liberty;—that the bulk of mankind are not fit to govern themselves, that they must have a
master, and were only made for the rein and the spur: We shall
then see the final triumph of despotism over liberty—The advocates of the latter must acknowledge it to be an *ignis fatuus*,
and abandon the pursuit. With the greatest advantages for promoting it, that ever a people had, we shall have betrayed the
cause of human nature.
. . . . .

66

ACT TO DISENFRANCHISE LOYALISTS May 12, 1784

WHEREAS It is of great importance to the safety of a free government, that persons holding principles inimical to the Constitution, should not be admitted into offices or places of trust, whereby they might acquire an immediate influence in the direction of its councils. And whereas some of the citizens of this State, entertaining sentiments hostile to its independence have taken an active part in the late war in opposition to the present government, and it would be improper and dangerous that such persons should be suffered to hold or enjoy any such office or place of trust within this State. *And whereas* it is the duty of the legislature to pursue every reasonable and proper measure to secure the government from being disturbed and endangered.

Be it therefore enacted . . . That all and every person or persons, natives or others, who being resident in this State, or any other of the United States, on [July 9, 1776] and who have at any time since . . . accepted, received, held or exercised, any military commission or commissions whatsoever, by or under any authority derived from the king of Great Britain; . . . have armed or fitted out, or who have been concerned in fitting out, any privateer or privateers, or vessels of war, to cruise against or commit hostilities upon the vessels, property and persons of any of the citizens of the United States, or against their allies; . . . have served on board such privateers or vessels of war, in the condition or capactity of captain lieutenant or master; . . . have accepted, held or exercised any official commission or appointment, in the board or boards of police instituted and established in the southern district of this State, during the late war, by virtue of, and under authority derived from the king of Great Britain; . . . have accepted, received, held or exercised any office commission or appointment whatsoever, in the court of admiralty instituted and established in the southern district of this State, during the late war, by virtue of authority derived from the king of Great Britain as aforesaid; and also all and every person or persons whatsoever, who being resident in any of the United States, except this State, on [July 9, 1776]; and who at

---

AN ACT to preserve the freedom and independence of this State, and for other purposes therein mentioned. *Laws of the State of New York*, 1: 772-74.

any time since that day and during the late war, have fled or
removed from such of the said states of which such person or
persons were respectively resident, on the 9th day of July
aforesaid, and who have gone over to, joined or put himself or
themselves under the power and protection of the fleets or armies of the king of Great Britain aforesaid; and all and every
person and persons who being resident in this State on [July 9,
1776] and who since that day, have voluntarily gone over to,
remained with, or joined the fleets and armies of the king of
Great Britain aforesaid at any time during the late war; who
has or have left this State on or before [December 10, 1783]
and who have not returned and who shall hereafter be found
within this State, such person or persons so found, shall be,
on conviction thereof, adjudged guilty of misprision of treason. . . .

And be it further enacted . . . That all and every person
or persons falling under any of the descriptions herein before
mentioned and the descriptions mentioned in the twelfth section
of the act entitled "An act to regulate elections within this
State," [March 27, 1778] and who has or have not left this
State, are hereby for ever disqualified and rendered incapable
of holding, exercising or enjoying any legislative, judicial or
executive office or place, whatsoever within this State; and
shall and hereby is and are, for every disqualified and incapacitated to elect or vote either by ballot or *viva voce* at any
election fo fill any office or place whatsoever within this
State, and if any person shall offer himself as an elector, at
any election hereafter to be holden for an office or place
within this State, and shall be suspected of, or charged to be
within any of the descriptions aforesaid, it shall be lawful
for the inspectors or superintendants (as the case may be) to
inquire into and determine the fact whereof such person shall
be suspected or wherewith he shall be charged as the cause of
disqualification aforesaid on the oath of one or more witness
or witnesses, or on the oath of the party so suspected or
charged, at their discretion; and if such fact shall in the
judgment of the inspectors or superintendants, be established,
it shall be lawful for them and they are hereby required to reject the vote of such persons at such election. Provided always, that if it shall appear to the satisfaction of the inspectors or superintendants at any election, that any person
offering himself as an elector, has, during the late war, within the southern district by fear or compulsion accepted held or
exercised any such office commission or appointment, or may
have involuntarily done any act or acts which by the said section would have disqualified him from holding any office or
from being an elector had the same been voluntarily done, and
that such person otherwise has uniformly behaved as a friend to
the freedom and independence of the United States, the inspec-

tors shall admit such persons to give his note at any such election, any thing in this act to the contrary notwithstanding.

Whereas a very respectable number of citizens of this State, well attached to the freedom and independence thereof, have entreated the legislature to extend mercy to persons herein after mentioned, and to restore them to their country.

Be it therefore enacted . . . That [27 names] shall be and every of them are hereby permitted to return to and reside within this State without any molestation, and therein to remain until the end of the next meeting of the legislature, or until further legislative provision shall be made in the premises, anything in the act entitled "An act more effectually to prevent the mischiefs arising from the influence and example of persons of equivocal and suspected characters in this State," passed the 30th day of June 1778, to the contrary thereof if anywise notwithstanding.

67

ALEXANDER HAMILTON TO ROBERT LIVINGSTON
New York, April 25, 1785

. . . . .

It may appear to you, Sir, a little extraordinary that I should take occasion in this professional letter to mention politics; but the situation of the state at this time is so critical that it is become a serious object of attention to those who are concerned for the *security of property* or the prosperity of government, to endeavour to put men in the Legislature whose principles are not of the *levelling kind*. The spirit of the present Legislature is truly alarming, and appears evidently directed to the confusion of all property and principle. The truth is that the state is now governed by a couple of New

Emmet Collection (#9349), Manuscript Division, New York Public Library, Astor, Lenox and Tilden Foundations. Printed in Syrett and Cooke, eds., *Papers of Alexander Hamilton*, 3: 609. Livingston was the third proprietor of Livingston Manor, Albany County.

England adventureres—Ford and Adgate;[1] who make tools of the
Yates[2] and their Associates. A number of attempts have been
made by this junto to subvert the constitution and destroy the
rights of private property; which but for the Council of Revision would have had the most serious effects. All men of re-
spectability, in the city, of whatever party, who have been
witnesses of the despotism and iniquity of the Legislature, are
convinced, that the principal people in the community just for
their own defence, unite to overset the party I have alluded to.
I wish you to be persuaded, Sir, that I would not take the liberty to trouble you with these remarks with a view to serving
any particular turn; but, from a thorough conviction, that the
safety of all those who have any thing to lose calls upon them
to take care that the power of government is intrusted to proper hands. Much depends on the ensuing election. You, Sir,
have much in your power; and I have no doubt you will have
heared from other quarters and from your immediate connections,
a like account of public affairs to that which I have now given.

. . . . .

68

JOHN JAY TO GEORGE WASHINGTON Philadelphia, June 27, 1786

. . . . .
    Our affairs seem to lead to some crisis, some revolution—
something that I cannot foresee or conjecture. I am uneasy and
apprehensive; more so than during the war. Then we had a fixed
object, and though the means and time of obtaining it were of-

---

[1]Mathew Ford and Jacob Adgate represented Albany County in the
legislature.

[2]Abraham Yates, Jr., and Robert Yates, residents of Albany City,
were political allies of Governor George Clinton.

Henry P. Johnston, ed., *The Correspondence and Public Papers of
John Jay* . . . , 4 vols. (New York: G. P. Putnam's Sons, 1890-
93), 3: 204-5. Jay was America's premier diplomat during the
1780s, serving as one of the U.S. commissioners at the Paris
peace conference of 1782-83, minister to Spain, and negotiator

ten problematical yet I did firmly believe we should ultimately
succeed, because I was convinced that justice was with us. The
case is now altered; we are going and doing wrong, and therefore I look forward to evils and calamities, but without being
able to guess at the instrument, nature, or measure of them.

That we shall again recover, and things again go well, I
have no doubt. Such a variety of circumstances would not, almost miraculously, have combined to liberate and make us a nation for transient and unimportant purposes. I therefore believe that we are yet to become a great and respectable people;
but when or how, the spirit of prophecy can only discern.

There doubtless is much reason to think and to say that we
are wofully and, in many instances, wickedly misled. Private
rage for property suppresses public considerations, and personal rather than national interests have become the great objects
of attention. Representative bodies will ever be faithful
copies of their originals, and generally exhibit a checkered
assemblage of virtue and vice, of abilities and weakness.

The mass of men are neither wise nor good, and the virtue
like the other resources of a country, can only be drawn to a
point and exerted by strong circumstances ably managed, or a
strong government ably administered. New governments have not
the aid of habit and hereditary respect, and being generally
the result of preceding tumult and confusion, do not immediately acquire stability or strength. Besides, in times of commotion, some men will gain confidence and importance, who merit
neither, and who, like political mountebanks, are less solici-
tous about the health of the credulous crowd than about making
the most of their nostrums and prescriptions.

. . . . .

What I most fear is, that the better kind of people, by
which I mean the people who are orderly and industrious, who
are content with their situations and not uneasy in their cir-
cúmstances, will be led by the insecurity of property, the loss
of confidence in their rulers, and the want of public faith and
rectitude, to consider the charms of liberty as imaginary and
delusive. A state of fluctuation and uncertainty must disgust
and alarm such men, and prepare their minds for almost any
change that may promise them quiet and security.

. . . . .

(Cont'd.) of the Jay-Gardoqui Treaty of 1785. Conservative
and nationalistic, he politically opposed the regime of Govern-
or George Clinton.

Chapter five:

Toward "A More Perfect Union," 1787-88

From a conference held at Annapolis in September 1786 to discuss interstate commerce emanated an invitation, written by Alexander Hamilton, for the states to send representatives to Philadelphia in May 1787 to discuss means of rendering the Articles of Confederation adequate to the exigencies of the nation. The New York legislature initially disavowed the action of the Annapolis Convention but acquiesced when the Continental Congress sanctioned the meeting for the sole purpose of revising the Articles. But the delegates deviated from their instructions, and ignored the provisions of the Articles, and subsequently transformed themselves into a constitutional convention and fashioned an entirely new instrument of national government. Faced with a fait accompli, the congress referred the document to the states for ratification or rejection in September 1787.

The contest over the Constitution was especially heated in New York, where for nine months it was the subject of an intense debate between the federalists, led by Alexander Hamilton, and the antifederalists, led by Governor George Clinton. The state legislature met in January 1788 and promptly called for the election of a ratifying convention to decide the issue. By the time the antifederalist-dominated gathering convened in Poughkeepsie on June 17, eight states had ratified the Constitution; the accession of New Hampshire on June 21 and Virginia four days later assured the future of the national union, with only New York, North Carolina, and Rhode Island outside the fold. The proceedings at Poughkeepsie were thus anticlimactic, for the question was not whether but when and in what manner New York would ratify the Constitution. Finally, after the defection of twelve antifederalists led by Melancton Smith and the adoption of thirty-two proposed amendments to the document, the convention endorsed the new instrument of government on July 26 by the narrowest margin in any state, thirty to twenty-seven. New York and the nation had taken a momentous step toward the consolidation of independence.

69

THE NEW YORK BILL OF RIGHTS   January 26, 1787

Be it enacted . . .

First, That no authority shall, on any pretence whatsoever be exercised over the citizens of this State but such as is or shall be derived from and granted by the people of this State.

Second, That no citizen of this State shall be taken or imprisoned or be disseised of his or her freehold or liberties of free customs or outlawed or exiled or condemned or otherwise destroyed, but by lawful judgment of his or her peers or by due process of law.

Third, That no citizen of this State shall be taken or imprisoned for any offence upon petition or suggestion unless it be by indictment or presentment of good and lawful men of the same neighbourhood where such deeds be done, in due manner or by due process of law.

Fourth, That no person shall be put to answer without presentment before justices, or matter of record, or due process of law according to the law of the land and if any thing be done to the contrary it shall be void in law and holden for error.

Fifth, That no person, of what estate or condition soever shall be taken or imprisoned, or disinherited or put to death without being brought to answer by due process of law, and that no person shall be put out of his or her franchise or freehold or lose his or her life or limb, or goods and chattels, unless he or she be duly brought to answer and be forejudged of the same by due course of law and if any thing be done contrary to the same it shall be void in law and holden for none.

Sixth, That neither justice, nor right shall be sold to any person, nor denied nor deferred; and that writs and process shall be granted freely and without delay to all persons requiring the same and nothing from henceforth shall be paid or taken for any writ or process but the accustomed fee for writing and for the seal of the same writ or process and all fines duties and impositions whatsoever heretofore taken or demanded under what name or description soever, for or upon granting any writs, inquests, commissions or process to suitors in their causes shall be and hereby are abolished.

AN ACT concerning the rights of the citizens of this State. *Laws of the State of New York*, 2: 344-45.

Seventh, That no citizens of this State shall be fined or amerced without reasonable cause and such fine or amerciament shall always be according to the quantity of his or her trespass or offence and saving to him or her, his or her contenement; That is to say every freeholder saving his freehold, a merchant saving his merchandize and a mechanick saving the implements of his trade.

Eighth, That excessive bail ought not be required, nor excessive fines imposed, nor cruel and unusual punishments inflicted.

Ninth, That all elections shall be free and that no person by force of arms nor by malice or menacing or otherwise presume to disturb or hinder any citizen of this State to make free election upon pain of fine and imprisonment and trebel damages to the party grieved.

Tenth, That it is the right of the citizens of this State to petition the person administering the government of this State for the time being, or either house of the legislature and all commitments and prosecutions for such petitioning are illegal.

Eleventh, That the freedom of speech and debates and proceedings in the senate and assembly shall not be impeached or questioned in any court or place out of the senate or assembly.

Twelfth, That no tax duty aid or imposition whatsoever shall be taken or levied within this State without the grant and assent of the people of this State by their representatives in senate and assembly and that no citizen of this State shall be by any means compelled to contribute to any gift loan tax or other like charge not set laid or imposed by the legislature of this State: *And further*, that no citizen of this State shall be constrained to arm himself or to go out of this State or to find soldiers or men of arms either horsemen or footmen, if it be not by assent and grant of the people of this State by their representatives in senate and assembly.

Thirteenth, That by laws and customs of this State the citizens and inhabitants thereof cannot be compelled against their wills to receive soldiers into their houses and to sojourn them there and therefore no officer military or civil nor any other person whatsoever shall from henceforth presume to place, quarter or billet any soldier or soldiers upon any citizen or inhabitant of this State of any degree or profession whatever without his or her consent and that it shall and may be lawful for every such citizen and inhabitant to refuse to sojourn or quarter any soldier or soldiers notwithstanding any command order warrant or billetting whatever.

70

ROBERT YATES AND JOHN LANSING
TO GOVERNOR GEORGE CLINTON   Albany, December 21, 1787

We do ourselves the honor to advise your excellency that,
in pursuance to concurrent resolutions of the honorable Senate
and Assembly, we have, together with Mr. Hamilton, attended the
Convention appointed for revising the Articles of Confederation,
and reporting amendments to the same.

It is with the sincerest concern we observe that, in the
prosecution of the important objects of our mission, we have
been reduced to the disagreeable alternative of either exceeding the powers delegated to us, and giving assent to measures
which we conceive destructive to the political happiness of the
citizens of the United States, or opposing our opinions to that
of a body of respectable men, to whom these citizens had given
the most unequivocal proofs of confidence. Thus circumstanced,
under these impressions, to have hesitated would have been to
be culpable. We therefore gave the principles of the Constitution, which has received the sanction of a majority of the Convention, our decided and unreserved dissent; but we must candidly confess that we should have been equally opposed to any

Jonathan Elliot, comp., *The Debates in the Several State Conventions on the Adoption of the Federal Constitution . . . ,*
5 vols., 2d ed. (Philadelphia: J. B. Lippincott & Co., 1863),
1: 480–81. First published in the *New York Journal*, January 14,
1788. Lansing (1754–1829?) and Yates (1738–1801), both of Albany, and Alexander Hamilton (1757–1804) represented New York
in the Federal Convention; however, only the latter signed the
Constitution and championed its ratification. Hamilton, a New
York City lawyer, favored from the outset a marked augmentation
of federal authority. The early views of Lansing and Yates are
uncertain, but they probably leaned toward antifederalism because the two men were political associates of Governor Clinton,
an outspoken opponent of the convention and its work. Lansing,
an attorney, had served in the assembly (1780–84, 1786), the
Congress (1784–85), and as mayor of Albany since 1786. Also a
lawyer, Yates had been a member of the committee that drafted
the state constitution and was a judge of the supreme court
(1777–98). They left Philadelphia soon after July 10 for professional reasons; in late August they decided not to return.
Both were members of the ratifying convention, where they ada-
mantly opposed adoption of the Constitution.

system however, modified, which had in object the consolidation of the United States into one government.

We beg leave, briefly, to state some cogent reasons, which, among others, influenced us to decide against a consolidation of the states. These are reducible into two heads:—

1st. The limited and well-defined powers under which we acted, and which could not, on any possible construction, embrace an idea of such magnitude as to assent to a general Constitution, in subversion of that of the state.

2d. A conviction of the impracticability of establishing a general government, pervading every part of the United States, and extending essential benefits to all.

Our powers were explicit, and confined to ["]the sole and express purpose of revising the Articles of Confederation,["] and reporting such alterations and provisions therein as should ["]render the Federal Constitution adequate to the exigencies of government and the preservation of the Union.["]

From these expressions, we were led to believe that a system of consolidated government could not, in the remotest degree, have been in contemplation of the legislature of this state; for that so important a trust as the adopting measures which tended to deprive the state government of its most essential rights of sovereignty, and to place it in a dependent situation, could not have been confided by implication; and the circumstance, that the acts of the Convention were to receive a state approbation in the last resort, forcibly corroborated the opinion that our powers could not involve the subversion of a Constitution which, being immediately derived from the people, could only be abolished by their express consent, and not by a legislature possessing authority vested in them for its preservation. Nor could we suppose that, if it has been the intention of the legislature to abrogate the existing Confederation, they would, in such pointed terms, have directed the attention of their delegates to the revision and amendment of it, in total exclusion of every other idea.

Reasoning in this manner, we were of opinion that the leading feature of every amendment ought to be the preservation of the individual states in their uncontrolled constitutional rights; and that, in reserving these, a mode might have been devised of granting to the Confederacy the moneys arising from a general system of revenue, the power of regulating commerce and enforcing the observance of foreign treaties, and other necessary matters of less moment.

Exclusive of our objections originating from the want of power, we entertained an opinion that a general government, however guarded by declarations of rights, or cautionary provisions, must unavoidably, in a short time, be productive of the destruction of the civil liberty of such citizens who could be effectually coerced by it, by reason of the extensive territory

of the United States, the dispersed situation of its inhabitants, and the insuperable difficulty of controlling or coun-
teracting the views of a set of men (however unconstitutional
and oppressive their acts might be) possessed of all the powers
of government, and who, from their remoteness from their constituents, and necessary permanency of office, could not be
supposed to be uniformly actuated by an attention to their welfare and happiness; that, however wise and energetic the prin-
iples of the general government might be, the extremities of
the United States could not be kept in due submission and obedience to its laws, at the distance of many hundred miles from
the seat of government; that, if the general legislature was
composed of. so numerous a body of men as to represent the interests of all the inhabitants of the United States, in the
usual and true ideas of representation, the expense of supporting it would become intolerably burdensome; and that, if
a few only were vested with a power of legislation, the interests of a great majority of the inhabitants of the United
States must necessarily be unknown; or, if known, even in the
first stages of the operations of the new government, unattend-
ed to.

These reasons were, in our opinion, conclusive against any
system of consolidated government. . . .

. . . . .

71

CALL FOR THE ELECTION OF A RATIFYING CONVENTION
February 1, 1788

Whereas the United States, in Congress assembled, did, on
the 28th day of September last unanimously resolve, that the
report of the Convention of the states lately assembled in

Elliot, comp., *Debates . . . on the Adoption of the Federal
Constitution*, 2: 18. Suffrage in most states for the election
of ratifying conventions was restricted to those who were qualified to vote for members of the lower house of the legislature.
There was virtually no debate in the New York General Assembly
on the suffrage qualifications contained in the resolution
calling for the election of the convention.

Philadelphia, with the resolutions and letter accompanying the same, be transmitted to the several legislatures, in order to be submitted to a Convention of delegates, chosen in each state by the people thereof, in conformity to the resolves of the Convention, made and provided in that case,—Therefore,

Resolved, as the sense of the legislature, that the said report, with the said resolutions and letter accompanying the same, be submitted to a Convention of delegates to be chosen by the people of this state; that it be recommended to the people of this state to choose, by ballot, delegates to meet in Convention for the purpose aforesaid; that the number of delegates to be elected be the same as the number of members of Assembly from the respective cities and counties; that all free male citizens of the age of twenty-one years and upwards be admitted to vote, and that any person of that description be eligible; that the election be held on the last Tuesday in April next, at the same respective places where the elections for members of Assembly shall be held, and be continued by adjournment from day to day, until the same shall be completed, not exceeding five days; that the inspectors, who shall inspect the election for members of Assembly, be also inspectors of the election of delegates. . . .

72

THE NEW YORK SLAVE CODE   February 22, 1788

WHEREAS in consequence of the act directing a revision of the laws of this State, it is expedient that the several existing laws relative to slaves, should be revised, and comprized in one.   Therefore,

---

AN ACT concerning slaves. *Laws of the State of New York*, 2: 675-79. On the eve of the Revolution New York had more slaves (approximately 20,000 or about 14 percent of its population) than any other colony north of Maryland. Although the slave trade had been ended by congressional resolution at the time of the Continental Association in 1774, by the end of the war the only provisions to liberate the black population were laws providing for the emancipation of slaves who had served in the rebel army with the consent of their owners and those who were

Be it enacted . . . That every negro, mulatto or mestee,
within this State, who at the time of the passing of this act,
is a slave, for his or her life, shall continue such, for and
during his or her life, unless he or she, shall be manumitted
or set free, in the manner prescribed in and by this act, or in
and by some future law of this State.

And be it further enacted . . . That the children of every
negro, mulatto or mestee woman, being a slave, shall follow the
state and condition of the mother, and be esteemed, reputed,
taken and adjudged slaves to all intents and purposes whatsoever.

. . . . .

And to prevent the further importation of slaves into this
State, *Be it further enacted* . . . That if any person shall
sell as a slave within this State, any negro, or other person,
who has been imported or brought into this State, after [June 1,
1785] or who shall be imported or brought into this State, after the passing of this act, such seller, or his or her factor
or agent, making such sale, shall be deemed guilty of a public
offence, and shall for every such offence, forfeit the sume of
one hundred pounds. . . . *And further*, That every person so imported or brought into this State, and sold contrary to the
true intent and meaning of this act, shall be free.

And be it further enacted . . . That if any person shall,
at any time purchase or buy, or shall, as factor or agent to
another, take or receive any slave, with intent to remove, export, or carry such slave from this State, to any other place
without this State, and there to be sold, the person so pur-
chasing or buying, or so as factor or agent, receiving or taking a slave, with such intent as aforesaid, shall be deemed to
have committed an offence, against the people of this State,
and shall for every such offence, forfeit the sume of one hundred pounds . . . and the slave so purchased, bought, taken, or
received, shall be, immediately after he or she shall be so
purchased, bought, received, or taken, and hereby is declared
to be, free.

And be it further enacted . . . That if any person or persons, shall, after the passing of this act, employ, harbour,

---

(Cont'd.) part of confiscated loyalist estates. Antislavery
agitation (largely by Quakers) resulted in the formation of the
New York Manumission Society in 1785; that same year a bill
providing for gradual abolition was narrowly defeated in the
legislature. Subsequent attempts to effect emancipation
reached fruition in 1799 with the enactment of a gradual abolition statute; in 1817 New York became the first state to invoke
a total abolition of slavery (as of July 4, 1827). The law of
1788 was the first general slave code adopted since 1730.

conceal or entertain, any negro or other slave, knowing such negro or other slave, to be the slave of any other person or persons, without the consent of the owner or owners of such slave, he, she or they shall forfeit, to the owner or owners of such slave, the sume of five pounds, for every twenty four hours, and in that proportion, for a greater or less time, while such slave shall have been employed, harboured, concealed or entertained as aforesaid; but that such forfeiture, shall not in the whole, exceed the value of such slave. *And further*, that if any person or persons, shall be found guilty of harbouring, entertaining, or concealing any slave, or of assisting to convey him or her away, and if such slave shall be lost, die or be otherwise destroyed, the person or persons so harbouring, entertaining, concealing, assisting or conveying away such slave, shall be liable to pay to the owner or owners of such slave, the value thereof. . . .

And be it further enacted . . . That if any slave shall strike a white person, it shall be lawful for any justice of the peace, to commit such slave to prison; and such slave, shall thereupon be tried and punished in the manner directed in cases of petit larceny. . . .

And be it further enacted . . . That all negroes and other persons whatsoever, commonly reputed and deemed slaves, shall forever hereafter, have the privilege of being tried by a jury in all capital cases, according to the course of the common law.

And be it further enacted . . . That from and after the passing of this act, no slave shall be admitted a witness, for or against any person, in any matter, cause or thing whatsoever, civil or criminal, except in criminal cases, in which the evidence of one slave, shall be admitted for or against another slave.

. . . . .

And be it further enacted . . . That when the owner or owners of any slave, under fifty years of age, and of sufficient ability to provide for himself, or herself, shall be disposed to manumit such slave, he, she or they, shall previous thereto, procure a certificate, signed by the overseers of the poor, or the major part of them, of the city, town or place, and of two justices of the peace of the county, where such person or persons shall dwell or reside; and if in the cities of New York or Albany, then from the mayor or recorder, and any two of the aldermen, certifying that such slave appears to be under fifty years of age, and of sufficient ability to provide for himself or herself . . . that then it shall be lawful for such person or persons, to manumit such slave, without giving or providing any security, to indemnify such city, town or place. . . .

And be it further enacted . . . That if any person, by his or her last will and testament, shall give his or her slave, freedom, such slave being at the death of the testator or testatrix, under fifty years of age, and also of sufficient ability of provide for himself, or herself, to be certified in manner aforesaid, such freedom given as aforesaid, shall without any security to indemnify the city, town or place, be deemed, taken and adjuged to be good and valid, to all intents and purposes. And further, that if the owner or owners of any other slave, shall be disposed, to manumit and set at liberty, such slave, and such owner or owners, or any other sufficient person, for, or in behalf of such slave, shall and do, at the court of general sessions of the peace, for the city or county, where such negro or other slave shall dwell or reside, enter into a bond, to the people of the State of New York, with one or more surety or sureties, to be approved by such court, in a sum, not less than two hundred pounds, to keep and save such slave from becoming or being any charge to the city, town or place within this State, wherein such slave shall at any time, after such manumission, live, the said slave shall be free, according to such manumission of the owner or owners of such slave. And further, if any such slave hath been, or hereafter shall be made free, by the last will and testament of any person deceased, and if the executor or executors of such person so deceased, or in case of the neglect or refusal of such executor or executors, if any other sufficient person, for, and in behalf of such slave, shall and do, enter into such surety as aforesaid, in manner aforesaid, then the said slave shall be free, according to the true intent and meaning of such last will and testament. And moreover, that if any person shall, by last will or otherwise, manumit or set free, his or her slave, and no such certificate or security as aforesaid be given or obtained, such slave shall nevertheless, be considered as freed from such owner, his or her executors, administrators and assigns. But such owner, his and her heirs, executors, and administrators, shall remain and be liable, to support and maintain, such slave, if the same slave shall become unable to support and maintain himself or herself.

73

ALEXANDER HAMILTON, *THE FEDERALIST*, NO. 85
New York, May 28, 1788

ACCORDING to the formal division of the subject of these
papers, announced in my first number, there would appear still
to remain for discussion, two points, "the analogy of the proposed government to your own state constitution," and "the additional security, which its adoption will afford to republican
government, to liberty and to property." But these heads have
been so fully anticipated and exhausted in the progress of the
work, that it would now scarcely be possible to do any thing
more than repeat, in a more dilated form, what has been heretofore said; which the advanced stage of the question, and the
time already spent upon it conspire to forbid.
    It is remarkable, that the resemblance of the plan of the
convention to the act which organizes the government of this
state holds, not less with regard to many of the supposed defects, than to the real excellencies of the former. Among the
pretended defects, are the re-eligibility of the executive, the
want of a council, the omission of a formal bill of rights, the
omission of a provision respecting the liberty of the press:
These and several others, which have been noted in the course
of our inquiries, are as much chargeable on the existing constitution of this state, as on the one proposed for the Union.
And a man must have slender pretensions to consistency, who can
rail at the latter for imperfections which he finds no difficulty in excusing in the former. Nor indeed can there be a
better proof of the insincerity and affectation of some of the
zealous adversaries of the plan of the convention among us, who
profess to be the devoted admirers of the government under
which they live, than the fury with which they have attacked

Jacob E. Cooke, ed., *The Federalist* (Middletown, Conn.: Wesleyan University Press, 1961), pp. 587-95. The leading pro-Con-
stitution publication to emerge during the pamphlet war engendered by the ratification campaign was *The Federalist*, which
appeared in eighty-five installments between October 27, 1787,
and May 28, 1778, under the pseudonym "Publius" (after Publius
Valerius, who, according to Plutarch, established a republican
government in Rome after the downfall of Tarquin). Written by
Hamilton, Jay, and Madison (the latter was called in when Jay
became incapacitated in November), the papers seem to have had
little impact outside New York City.

that plan, for matters in regard to which our own constitution
is equally, or perhaps more vulnerable.

The additional securities to republican government, to
liberty and to property, to be derived from the adoption of the
plan under consideration, consist chiefly in the restraints
which the preservation of the union will impose on local factions and insurrections, and on the ambition of powerful individuals in single states, who might acquire credit and influence enough, from leaders and favorites, to become the despots
of the people; in the diminution of the opportunities to foreign intrigue, which the dissolution of the confederacy would
invite and facilitate; in the prevention of extensive military
establishments, which could not fail to grow out of wars between the states in a disunited situation; in the express guar-
antee of a republican form of government to each; in the absolute and universal exclusion of titles of nobility; and in the
precautions against the repetition of those practices on the
part of the state governments, which have undermined the foundations of property and credit, have planted mutual distrust in
the breasts of all classes of citizens, and have occasioned an
almost universal prostration of morals.

. . . The charge of a conspiracy against the liberties of
the people, which has been indiscriminately brought against the
advocates of the plan, has something in it too wanton and too
malignant not to excite the indignation of every man who feels
in his own bosom a refutation of the calumny. The perpetual
charges which have been rung upon the wealthy, the well-born
and the great, have been such as to inspire the disgust of all
sensible men. And the unwarrantable concealments and misrepresentations which have been in various ways practiced to keep
the truth from the public eye, have been of a nature to demand
the reprobation of all honest men. . . .

. . . . .

I shall not dissemble, that I feel an intire confidence in
the arguments, which recommend the proposed system to your
adoption; and that I am unable to discern any real force in
those by which it has been opposed. I am persuaded, that it is
the best which our political situation, habits and opinions
will admit, and superior to any the revolution has produced.

Concessions on the part of the friends of the plan, that
it has not a claim to absolute perfection, have afforded matter
of no small triumph to its enemies. Why, say they, should we
adopt an imperfect thing? Why not amend it, and make it perfect before it is irrevocably established? This may be plausible enough, but it is only plausible. In the first place I remark, that the extent of these concessions has been greatly
exaggerated. They have been stated as amounting to an admis-
sion, that the plan is radically defective; and that, without
material alterations, the rights and the interests of the com-

munity cannot be safely confided to it. This, as far as I have understood the meaning of those who make the concessions, is an intire perversion of their sense. No advocate of the measure can be found who will not declare as his sentiment, that the system, though it many not be perfect in every part, is upon the whole a good one, is the best that the present views and circumstances of the country will permit, and is such an one as promises every species of security which a reasonable people can desire.

I answer in the next place, that I should esteem it the extreme of imprudence to prolong the precarious state of our national affairs, and to expose the union to the jeopardy of successive experiments, in the chimerical pursuit of a perfect plan. I never expect to see a perfect work from imperfect man. The result of the deliberations of all collective bodies must necessarily be a compound as well of the errors and prejudices, as of the good sense and wisdom of the individuals of whom they are composed. The compacts which are to embrace thirteen distinct states, in a common bond of amity and union, must as necessarily be a compromise of as many dissimilar interests and inclinations. How can perfection spring from such materials?

. . . . .

It appears to me susceptible of absolute demonstration, that it will be far more easy to obtain subsequent than previous amendments to the constitution. The moment an alteration is made in the present plan, it becomes, to the purpose of adoption, a new one, and must undergo a new decision of each state. To its complete establishment throughout the union, it will therefore require the concurrence of thirteen states. If, on the contrary, the constitution proposed should once be ratified by all the states as it stands, alterations in it may at any time be effected by nine states. Here then the chances are as thirteen to nine in favour of subsequent amendments, rather than of the original adoption of an intire system.

In opposition to the probability of subsequent amendments it has been urged, that the persons delegated to the administration of the national government, will always be disinclined to yield up any portion of the authority of which they were once possessed. For my own part I acknowledge a thorough conviction that any amendments which may, upon mature consideration, be thought useful, will be applicable to the organization of the government, not to the mass of its powers; and on this account alone, I think there is no weight in the observation just stated. I also think there is little weight in it on another account. The intrinsic difficulty of governing THIRTEEN STATES at any rate, independent of calculations upon an ordinary degree of public spirit and integrity, will, in my opinion, constantly *impose* on the national rulers the *necessity* of a spirit of accommodation to the reasonable expectations of their

constituents. But there is yet a further consideration, which
proves beyond the possibility of doubt, that the observation is
futile. It is this, that the national rulers, whenever nine
states concur, will have no option upon the subject. By the
fifth article of the plan the congress will be *obliged*, "on the
application of the legislatures of two-thirds of the states,
(which at present amounts to nine) to call a convention for
proposing amendments, which *shall be valid* to all intents and
purposes, as part of the constitution, when ratified by the
legislatures of three-fourths of the states, or by conventions
in three-fourths thereof." The words of this article are per-
emptory. The congress "*shall* call a convention." Nothing in
this particular is left to the discretion of that body. And of
consequence all the declamation about their disinclination to a
change, vanishes in air. Nor however difficult it may be supposed to unite two-thirds or three-fourths of the state legislatures, in amendments which may affect local interests, can
there by any room to apprehend any such difficulty in a union
on points which are merely relative to the general liberty or
security of the people. We may safely rely on the disposition
of the state legislatures to erect barriers against the encroachments of the national authority.

The zeal for attempts to amend, prior to the establishment
of the constitution, must abate in every man, who, is ready to
accede to the truth of the following observations of a writer,
equally solid and ingenious: "To balance a large state or society (says he) whether monarchial or republican, on general laws,
is a work of so great difficulty, that no human genius, however
comprehensive, is able by the mere dint of reason and reflection, to effect it. The judgments of many must unite in the
work: EXPERIENCE must guide their labour: TIME must bring it to
perfection: And the FEELING of inconveniences must correct the
mistakes which they *inevitably* fall into, in their first trials
and experiments." These judicious reflections contain a lesson
of moderation to all the sincere lovers of the union, and ought
to put them upon their guard against hazarding anarchy, civil
war, a perpetual alienation of the states from each other, and
perhaps the military despotism of a victorious demagogue, in
the pursuit of what they are not likely to obtain, but from
TIME and EXPERIENCE. It may be in me a defect of political
fortitude, but I acknowledge, that I cannot entertain an equal
tranquillity with those who affect to treat the dangers of a
longer continuance in our present situation as imaginary. A
NATION without a NATIONAL GOVERNMENT is, in my view, an awful
spectacle. The establishment of a constitution, in time of
profound peace, by the voluntary consent of a whole people, is
a PRODIGY, to the completion of which I look forward with trembling anxiety. I can reconcile it to no rules of prudence to
let go the hold we now have, in so arduous an enterprise, upon

seven out of the thirteen states; and after having passed over
so considerable a part of the ground to recommence the course.
I dread the more the consequences of new attempts, because I
KNOW that POWERFUL INDIVIDUALS, in this and in other states,
are enemies to a general national government, in every possible
shape.

74

ALEXANDER HAMILTON TO JAMES MADISON New York, June 8, 1788

    In my last, I think, I informed you that the elections had
turned out, beyond expectation, favorable to the Antifederal
party. They have a majority of two thirds in the Convention,
and, according to the best estimate I can form, of about four
sevenths in the community. The views of the leaders in this
city are pretty well ascertained to be turned towards a *long*
adjournment—say, till next spring or summer. Their incautious
ones observe that this will give an opportunity to the State to
see how the government works, and to act according to *circumstances.*
    My reasonings on the fact are to this effect: The leaders
of the party hostile to the Constitution are equally hostile to
the Union. They are, however, afraid to reject the Constitution at once, because that step would bring matters to a crisis
between this State and the States which had adopted the Constitution, and between the parties in the State. A separation of
the Southern District from the other parts of the State, it is
perceived, would become the object of the Federalists and of
the neighboring States. They therefore resolve upon a long adjournment as the safest and most artful course to effect their
final purpose. They suppose that when the government gets into
operation, it will be obliged to take some steps in respect to
revenue, etc., which will furnish topics of declamation to its
enemies in the several States, and will strengthen the minori-
ties. If any considerable discontent should show itself, they

Manuscript Division, Library of Congress. Printed in Henry
Cabot Lodge, ed., *The Works of Alexander Hamilton*, 8: 187–88,
and Syrett and Cooke, eds., *Papers of Alexander Hamilton*, 5:
2–3.

will stand ready to head the opposition. If, on the contrary, the thing should go on smoothly, and the sentiments of our own people should change, they can elect to come into the Union. They, at all events, take the chances of time and the chapter of accidents.

How far their friends in the country will go with them, I am not able to say, but, as they have always been found very obsequious, we have little reason to calculate upon an uncompliant temper in the present instance. For my own part, the more I can penetrate the views of the Anti-federal party in this State, the more I dread the consequences of the non-adoption of the Constitution by any of the other States—the more I fear an eventual disunion and civil war. God grant that Virginia may accede. The example will have a vast influence on our politics. New Hampshire, all accounts give us to expect, will be an assenting State.

The number of the volumes of the Federalist which you desired have been forwarded, as well the second as the first, to the care of Governor Randolph. It was impossible to correct a certain error.

In a former letter, I requested you to communicate to me, by express, the event of any decisive question in favor of the Constitution, authorizing changes of horses, etc., with an assurance to the person that he will be liberally paid for his diligence.

75

ROBERT YATES, COMPARISON OF THE
FEDERAL AND STATE CONSTITUTIONS   June 13-14, 1788

. . . . .

Although a variety of objections to the proposed new constitution for the government of the United States have been laid before the public by men of the best abilities, I am led to believe that representing it in a point of view which has

---

Writing under the pen name "Sydney," Yates was a prolific anti-federalist publicist. The comparison of the state and federal constitutions appeared in two essays in the *Daily Patriotic Register* on June 13 and 14, 1788. This excerpt, which omits

escaped their observation may be of use, that is, by comparing
it with the constitution of the State of New York.

. . . . .

It may be proper to premise that the pressure of necessity
and distress (and not corruption) had a principal tendency to
induce the adoption of the state constitutions and the existing
confederation, that power was even then vested in the rulers
with the greatest caution, and that, as from every circumstance
we have reason to infer that the new constitution does not
originate from a pure source, we ought deliberately to trace
the extent and tendency of the trust we are about to repose,
under the conviction that a reassumption of that trust will at
least be difficult, if not impracticable. If we take a retro-
spective view of the measures of Congress . . . we can scarcely
entertain a doubt but that a plan has long since been framed to
subvert the confederation; that that plan has been matured with
the most perservering industry and unremitted attention; and
that the objects expressed in the preamble to the constitution,
that is "to promote the general welfare and secure the blessings of liberty to ourselves and our posterity," were merely
the ostensible, and not the real reasons of its framers . . . .

. . . . .

. . . The state governments are considered in [the proposed constitution] as mere dependencies, existing solely by
its toleration, and possessing powers of which they may be deprived whenever the general government is disposed so to do.
If then the powers of the state governments are to be totally
absorbed, in which all agree, and only differ as to the mode,
whether it will be effected by a rapid progression, or by as
certain, but slower, operations: what is to limit the oppression of the general government? Where are the rights, which
are declared to be incapable of violation? And what security
have people against the wanton oppression of unprincipled governors? No constitutional redress is pointed out, and no express declaration is contained in it, to limit the boundaries
of their rulers; beside which the mode and period of their being elected tends to take away their responsibility to the people over whom they may, by the power of the purse and sword,
domineer at discretion. . . .

I shall now proceed to compare the constitution of the
state of New York with the proposed federal government, distin-
guishing the paragraphs in the former, which are rendered nuga-

---

(Cont'd.) the detailed comparison of the two instruments of
government, is from Paul L. Ford, ed., *Essays on the Constitution of the United States Published During its Discussion by
the People, 1787-1788* (Brooklyn: Historical Printing Club 1892),
pp. 297-98, 300, 313-14.

tory by the latter; those which are in a great measure ener-
vated, and such as are in the discretion of the general government to permit or not. . . .

. . . . .

From this contrast it appears that the general government,
when completely organized, will absorb all those powers of the
state which the framers of its constitution had declared should
be only exercised by the representatives of the people of the
state; that the burdens and expense of supporting a state establishment will be perpetuated; but its operations to ensure
or contribute to any essential measures promotive of the happiness of the people may be totally prostrated, the general
government arrogating to itself the right of interfering in the
most minute objects of internal police, and the most trifling
domestic concerns of every state, by possessing a power of
passing laws "to provide for the general welfare of the United
States," which may affect life, liberty and property in every
modification they may think expedient, unchecked by cautionary
reservations, and unrestrained by a declaration of any of those
rights which the wisdom and prudence of America in the year
1776 held ought to be at all events protected from violation.

In a word, the new constitution will prove finally to dissolve all the power of the several state legislatures, and destroy the rights and liberties of the people; for the power of
the first will be all in all, and of the latter a mere shadow
and form without substance, and if adopted we may (in imitation
of the Carthagenians) say, Delenda vit Americae.

76

JOHN WILLIAMS, RATIFYING CONVENTION SPEECH   June 21, 1788

. . . . .

I believe that this country has never before seen such a
critical period in political affairs. We have felt the feeble-

---

Elliot, comp., *Debates . . . on the Adoption of the Federal
Constitution*, 2: 240-41. Williams was a physician and large
landowner in frontier Washington County, located in the extreme
northeast corner of the state. He ultimately voted against
ratification.

ness of those ties by which the states are held together, and
the want of that energy which is necessary to manage our general concerns. Various are the expedients which have been proposed to remedy these evils; but they have been proposed without effect; though I am persuaded that, if the Confederation
had been attended to as its value justly merited, and proper
attention paid to a few necessary amendments, it might have
carried us on for a series of years, and probably have been in
as great estimation with succeeding ages as it was in our long
and painful war, notwithstanding the frightful picture that has
been drawn of our situation, and the imputation of all our difficulties to the want of an energetic government. Indeed, sir,
it appears to me that many of our present distresses flow from
a source very different from the defects in the Confederation.
Unhappily for us, immediately after our extrication from a
cruel and unnatural war, luxury and dissipation overran the
country, banishing all that economy, frugality, and industry,
which had been exhibited during the war.

Sir, if we were to reassume all our old habits, we might
expect to prosper. Let us, then, abandon all those foreign
commodities which have hitherto deluged our country, which have
loaded us with debt, and which, if continued, will forever involve us in difficulties. How many thousands are daily wearing
the manufactures of Europe, when, by a little industry and frugality, they might wear those of their own country! One may
venture to say, sir, that the greatest part of the goods are
manufactured in Europe by persons who support themselves by our
extravagance. And can we believe a government ever so well
formed can relieve us from these evils? What dissipation is
there from the immoderate use of spirits! Is it not notorious
that men cannot be hired, in time of harvest, without giving
them, on an average, a pint of rum per day? so that, on the
lowest calculation, every twentieth part of the grain is expended on that article; and so, in proportion, all the farmer's
produce. And what is worse, the disposition of eight tenths of
the commonalty is such, that, if they can get credit, they will
purchase unnecessary articles, even to the amount of their crop,
before it becomes merchantable. And therefore it is evident
that the best government ever devised, without economy and frugality, will leave us in a situation no better than the present.

Sir, the enormous expense of the article of tea will
amount, in two years, to our whole foreign debt. Much more
might be said on the subject; but I fear I have trespassed on
your patience already. The time of the committee would not
have been so long taken up, had there not appeared a propriety
in showing that all our present difficulties are not to be at-
tributed to the defects in the Confederation; and, were the
real truth known, part of its defects have been used as an instrument to make way for the proposed system; and whether or

not it is calculated for greater emoluments and more placemen
the committee will determine. However, from what has been said,
and the mode agreed on for our proceedings, it appears probable
that the system of government under consideration is preferred
before the Confederation. This being the case, let us examine
whether it be calculated to preserve the invaluable blessings
of liberty, and secure the inestimable rights of mankind. If
it be so, let us adopt it. But if it be found to contain principles that will lead to the subversion of liberty,—if it
tends to establish a despotism, or, what is worse, a tyrannical
aristocracy,—let us insist upon the necessary alterations and
amendments.

. . . . .

77

MELANCTON SMITH, RATIFYING CONVENTION SPEECH June 21, 1788

. . . . .
To determine whether the number of representatives proposed by this Constitution is sufficient, it is proper to examine the qualifications which this house ought to possess, in
order to exercise their power discreetly for the happiness of
the people. The idea that naturally suggests itself to our
minds, when we speak of representatives, is, that they resemble
those they represent. They should be a true picture of the
people, possess a knowledge of their circumstances and their
wants, sympathize in all their distresses, and be disposed to
seek their true interests. The knowledge necessary for the
representative of a free people not only comprehends extensive
political and commercial information, such as is acquired by
men of refined education, who have leisure to attain to high

Elliot, comp., *Debates . . . on the Adoption of the Federal
Constitution*, 2: 245–50. Smith (1744–98) was a prominent merchant, land speculator, and lawyer from Poughkeepsie in
Dutchess County. A member of the congress from 1785 to 1788,
he was a staunch antifederalist and a political ally of George
Clinton. Smith led the defection of a group of antifederalists
that broke the convention stalemate and made ratification possible.

degrees of improvement, but it should also comprehend that kind of acquaintance with the common concerns and occupations of the people, which men of the middling class of life are, in general, more competent to than those of a superior class. To understand the true commercial interests of a country, not only requires just ideas of the general commerce of the world, but also, and principally, a knowledge of the productions of your own country, and their value, what your soil is capable of producing, the nature of your manufactures, and the capacity of the country to increase both. To increase the power of laying taxes, duties, and excises, with discretion, requires something more than an acquaintance with the abstruse parts of the system of finance. It calls for a knowledge of the circumstances and ability of the people in general—a discernment how the burdens imposed will bear upon the different classes.

From thse observations results this conclusion—that the number of representatives should be so large, as that, while it embraces the men of the first class, it should admit those of the middling class of life. I am convinced that this government is so constituted that the representatives will generally be composed of the first class in the community, which I shall distinguish by the name of the *natural aristocracy* of the country. I do not mean to give offence by using this term. I am sensible this idea is treated by many gentlemen as chimerical. I shall be asked what is meant by the *natural aristocracy*, and told that no such distinction of classes of men exists among us. It is true, it is our singular felicity that we have no legal or hereditary distinctions of this kind; but still there are real differences. Every society naturally divides itself into classes. The Author of nature has bestowed on some greater capacities than others; birth, education, talents, and wealth, create distinctions among men as visible, and of as much influence, as titles, stars, and garters. In every society, men of this class will command a superior degree of respect; and if the government is so constituted as to admit but few to exercise the powers of it, it will, according to the natural course of things, be in their hands. Men in the middling class, who are qualified as representatives, will not be so anxious to be chosen as those of the first. When the number is so small, the office will be highly elevated and distinguished; the style in which the members live will probably be high; circumstances of this kind will render the place of a representative not a desirable one to sensible, substantial men, who have been used to walk in the plain and frugal paths of life.

Besides, the influence of the great will generally enable them to succeed in elections. It will be difficult to combine a district of country containing thirty or forty thousand inhabitants,—frame your election laws as you please,—in any other character, unless it be in one of conspicuous military,

popular, civil, or legal talents. The great easily form associations; the poor and middling class form them with difficulty.
If the elections be by plurality,—as probably will be the case
in this state,—it is almost certain none but the great will be
chosen, for they easily unite their interests: the common people will divide, and their divisions will be promoted by the
others. There will be scarcely a chance of their uniting in
any other but some great man, unless in some popular demagogue,
who will probably be destitute of principle. A substantial
yeoman, of sense and discernment, will hardly ever be chosen.
From these remarks, it appears that the government will fall
into the hands of the few and the great. This will be a government of oppression. I do not mean to declaim against the
great, and charge them indiscriminately with want of principle
and honesty. The same passions and prejudices govern all men.
The circumstances in which men are placed in a great measure
give a cast to the human character. Those in middling circumstances have less temptation; they are inclined by habit, and
the company with whom they associate, to set bounds to their
passions and appetites.   If this is not sufficient, the want
of means to gratify them will be a restraint: they are obliged
to employ their time in their respective callings; hence the
substantial yeomanry of the country are more temperate, of better morals, and less ambition, than the great. The latter do
not feel for the poor and middling class; the reasons are obvious—they are not obliged to use the same pains and labor to
procure property as the other. They feel not the inconveniences arising from the payment of small sums. The great consider themselves above the common people, entitled to more respect, do not associate with them; they fancy themselves to
have a right of preëminence in every thing. In short, they
possess the same feelings, and are under the influence of the
same motives, as an hereditary nobility. I know the idea that
such a distinction exists in this country is ridiculed by some;
but I am not the less apprehensive of danger from their influence on this account. Such distinctions exist all the world
over, have been taken notice of by all writers on free government, and are founded in the nature of things. It has been the
principal care of free governments to guard against the encroachments of the great. Common observation and experience
prove the existence of such distinctions. Will any one say
that there does not exist in this country the pride of family,
of wealth, of talents, and that they do not command influence
and respect among the common people? . . . We ought to guard
against the government being placed in the hands of this class.
They cannot have that sympathy with their constituents which is
necessary to connect them closely to their interests. Being in
the habit of profuse living, they will be profuse in the public
expenses. They find no difficulty in paying their taxes, and

therefore do not feel public burdens. Besides, if they govern,
they will enjoy the emoluments of the government. The middling
class, from their frugal habits, and feeling themselves the
public burdens, will be careful how they increase them.

But I may be asked, Would you exclude the first class in
the community from any share in legislation? I answer, By no
means. They would be factious, discontented, and constantly
disturbing the government. It would also be unjust. They have
their liberties to protect, as well as others, and the largest
share of property. But my idea is, that the Constitution
should be so framed as to admit this class, together with a
sufficient number of the middling class to control them. You
will then combine the abilities and honesty of the community,
a proper degree of information, and a disposition to pursue the
public good. A representative body, composed principally of
respectable yeomanry, is the best possible security to liberty.
When the interest of this part of the community is pursued, the
public good is pursued, because the body of every nation consists of this class, and because the interest of both the rich
and the poor are involved in that of the middling class. No
burden can be laid on the poor but what will sensibly affect
the middling class. Any law rendering property insecure would
be injurious to them. When, therefore, this class in society
pursue their own interest, they promote that of the public, for
it is involved in it.

In so small a number of representatives, there is great
danger from corruption and combination. A great politician has
said that every man has his price. I hope this is not true in
all its extent; but I ask the gentleman to inform me what government there is in which it has not been practised. Notwithstanding all that has been said of the defects in the constitution of the ancient confederacies in the Grecian republics,
their destruction is to be imputed more to this cause than to
any imperfection in their forms of government. This was the
deadly poison that effected their dissolution. This is an extensive country, increasing in population and growing in consequence. Very many lucrative offices will be in the grant of
the government, which will be objects of avarice and ambition.
How easy will it be to gain over a sufficient number, in the
bestowment of offices, to promote the views and the purposes of
those who grant them! Foreign corruption is also to be guarded
against. A system of corruption is known to be the system of
government in Europe. It is practised without blushing; and we
may lay it to our account, it will be attempted amongst us.
The most effectual as well as natural security against this is
a strong democratic branch in the legislature, frequently chosen, including in it a number of the substantial, sensible,
yeomanry of the country. Does the House of Representatives
answer this description? I confess, to me they hardly wear the

complexion of a democratic branch; they appear the mere shadow
of representation. The whole number, in both houses, amounts
to ninety-one; of these forty-six make a quorum; and twenty-
four of those, being secured, may carry any point. Can the
liberties of three millions of people be securely trusted in
the hands of twenty-four men? Is it prudent to commit to so
small a number the decision of the great questions which will
come before them? Reason revolts at the idea.

. . . We certainly ought to fix, in the Constitution,
those things which are essential to liberty. If any thing
falls under this description, it is the number of the legislature. To say, as this gentleman does, that our security is to
depend upon the spirit of the people, who will be watchful of
their liberties, and not suffer them to be infringed, is absurd. . . . Government operates upon the spirit of the people,
as well as the spirit of the people operates upon it; and if
they are not conformable to each other, the one or the other
will prevail. In a less time than twenty-five years, the government will receive its tone. What the spirit of the country
may be at the end of that period, it is impossible to foretell.
Our duty is to frame a government friendly to liberty and the
rights of mankind, which will tend to cherish and cultivate a
love of liberty among our citizens. If this government becomes oppressive, it will be by degrees: it will aim at its end
by disseminating sentiments of government opposite to republicanism, and proceed from step to step in depriving the people
of a share in the government. A recollection of the change
that has taken place in the minds of many in this country in
the course of a few years, ought to put us on our guard. Many,
who are ardent advocates for the new system, reprobate republican principles as chimerical, and such as ought to be expelled
from society. Who would have thought, ten years ago, that the
very men, who risked their lives and fortunes in support of
republican principles, would now treat them as the fictions of
fancy? A few years ago, we fought for liberty; we framed a
general government on free principles; we placed the state legislatures, in whom the people have a full and a fair representation, between Congress and the people. We were then, it is
true, too cautious, and too much restricted the powers of the
general government. But now it is proposed to go into the contrary, and a more dangerous extreme—to remove all barriers, to
give the new government free access to our pockets, and ample
command of our persons, and that without providing for a genuine and fair representation of the people.

. . . . .

78

ALEXANDER HAMILTON, RATIFYING CONVENTION SPEECH

June 21, 1788

. . . . .

It was remarked yesterday, that a numerous representation was necessary to obtain the confidence of the people. This is not generally true. The confidence of the people will easily be gained by a good administration. This is the true touchstone. . . . Probably the public attachment is more strongly secured by a train of prosperous events, which are the result of wise deliberation and vigorous execution, and to which large bodies are much less competent than small ones. If the representative conducts with propriety, he will necessarily enjoy the good-will of the constituent. It appears, then, if my reasoning be just, that the clause is perfectly proper, upon the principles of the gentleman who contends for the amendment; as there is in it the greatest degree of present security, and a moral certainty of an increase equal to our utmost wishes.

It has been further, by the gentlemen in the opposition, observed, that a large representation is necessary to understand the interests of the people. This principle is by no means true in the extent to which the gentlemen seem to carry it. I would ask, Why may not a man understand the interests of thirty as well as twenty? The position appears to be made upon the unfounded presumption that all the interests of all parts of the community must be represented. No idea is more erroneous than this. Only such interests are proper to be represented as are involved in the powers of the general government. These interests come completely under the observation of one or a few men; and the requisite information is by no means augmented in proportion to the increase of number . . . .

Sir, we hear constantly a great deal which is rather calculated to awake our passions, and create prejudices, than to conduct us to the truth, and teach us our real interests. I do not suppose this to be the design of the gentlemen. Why, then, are we told so often of an aristocracy? For my part, I hardly know the meaning of this word, as it is applied. If all we hear be true, this government is really a very bad one. But who are the aristocracy among us? Where do we find men elevated to a perpetual rank above their fellow-citizens, and pos-

Elliot, comp., *Debates . . . on the Adoption of the Federal Constitution*, 2: 254-58.

sessing powers entirely independent of them? The arguments of
the gentlemen only go to prove that there are men who are rich,
men who are poor, some who are wise, and others who are not;
that, indeed, every distinguished man is an aristocrat. This
reminds me of a description of the aristocrats I have seen in
a late publication styled the Federal Farmer. The author reck-
ons in the aristocracy all governors of states, members of Congress, chief magistrates, and all officers of the militia.
This description, I presume to say, is ridiculous. The image
is a phantom. Does the new government render a rich man more
eligible than a poor one? No. It requires no such qualifica-
tion. It is bottomed on the broad and equal principle of your
state constitution.

Sir, if the people have it in their option to elect their
most meritorious men, is this to be considered as an objection?
Shall the Constitution oppose their wishes, and abridge their
most invaluable privilege? While property continues to be pretty equally divided, and a considerable share of information
pervades the community, the tendency of the people's suffrages
will be to elevate merit even from obscurity. As riches increase and accumulate in few hands, as luxury prevails in society, virtue will be in a greater degree considered as only a
graceful appendage of wealth, and the tendency of things will
be to depart from the republican standard. This is the real
disposition of human nature: it is what neither the honorable
member nor myself can correct; it is a common misfortune, that
awaits our state constitution as well as all others.

. . . . .

It is a harsh doctrine that men grow wicked in proportion
as they improve and enlighten their minds. Experience has by
no means justified us in the supposition that there is more virtue in one class of men than in another. Look through the rich
and the poor of the community, the learned and the ignorant.
Where does virtue predominate? The difference indeed consists,
not in the quantity, but kind, of vices which are incident to
various classes; and here the advantage of character belongs to
the wealthy. Their vices are probably more favorable to the
prosperity of the state than those of the indigent, and partake
less of moral depravity.

. . . . .

Suggestions, sir, of an extraordinary nature, have been
frequently thrown out in the course of the present political
controversy. It gives me pain to dwell on topics of this kind,
and I wish they might be dismissed. We have been told that the
old Confederation has proved inefficacious, only because in-
triguing and powerful men, aiming at a revolution, have been
forever instigating the people, and rendering them disaffected
with it. This, sir, is a false insinuation. The thing is impossible. I will venture to assert, that no combination of

designing men under heaven will be capable of making a government unpopular which is in its principles a wise and good one, and vigorous in its operations.

The Confederation was framed amidst the agitation and tumults of society. It was composed of unsound materials, put together in haste. Men of intelligence discovered the feebleness of the structure, in the first stages of its existence; but the great body of the people, too much engrossed with their distresses to contemplate any but the immediate causes of them, were ignorant of the defects of their constitution. But when the dangers of war were removed, they saw clearly what they had suffered, and what they had yet to suffer, from a feeble form of government. There was no need of discerning men to convince the people of their unhappy situation; the complaint was coëxtensive with the evil, and both were common to all classes of the community. We have been told that the spirit of patriotism and love of liberty are almost extinguished among the people, and that it has become a prevailing doctrine that republican principles ought to be hooted out of the world. Sir, I am confident that such remarks as these are rather occasioned by the heat of argument than by a cool conviction of their truth and justice. As far as my experience has extended, I have heard no such doctrine; nor have I discovered any diminution of regard for those rights and liberties, in defence of which the people have fought and suffered. . . . I trust that the proposed Constitution affords a genuine specimen of representative and republican government, and that it will answer, in an eminent degree, all the beneficial purposes of society.

79

RATIFICATION OF THE CONSTITUTION   July 26, 1788

We, the delegates of the people of the state of New York, duly elected and met in Convention, having maturely considered

---

Elliot, comp., *Debates . . . on the Adoption of the Federal Constitution*, 1: 327-331. The ratifying convention commenced deliberations in Poughkeepsie on June 17, with the antifederalists, who carried nine of thirteen counties in the election, occupying forty-six of the sixty-five seats. The popular vote

the Constitution for the United States of America . . . and
having also seriously and deliberately considered the present
situation of the United States,—Do declare and make known,—

That all power is originally vested in, and consequently
derived from, the people, and that government is instituted by
them for their common interest, protection, and security.

That the enjoyment of life, liberty, and the pursuit of
happiness, are essential rights, which every government ought
to respect and preserve.

That the powers of government may be reassumed by the people whensoever it shall become necessary to their happiness;
that every power, jurisdiction, and right, which is not by the
said Constitution clearly delegated to the Congress of the
United States, or the departments of the government thereof,
remains to the people of the several states, or to their respective state governments, to whom they may have granted the
same; and that those clauses in the said Constitution, which
declare that Congress shall not have or exercise certain powers,
do not imply that Congress is entitled to any powers not given
by the said Constitution; but such clauses are to be construed
either as exceptions to certain specified powers, or as inserted merely for greater caution.

That the people have an equal, natural, and unalienable
right freely and peaceably to exercise their religion, according to the dictates of conscience; and that no religious sect
or society ought to be favored or established by law in preference to others.

That the people have a right to keep and bear arms; that a
well-regulated militia, including the body of the people *capable of bearing arms*, is the proper, natural, and safe defence
of a free state.

. . . . .

That standing armies, in time of peace, are dangerous to
liberty, and ought not to be kept up, except in cases of necessity; and that at all times the military should be under strict
subordination to the civil power.

(Cont'd.) was closer, however; the antifederalists received
12,347 of the 22,088 known ballots (56 percent). New York has
the distinction of being the only state to stipulate condition-
al ratification. Adoption of the Constitution was contingent
upon the twenty-three declarations of rights affixed to the
statement of ratification being held inviolate by the federal
government. The delegates also drafted thirty-two amendments
to be considered by a second constitutional convention, which
they were confident would be summoned to resolve the objections
registered against the Constitution.

That, in time of peace, no soldier ought to be quartered in any house without the consent of the owner, and in time of war only by the civil magistrate, in such manner as the laws may direct.

That no person ought to be taken, imprisoned, or disseized of his freehold, or be exiled, or deprived of his privileges, franchises, life, liberty, or property, but by due process of law.

That no person ought to be put twice in jeopardy of life or limb, for one and the same offence; nor, unless in case of impeachment, be punished more than once for the same offence.

That every person restrained of his liberty is entitled to an inquiry into the lawfulness of such restraint, and to a removal thereof if unlawful; and that such inquiry or removal ought not to be denied or delayed, except when, on account of public danger, the Congress shall suspend the privilege of the writ of *habeas corpus*.

That excessive bail ought not to be required, nor excessive fines imposed, nor cruel or unusual punishments inflicted.

That (except in the government of the land and naval forces, and of the militia when in actual service, and in cases of impeachment) a presentment or indictment by a grand jury ought to be observed as a necessary preliminary to the trial of all crimes cognizable by the judiciary of the United States; and such trial should be speedy, public, and by an impartial jury of the county where the crime was committed; and that no person can be found guilty without the unanimous consent of such jury . . . and that, in all criminal prosecutions, the accused ought to be informed of the cause and nature of his accusation, to be confronted with his accusers and the witnesses against him, to have the means of producing his witnesses, and the assistance of counsel for his defence; and should not be compelled to give evidence against himself.

That the trial by jury, in the extent that it obtains by the common law of England, is one of the greatest securities to the rights of a free people, and ought to remain inviolate.

That every freeman has a right to be secure from all unreasonable searches and seizures of his person, his papers, or his property; and therefore, that all warrants to search suspected places, or seize any freeman, his papers, or property, without information, upon oath or affirmation, of sufficient cause, are grievous and oppressive; and that all general warrants (or such in which the place or person suspected are not particularly designated) are dangerous, and ought not to be granted.

That the people have a right peaceably to assemble together to consult for their common good, or to instruct their representatives, and that every person has a right to petition or apply to the legislature for redress of grievances.

That the freedom of the press ought not to be violated or
restrained.

. . . . .

Under these impressions, and declaring that the rights
aforesaid cannot be abridged or violated, and that the explana-
tions aforesaid are consistent with the said Constitution, and
in confidence that the amendments which shall have been proposed to the said Constitution will receive an early and mature
consideration,—We, the said delegates, in the name and in the
behalf of the people of the state of New York, do, by these
presents, assent to and ratify the said Constitution.

And the Convention do, in the name and behalf of the people of the state of New York, enjoin it upon their representatives in Congress to exert all their influence, and use all
reasonable means, to obtain a ratification of the following
amendments to the said Constitution, in the manner prescribed
therein; and in all laws to be passed by the Congress, in the
mean time, to conform to the spirit of the said amendments, as
far as the Constitution will admit.

That there shall be one representative for every thirty
thousand inhabitants, according to the enumeration or census
mentioned in the Constitution, until the whole number of representatives amounts to two hundred, after which that number
shall be continued or increased, but not diminished, as the
Congress shall direct, and according to such ratio as the Congress shall fix, in conformity to the rule prescribed for the
apportionment of representatives and direct taxes.

That the Congress do not impose any excise on any article
(ardent spirits excepted) of the growth, production, or manu-
facture of the United States, or any of them.

That Congress do not lay direct taxes but when the moneys
arising from the impost and excise shall be insufficient for
the public exigencies, nor then, until Congress shall first
have made a requisition upon the states to assess, levy, and
pay, their respective proportions of such requisition, agreeably to the census fixed in the said Constitution, in such way
and manner as the legislatures of the respective states shall
judge best; and in such case, if any state shall neglect or
refuse to pay its proportion, pursuant to such requisition,
then Congress may assess and levy such state's proportion, together with interest at the rate of six per centum per annum,
from the time of payment prescribed in such requisition.

That the Congress shall not make or alter any regulation,
in any state, respecting the times, places, and manner, of
holding elections for senators and representatives, unless the
legislature of such state shall neglect or refuse to make laws
or regulations for the purpose, or from any circumstance be incapable of making the same, and then only until the legislature
of such state shall make provision in the premises; provided

that Congress may prescribe the time of the election of representatives.

That no persons, except natural-born citizens, or such as were citizens on or before the 4th day of July, 1776, or such as held commissions under the United States during the war, and have at any time since the 4th day of July, 1776, become citizens of one or other of the United States, and who shall be freeholders, shall be eligible to the places of President, Vice-President, or members of either house of the Congress of the United States.

That the Congress do not grant monopolies, or erect any company with exclusive advantages of commerce.

That no standing army or regular troops shall be raised, or kept up, in time of peace, without the consent of two thirds of the senators and representatives present in each house.

That no money be borrowed on the credit of the United States without the assent of two thirds of the senators and representatives present in each house.

That the Congress shall not declare war without the concurrence of two thirds of the senators and representatives present in each house.

. . . . .

That no capitation tax shall ever by laid by Congress.

That no person be eligible as a senator for more than six years in any term of twelve years; and that the legislatures of the respective states may recall their senators, or either of them, and elect others in their stead, to serve the remainder of the time for which the senators so recalled were appointed.

That no senator or representative shall, during the time for which he was elected, be appointed to any office under the authority of the United States.

That the authority given to the executives of the states to fill up the vacancies of senators be abolished, and that such vacancies be filled by the respective legislatures.

. . . . .

That no person shall be eligible to the office of President of the United States a third time.

. . . . .

That the President, or person exercising his powers for the time being shall not command an army in the field in person, without the previous desire of the Congress.

. . . . .

That the senators and representatives, and all executive and judicial officers of the United States, shall be bound by oath or affirmation not to infringe or violate the constitutions or rights of the respective states.

80

CALL FOR A SECOND CONSTITUTIONAL CONVENTION   July 28, 1788

We, the members of the convention of this State, have deliberately and maturely considered the Constitution proposed for the United States.

Several articles in it appear so exceptionable to a majority of us, that nothing but the fullest confidence of obtaining a revision of them by a general convention, and an invincible reluctance to separating from our sister States, could have prevailed upon a sufficient number to ratify it, without stipulating for previous amendments.

We all unite in opinion that such a revision will be necessary to recommend it to the approbation and support of a numerous body of our constituents.

We observe that amendments have been proposed, and are anxiously desired by several of the States as well as by this, and we think it of great importance that effectual measures be immediately taken for calling a convention to meet at a period not far remote; for we are convinced, that the apprehensions and discontents which those articles occasion cannot be removed or allowed, unless an act to provide for it be among the first that shall be passed by the new Congress.

As it is essential that an application for the purpose should be made to them by two thirds of the States, we earnestly exhort and request the legislature of your State (or Commonwealth) to take the earliest opportunity of making it. We are persuaded that a similar one will be made by our legislature at their next session; and we ardently wish and desire that the other States may concur in adopting and promoting the measure.

It cannot be necessary to observe that no government, however constructed, can operate well unless it possesses the confidence and good-will of the great body of the people; and as we desire nothing more than that the amendments proposed by this or other States be submitted to the consideration and decision of a general convention, we flatter ourselves that motives of mutual affection and conciliation will conspire with the obvious dictates of sound policy, to induce even such of

---

"The Circular Letter, from the Convention of the State of New York to the governors of the several states in the Union," in Elliot, comp., *Debates . . . on the Adoption of the Federal Constitution*, 2: 413-14. Johy Jay wrote the letter, signed by George Clinton, president of the convention.

the States as may be content with every article in the Constitution to gratify the reasonable desires of that numerous class of American citizens who are anxious to obtain amendments of some of them.

Our amendments will manifest that none of them originated in local views, as they are such as if acceded to must equally affect every State in the Union.

Our attachment to our sister States, and the confidence we repose in them, cannot be more forcibly demonstrated than by acceding to a government which many of us think imperfect, and devolving the power of determining whether that government shall be rendered perpetual in its present form, or altered agreeable to our wishes or a minority of the States with whom we unite.

We request the favour of your Excellency to lay this letter before the legislature of your State (or Commonwealth), and we are persuaded that your regard for our national harmony and good government will induce you to promote a measure which we are unanimous in thinking very conducive to those interesting objects.

. . . . .

81

GILBERT LIVINGSTON TO GEORGE CLINTON
Poughkeepsie, July 29, 1788

. . . . .
Permit me sir again to say, that I have had a severe struggle in my mind between *duty* and *prejudice*.

I entered this house, as fully determined on previous amendments (I sincerely believe) as any one member in it. Nothing sir, but a conviction that I am serving the most essential interests of my country, could ever induce me to take another ground, and differ from so many of my friends on this floor. . . . With respect to the constitution itself, I have

---

Poughkeepsie Country Journal, July 29, 1788. Livingston, a Dutchess County lawyer, was one of the antifederalists who voted with the federalists on the final question of ratification.

the same idea of it I ever had—that is, that there is not
safety under it, unless amended. Some time after we first met
sir, a majority of those in this house who opposed it, did determine not to reject it. Only one question then remained—
which was the most eligible mode, to ensure a general convention of the States, to reconsider it, [or] to have the essential amendments ingrafted into it? [After] the most mature
and deliberate consideration . . . the result of my judgment
is—that the adoption on the table, with the bill of rights and
amendments contained in it, and the circular letter to the different States accompanying it, is, considering our *present* situation with respect to our sister States, the wisest and best
measure, we can possibly pursue. I shall therefore vote for it
[but] I will steadily persevere, in every possible means to
procure this desirable object, a revision of the Constitution.

. . . . .

Postscript:

"Truth and error...imperceptibly...mixed"

82

JOHN JAY TO THE REVEREND JEDEDIAH MORSE
Albany, February 28, 1797

. . . . .
It gives me pleasure to learn that you will endeavour at
least to prepare for a history of the American Revolution. To
obtain competent and exact information on the subject is not
the least arduous part of the task; it will require much time,
patient perseverance, and research. As the Revolution was accomplished by the councils and efforts of the *Union*, and by the
auxiliary councils and efforts of each individual *State or col-*
ony, it appears to me that your inquiries will necessarily be
divided into those *two departments*. The first of them will of
course include foreign affairs, and both of them will naturally
divide into two others—viz., the *civil* and the *military*. Each
of these, you know, comprehends several distinct heads, which
are obvious.
So much of our colonial history as casts light on the Revolution, viewed under its different aspects, and considered in
all its anterior relations, will be essential. I think our
colonial history is strongly marked by discriminating circumstances relative to our political situation and feelings, at

---

Johnston, ed., *Jay Papers*, 4: 224-25. Morse (1761-1826), a
conservative Congregationalist minister, is best known as "the
father of American geography." His projected history of the
Revolution reached fruition in 1824 with the publication of the
Annals of the American Revolution.

181

three different periods: 1st, down to the revolution under King William; 2d, from thence to the year 1763; and 3d, from that year to the union of the colonies in 1774. Want of leisure will not permit me to go into details.

As to documents— *public* and *private* journals of Congress; the papers mentioned or alluded to in them, such as certain reports of committees; letters to and from civil and military officers, ministers, agents, State governors, etc.; the proceedings of the standing committees for marine, commercial, fiscal, political, and foreign affairs,—all merit attention.

The journals and papers of State conventions, and councils of safety, and of some of the standing and other committees, during the revolutionary government, contain much interesting information.

There are also diaries and memoirs and private letters, which would give some aid and light to a sagacious and cautious inquirer; for experience has convinced me that they are entitled to no other respect or attention than what they derive from the well established characters of the writers for judgment, accuracy, and candour. As to characters, I have, throughout the Revolution, known some who passed for more than they were worth, and others who passed for less. On this head great circumspection is particularly requisite. It is to be regretted, but so I believe the fact to be, that except the Bible there is not a true history in the world. Whatever may be the virtue, discernment, and industry of the writers, I am persuaded that truth and error (though in different degrees) will imperceptibly become and remain mixed and blended until they shall be separated forever by the great and last refining fire.

Selected Bibliograhy
of Published Primary Materials

There are two invaluable sources for the study of the American Revolution in New York—and elsewhere. First, "Early American Imprints," an ambitious microcard series prepared by Clifford K. Shipton under the auspices of the American Antiquarian
Society, makes readily available most of the nonserial items
listed in Charles Evans et al., comps., *American Bibliography:
A Chronological Dictionary of All Books, Pamphlets, and Period-
ical Literature Published in the United States of America
from . . . 1639 to . . . 1820*, 14 vols. (Chicago, New York, and
Worcester, Mass., 1903-59). Clifford K. Shipton and James E.
Mooney, comps., *National Index of American Imprints through
1800: The Short-Title Evans*, 2 vols. (Worcester, Mass.: American Antiquarian Society and Barre Publishers, 1969), contains
additions and corrections to Evans. Second, newspapers provide
not only substantive data but also provide empathy for the
times as no other source can. For information about the New
York press, consult Clarence S. Brigham's *History and Bibliography of American Newspapers, 1690-1820*, 2 vols. (Worcester,
Mass.: American Antiquarian Society, 1947), and "Additions and
Corrections . . . ," *Proceedings of the American Antiquarian
Society*, n.s. 71 (April 1961): 15-62. For a partial listing of
the growing number of newspapers on microfilm see the latest
edition of *Newspapers on Microfilm* issued by the Library of
Congress.

Official records provide a wealth of information about the
transition from colony to state. For legislative activities
see the *Journal of the Votes and Proceedings of the General Assembly of the Colony of New-York, 1691-1765*, 2 vols. (New York:
Hugh Gaine, 1764-66); *Journal of the Votes and Proceedings of
the General Assembly of the Colony of New-York from 1766 to
1776* (Albany, N.Y.: J. Buel, 1820); *Journal of the Legislative
Council of the Colony of New-York . . . [1691-1775]*, 2 vols.
(Albany, N.Y.: Weed, Parsons and Co., 1861); and Victor Hugo
Paltsits, ed., *Minutes of the Executive Council of the Province*

of New-York . . . , 2 vols. (Albany, N.Y.: State of New York, 1910).   The journals of the Assembly and Senate for the years 1777-88 are available on "Early American Imprints" microcards. Charles Z. Lincoln et al., eds., *The Colonial Laws of New York from the Year 1664 to the Revolution*, 5 vols. (Albany, N.Y.: J. B. Lyon Company, 1894-96); *Laws of the State of New-York, Comprising the Constitution, and the Acts of the Legislature since the Revolution, from the First to the Twelfth Session, Inclusive*, 2 vols. (New York: Hugh Gaine, 1789); and volumes I (1777-84) and II (1785-88) of *Laws of the State of New York, 1777-1801*, 5 vols. (Albany, N.Y.: J. B. Lyon Co., 1886-88) reveal public policy.   The actions of the revolutionary government are chronicled in the *Journals of the Provincial Congress, Provincial Convention, Committee of Safety and Council of Safety of the State of New York, 1775-1777*, 2 vols. (Albany, N.Y.: T. Weed, 1842).   *Minutes of the Committee and of the First Commission for Detecting and Defeating Conspiracies in the State of New York, Dec. 11, 1776-Sept. 23, 1778; Collections*, 57-58 (New York: New-York Historical Society, 1924-1925); and Victor Hugo Paltsits, ed., *Minutes of the Commissioners for Detecting and Defeating Conspiracies in the State of New York: Albany County Sessions, 1778-1781*, 3 vols. (Albany, N.Y.: J. B. Lyon Co., 1909-10) provide insight into the operation of a key government agency.   The Revolution at the local level is reflected in Samuel L. Frey, ed., *The Minute Book of the Committee of Safety of Tryon County* . . . (New York: Dodd, Mead and Co., 1905), and James Sullivan, ed., *Minutes of the Albany Committee of Correspondence, 1775-1778, and Minutes of the Schenectady Committee, 1775-1779*, 2 vols. (Albany, N.Y.: The University of the State of New York, 1923, 1926.).   Also of value are John Austin Stevens, Jr., ed., *Colonial Records of the New York Chamber of Commerce, 1768-1784* . . . (New York: J. F. Trow & Co., 1867); Herbert Levi Osgood et al., eds., *Minutes of the Common Council of the City of New York, 1675-1776*, 8 vols. (New York: Dodd, Mead and Co., 1905); and *Minutes of the Council of Appointment, State of New York, April 2, 1778-May 3, 1779, Collections*, 58 (New York: New-York Historical Society, 1925). Taken together, the *Journal of the Convention of the State of New-York* . . . (Poughkeepsie, N.Y.: Nicholas Power, 1788), and *Debates and Proceedings of the Convention of the State of New-York* . . . (New York: Francis Childs, 1788) illuminate the work of the ratifying convention.

Because history is largely the result of actions taken or not taken by men, a careful perusal of the personal papers of public figures is indispensible for comprehending the Revolution.   Available printed correspondence, journals, and memoirs include Ross J.S. Hoffman, ed., *Edmund Burke, New York Agent, with His Letters to the New York Assembly* . . . *1761-1776* (Philadelphia: American Philosophical Society, 1956); Hugh Hastings

and J. A. Holden, eds., *Public Papers of George Clinton, First
Governor of New York, 1777-1795, 1801-1804 . . . ,* 10 vols.
(Albany, N.Y.: State of New York, 1899-1914); *The Colden Letter
Books* and *The Letters and Papers of Cadwallader Colden, 1711-
1775, Collections,* 9-10, 50-56, 67-68 (New York: New-York Historical Society, 1877-78, 1917-23, 1934-35); "The [James] Duane
Letters," *Publications* 7: 170-85, 247-56, 362-68, 8: 53-56,
377-90, 9: 393-400, 10: 299-310 (Washington, D.C.: Southern History Association, 1903-6); Clarence E. Carter, ed., *The Correspondence of General Thomas Gage with the Secretaries of
State, and with the War Office and the Treasury, 1763-1775,*
2 vols. (New Haven, Conn.: Yale University Press, 1931, 1933);
Harold C. Syrett and Jacob E. Cooke, eds., *The Papers of Alexander Hamilton,* 16 vols. to date (New York: Columbia University
Press, 1961-); William Jay, *The Life of John Jay. With Selections from his Correspondence and Miscellaneous Papers,* 2 vols.
(New York: J & J Harper, 1833); Henry P. Johnston, ed., *Correspondence of John Jay: New York City During the American Revolution. Being A Collection of Original Papers (Now First Published) From the Manuscripts in the Possession of the
Mercantile Library Association of New York City* (New York:
Mercantile Library Association, 1861), and *The Correspondence
and Public Papers of John Jay . . . ,* 4 vols. (New York: G. P.
Putnam's Sons, 1890-93); E. Edwards Beardsley, ed., *Life and
Correspondence of Samuel Johnson . . . ,* 2d ed. (New York: Hurd
and Houghton, 1874); James Sullivan et al., eds., *The Papers of
Sir William Johnson,* 12 vols. (Albany, N.Y.: The University of
the State of New York, 1921-57); Isaac Q. Leake, *Memoir of the
Life and Times of General John Lamb . . .* (Albany, N.Y.: J.
Munsell, 1850); [Charles] *Lee Papers, Collections,* 4-7 (New
York: New-York Historical Society, 1872-75); *Revolutionary Let-
ters of Importance: The Unpublished Correspondence of Robert R.
Livingston* (New York: American Art Association, 1918); *Papers
of the Lloyd Family of the Manor of Queens Village, Lloyd's
Neck, Long Island, New York, 1654-1826, Collections,* 59-60 (New
York: New-York Historical Society, 1927); G. D. Scull, ed., *The
[Capt. John] Montresor Journals, Collections,* 14 (New York:
New-York Historical Society, 1881); Jared Sparks, ed., *The Life
of Gouverneur Morris, with Selections from His Correspondence
and Miscellaneous Papers . . . ,* 3 vols. (Boston: Gray & Bowen,
1832); E. Edwards Beardsley, ed., *Life and Correspondence of
the Right Reverend Samuel Seabury . . . ,* 2d ed. (Boston:
Houghton Mifflin and Co., 1881); Edward H. Tatum, Jr., *The
American Journal of Ambrose Serle, Secretary to Lord Howe, 1776-
1778* (San Marino, Calif.: Huntington Library, 1940); William H.
W. Sabine, ed., *Historical Memoirs, from 16 March 1763 to 12
November 1783, of William Smith,* 3 vols. (New York: Colburn and
Tegg, Publishers, 1956, 1958, 1971); L. F. S. Upton, ed., *The
Diary and Selected Papers of Chief Justice William Smith, 1784-*

1793, Publications, 41-42 (Toronto: Champlain Society, 1963, 1965); Henry C. Van Schaack, *The Life of Peter Van Schaack, LL.D., Embracing Selections from His Correspondence and Other Writings During the American Revolution* . . . (New York: D. Appleton & Co., 1842), and *Memoir of Henry Van Schaack, Embracing Sections of His Correspondence and Other Writings* . . . (Chicago: A. C. McClurg & Co., 1892); and Dorothy C. Barck, ed., *Letter Book of John Watts, Merchant and Councillor of New York, January 1, 1762-December 22, 1765, Collections*, 61 (New York: New-York Historical Society, 1928).

Few systematic attempts have been made to collect, collate, and annotate the products of the pamphlet warfare that raged during the revolutionary era. Two notable exceptions are Clarence H. Vance, ed., *Letters of a Westchester Farmer (1774-1775) by the Reverend Samuel Seabury (1729-1796), Publications*, 8 (White Plains, N.Y.: Westchester County Historical Society, 1930), and Jacob E. Cooke, ed., *The Federalist* (Middletown, Conn.: Wesleyan University Press, 1961). Also valuable are Joseph Reese Strayer, ed., *The Delegate from New York, or Proceedings of the Federal Convention from the Notes of John Lansing, Jr.* (Princeton, N.J.: Princeton University Press, 1939), and Staughton Lynd, ed., "Abraham Yate's History of the Movement for the United States Constitution," *William and Mary Quarterly*, 3d ser. 20 (April 1963): 223-45. Thomas Jones's contemporary *History of New York During the Revolutionary War, and of the Leading Events in the Other Colonies*, 2 vols., edited by Edward F. de Lancey (New York: New-York Historical Society, 1879), must be used with caution.

Generations of students of New York History are indebted to Edmund Bailey O'Callaghan for, among others, his *Documentary History of the State of New York*, 4 vols. (Albany, N.Y.: Weed, Parsons and Co., 1849-51), *Documents Relative to the Colonial History of New York* . . . , 15 vols. (Albany, N.Y.: Weed, Parsons and Co., 1853-87), *Calendar of Historical Manuscripts Relating to the War of the Revolution, in the Office of the Secretary of State* . . . , 2 vols. (Albany, N.Y.: Weed, Parsons and Co., 1865-66), and *Calendar of New York Colonial Commissions, 1680-1770* (New York: New-York Historical Society, 1929). Much important material is contained in the *Aspinwall Papers, Collections*, 4th ser. 9-10 (Boston: Massachusetts Historical Society, 1871), and some unique items from the Thomlinson Papers appear in *New York City During the American Revolution; Being a Collection of Original Papers from the Manuscripts in the Possession of the Mercantile Library Association* (New York: Mercantile Library Association, 1861). Valuable for the study of politics are *The Burghers of New Amsterdam and the Freemen of New York, 1675-1866, Collections*, 18 (New York: New-York Historical Society, 1886) and Franklin B. Hough, comp., *The New-York Civil List from 1777 to 1855* (Albany, N.Y.: Weed, Par-

sons and Co., 1855). Still useful are Berthold Fernow, ed.,
New York in the Revolution (Albany, N.Y.: Weed, Parsons and Co.,
1887); James A. Roberts, comp., and Frederic G. Mather, ed.,
New York in the Revolution as Colony and State, 2d ed. (Albany,
N.Y.: Brandow Printing Co., 1898); Erastus C. Knight, comp.,
and Frederic G. Mather, ed., *New York in the Revolution as Col-*
ony and State, Supplement (Albany, N.Y.: O. A. Quayle, 1901).
The Roberts-Knight volumes were reissued as *New York in the*
Revolution as Colony and State . . . A Compilation of Documents
and Records from the Office of the State Comptroller, 2 vols.
(Albany, N.Y.: J. B. Lyon Co., 1904). Local histories are often neglected mines of information. Especially valuable for
the numerous documents that accompany the narrative are Henry
Onderdonk's *Documents and Letters Intended to Illustrate the*
the Revolutionary Incidents of Queens County . . . (New York:
Leavitt, Trow and Co., 1846), and *Revolutionary Incidents of*
Suffolk and Kings Counties . . . (New York: Leavitt and Co.,
1849); Henry B. Dawson's *Westchester County, New York, During*
the American Revolution (Morrisania, N.Y.: n.p., 1886); Joel
Munsell's *The Annals of Albany*, 10 vols. (Albany, N.Y.: J.
Munsell, 1850-59); and Isaac Newton Phelps Stokes's *The Iconog-*
raphy of Manhattan Island, 1498-1909, 6 vols. (New York: R. H.
Dodd, 1915-28). Civil and ecclesiastical affairs are treated
respectively by Charles Z. Lincoln, ed., *State of New York,*
Message from the Governors [1683-1906], 11 vols. (Albany, N.Y.:
J. B. Lyon Co., 1909), and Edward T. Corwin, ed., *Ecclesiasti-*
cal Records of the State of New York, 7 vols. (Albany, N.Y.: J.
B. Lyon Co., 1901-16). Interesting as well as informative
items can be gleaned from John Pintard, comp., *Broadsides, etc.,*
Consisting of Addresses, Advertisements, Ballads, Handbills . . .
Relating to America, 1700-1840, 2 vols. (New York: n.p., 1847),
and "New York Broadsides, 1762-1779," *Bulletin of the New York*
Public Library 3 (January 1899): 23-33.
     Several general documentary collections contain material
relative to New York. Foremost among these is Peter Force's
encyclopedic *American Archives . . . ,* 9 vols. (Washington,
D.C.: M. St. Clair and Peter Force, 1837-53), which contains
private correspondence, newspaper articles, pamphlet literature,
and the records of committees and congresses. More modest com-
pilations are Hezekiah Niles, *Principles and Acts of the Rev-*
olution in America . . . (Baltimore: William Ogden Niles, 1822),
and Frank Moore, *Diary of the American Revolution . . . ,* 2
vols. (New York: Charles Scribner, 1860). Margaret W. Willard,
ed., *Letters on the American Revolution, 1774-1776* (Boston:
Houghton Mifflin Co., 1925), provides excerpts of correspondence not printed elsewhere. Not to be overlooked, especially
for loyalist material, are Hugh Edward Egerton, ed., *The Royal*
Commission on the Losses and Services of American Loyalists,
1783 to 1785. Being the Notes of Mr. Daniel Parker Coke, M. P.

One of the Commissioners . . . (Oxford: Roxburghe Club, 1915);
*Calendar of Home Office Papers of the Reign of George III [1760-
1775]*, 4 vols. (London: Longmans, 1878-99); and two collections
of the Historical Manuscripts Commission: *Report on American
Manuscripts in the Royal Institution of Great Britain* 19 (Hereford: His Majesty's Stationery Office, 1904-9) and *Report on
the Manuscripts of Mrs. Stopford-Sackville* . . . 49 (Hereford:
His Majesty's Stationery Office, 1910). The actions of the New
York delegation in the Continental Congress can be followed
through Worthington C. Ford et al., eds., *Journals of the Continental Congress, 1774-1789*, 34 vols. (Washington, D.C.: U.S.
Government Printing Office, 1904-37), and Edmund Cody Burnett's
idiosyncratic and incomplete edition of *Letters of Members of
the Continental Congress*, 8 vols. (Washington, D.C.: Carnegie
Institution of Washington, 1921-36). The drafting and ratify-
ing of the Constitution is traceable in Max Farrand, ed., *The
Records of the Federal Convention of 1787*, 4 vols., rev. ed.
(New Haven, Conn.: Yale University Press, 1937); Paul Leicester
Ford, ed., *Pamphlets on the Constitution of the United States
Published During its Discussion by the People, 1787-1788* (Brook-
lyn, N.Y.: Historical Printing Club, 1888), and *Essays on the
Constitution of the United States Published During its Discus-
sion by the People, 1787-1788* (Brooklyn, N.Y.: Historical Print-
ing Club, 1892); Morton Borden, ed., *The Antifederalist Papers*
(East Lansing, Mich.: Michigan State University Press, 1965);
and Jonathan Elliot, comp., *The Debates in the Several State
Conventions on the Adoption of the Federal Constitution* . . . ,
5 vols., 2d ed. (Philadelphia: J. B. Lippincott and Co., 1863).